A People's History of the Cold War

A People's History of the Cold War

Stories From East and West

Colin Turbett

First published in Great Britain in 2023 by
Pen & Sword History
An imprint of
Pen & Sword Books Ltd
Yorkshire – Philadelphia

ISBN 978 1 39908 752 0

A CIP catalogue record for this book is available from the British Library.

Typeset by Mac Style
Printed in the UK by CPI Group (UK) Ltd, Croydon, CR0 4YY.

Pen & Sword Books Limited incorporates the imprints of Atlas, Archaeology, Aviation, Discovery, Family History, Fiction, History, Maritime, Military, Military Classics, Politics, Select, Transport, True Crime, Air World, Frontline Publishing, Leo Cooper, Remember When, Seaforth Publishing, The Praetorian Press, Wharncliffe Local History, Wharncliffe Transport, Wharncliffe True Crime and White Owl.

For a complete list of Pen & Sword titles please contact

PEN & SWORD BOOKS LIMITED
47 Church Street, Barnsley, South Yorkshire, S70 2AS, England
E-mail: enquiries@pen-and-sword.co.uk
Website: www.pen-and-sword.co.uk

Or

PEN AND SWORD BOOKS
1950 Lawrence Rd, Havertown, PA 19083, USA
E-mail: Uspen-and-sword@casematepublishers.com
Website: www.penandswordbooks.com

Contents

Foreword

I was born in Hanoi, capital of the Socialist Republic of Viêt Nam. The reason my family were here, is that my father, journalist Wilfred Burchett, met President Ho Chi Minh in his jungle headquarters in Thai Nguyen, in March 1954, on the eve of the historic battle of Dien Bien Phu that ended French colonial rule in Indochina. After that meeting – where Ho Chi Minh explained the military situation using his sun helmet – my father was able to report to the world, or at least to readers of the British *Daily Worker* and other "communist" publications the truth about this disaster for the colonial French army.

George Burchett is a visual artist now living in Hanoi, whose most recent work deals with narratives of resistance in Vietnam's long history as well as acts of resistance in general.

This book has quite a few references to Wilfred Burchett and an Appendix about his life. Its cover features a photo my father took in North Vietnam in 1966 and an atomic mushroom. The atomic mushroom reminds me of my father's solo train journey to Hiroshima in September 1945, almost exactly one month after the first atomic bomb was dropped on the Japanese city. You can read about it in Chapter 2.

But enough about Wilfred Burchett – this book is not about him – although he is the main reason I have been asked to write this preface. Another one is that I really like the book's title: I don't care much about Cold War history which, like most histories, is usually written by the victors, and we know who "won" the Cold War. I'm sure there are entire libraries dedicated to every facet and frankly, I couldn't care less about such accounts.

What I like in the title is "People's". It reminds me of Howard Zinn's *A People's History of the United States*. Colin Turbett gives us, the people – to those of us who care to try to understand the tectonic forces that have shaped much of the 20th century and are now again at play – a symmetrical overview of events from roughly the 1917 Bolshevik Revolution in Russia to today's increasingly dangerous confrontation between the forces of "freedom and democracy" and "authoritarianism" – as it is overwhelmingly presented by western corporate media.

You don't need to take sides to appreciate this book. In fact – and as the extensive bibliography at the end shows – these are many books in one. Turbett has done us – the people – a great service by digesting all this history and information – and presenting it almost as a chess game played by the opposing sides in the Cold War.

So read it and ponder: millions of lives lost, so many countries destroyed in the name of competing ideologies and interests, which, ultimately, only end up representing the interests of ruling elites, even though they may claim to work for the "People". There may not be anyone left to write *A People's History of the End of the World*. So it is time for us, the People, to show a collective finger to those who start wars in our name or in the name of this or that ideology, religion or whatever excuse – like the "war on terror". Reading this book would be a good start for understanding the folly of it all. And since I started with Wilfred Burchett, I would like to end with the closing paragraph of his autobiography, *At the Barricades*:

> It so happened that step by step and almost accidently, I had achieved a sort of journalistic Nirvana, free of any in-built loyalties to governments, parties or any organisations whatsoever. My loyalty was to my own convictions and my readers. This demanded freedom from any discipline except that of getting the facts on important issues back to the sort of people likely to act – often at great sacrifice – on the information they received. This was particularly so during my reporting in Vietnam, the most important of my career, far too important to be swayed by dictates from outside or above. Over the years, and in many countries, I had a circle of readers who did not buy papers for the stock market reports or strip cartoons, but for facts on vital issues affecting their lives and consciences. In keeping both eyes and both ears open during my forty years reporting from the world's hot spots, I had become more and more conscious of my responsibilities to my readers. The point of departure is a great faith in ordinary human beings and the sane and decent way they behave when they have the true facts of the case.

Amen!

George Burchett, Hanoi, July 2022

Acknowledgements

As the author, I am fully responsible for the contents of this book, and errors are mine alone. Wherever possible, images are credited and licences have been obtained for their use where this is required; some are from private collections in the ownership of the author and others, and for many of these, their exact origins are unknown. Should any image not have been credited correctly, please contact me via the publisher so the matter can be properly rectified.

Thanks to all those who have helped in any way with bringing this all together; particularly Valentina Kudinova from Kharkiv, Ukraine, who helped with research as she has done so faithfully in the past, Natalia McAllister who is patiently teaching me Russian language, and the team from Pen & Sword Publishing for their wonderful assistance with this, my fourth title for them. Also, thanks to all those friends and others who provided the stories for Chapters 8 and 9. George Burchett from Hanoi, Vietnam, was particularly helpful with photographs and permissions in respect of his late father Wilfred Burchett's work. As ever, my family – particularly my wife Diana – were supportive and helpful.

Author, Gdansk, Poland, 2011. (*Author*)

Key Definitions Used Throughout the Book

(Adapted from Wilczynski 1981 and Shaw & Pryce 1990)

Capitalism – a social system characterised by: ownership of the means of production being concentrated in the hands of private capitalists; a free market in an industrialised and well developed societal framework; individualism; democratic government based on multi-party politics and elections.

Communism – an ideology based on full social equality, but interpreted in at least seven different ways by its supporters and opponents: 1) idealistic self-managed communities (communalism); 2) a society based on Marxist philosophy, economic, political and sociological concepts; 3) a vague description of the social system that would follow the overthrow of capitalism; 4) the Marxist notion of the class-free society that would follow on from the transitional phase of socialism; 5) a totalitarian system of government based on the power of the ruling Communist Party; 6) the one party system described as 'the dictatorship of the proletariat' and exercised in the USSR, its satellites, China, Cuba etc; 7) the international ideology ascribed by its enemies to the foreign relations and expansionist practices of the USSR (and other socialist countries), aimed at destroying capitalism by any means necessary, including terrorism and subversion.

Détente – the relaxation of tension in attempts to defuse and end the Cold War.

Glasnost – the practice of 'openness' and honesty introduced by Gorbachev in his attempt to reform the USSR

Imperialism – used by Marxists to describe the highest stage of capitalism involving the concentrated ownership of capital and fierce competition; the rise of finance capitalism and monopoly of the banking system; the export of capital to underdeveloped countries and their exploitation; a division of the less developed world and struggle between the imperialist powers leading to trade and real wars.

Peaceful Co-existence – the acceptance of socialism and capitalism (i.e East and West) operating as parallel systems, and resolution of conflict through peaceful means and a renunciation of war.

Perestroika – Gorbachev's policy of restructuring the Soviet economy first proposed by Brezhnev in 1979; initially concerning automation and labour efficiency but developed to include the introduction of markets and the ending of central planning.

Politburo – the supreme policy-making body in the USSR (known as the praesidium between 1952 and 1966). Elected by the Central Committee at Party Congresses and directing the work of the Central Committee between them; its authority was binding on the Party as a whole. In 1976, it consisted of sixteen members and six candidate members, headed by the Secretary-General, Brezhnev.

Really Existing Socialism – the term used by the USSR and its satellites after the Second World War to describe their regimes.

Socialism – a term with multiple variants but generally used to describe a political and economic system emphasising social justice maintained by the state. In the USSR it described the transitional phase to the classless society of full communism. In the West it describes those who embrace social democracy as a choice exercised through free elections, but not necessarily challenging capitalism.

Abbreviations

ABM – Anti-Ballistic Missile
ALCM – Air Launched Cruise Missile
ANC – African National Congress (South Africa)
CIA – Central Intelligence Agency (USA)
CND – Campaign for Nuclear Disarmament (UK)
Comecon – Council for Mutual Economic Assistance
Comintern – Communist International (established 1920, dissolved 1943)
CPGB – Communist Party of Great Britain
CPSU – Communist Party of the Soviet Union
DDR – German Democratic Republic (East Germany)
DOSAAF – Volunteer Society for Cooperation with the Army, Aviation and Navy (USSR)
FDR – Federal German Republic (West Germany)
FLN – National Liberation Front (Algeria)
FNLA – National Liberation Front of Angola
FRELIMO – Liberation Front of Mozambique
GLCM – Ground Launched Cruise Missile
HUAC – House Un-American Activities Committee
ICBM – Inter-Continental Ballistic Missile
IRD – Information Research Department
KGB – Committee for State Security (USSR)
KOR – Workers Defence Committee (Poland)
MARV – Manoeuvrable Re-entry Vehicle
MCF – Movement for Colonial Freedom
MCP – Malayan Communist Party
MDP – Hungarian Workers Party
MK – Umkhonto we Sizwe ('Spear of the People')
MP – Member of Parliament (UK)
MPLA – People's Movement for the Liberation of Angola
MRLA – Malayan Races Liberation Army
MIC – Military-Industrial Complex
MIRV – Multiple Independently Targetable Re-entry Vehicle
NATO – North Atlantic Treaty Organisation
NBC – nuclear biological and chemical weapons

NLF – National Liberation Front (Aden)
OAS – Organisation Armée Secrète (Secret Army Organisation)
OSOAVIAKhIM – Union of Societies of Assistance to Defence and Aviation Chemical Construction of the USSR
PAIGC – African Party for the Independence of Guinea and Cape Verde
POW – Prisoner of War
PZPR – Polish United Workers Party
RAF – Royal Air Force
SALT – Strategic Arms Limitation Treaty
SANE – National Committee for a Sane Nuclear Policy
SDS – Students for a Democratic Society
SED – Socialist Unity Party (DDR)
SHAPE – Supreme Headquarters Allied Powers Europe
SLBM – Submarine Launched Ballistic Missile
SLCM – Submarine Launched Cruise Missile
SNCC – Student National Coordinating Committee
SSBN – Submersible Ship Ballistic Missile Nuclear
Stasi – Ministry for State Security (DDR)
SWAPO – South West Africa People's Organisation
UDI – unilateral declaration of independence
UK – United Kingdom
UN – United Nations
US/USA – United States / United States of America
USAF – United States Air Force
USSR – Union of Soviet Socialist Republics
YAR – Republic of Yemen
YCL – Young Communist League
ZANU-PF – Zimbabwe African National Union – Patriotic Front
ZAPU – Zimbabwe African People's Union

Introduction

Oh, show me round your snow-peaked mountains
Way down south
Take me to your daddy's farm
Let me hear the balalaikas ringing out
Come and keep your comrade warm

I'm back in the USSR
You don't know how lucky you are, boy
Back in the USSR

The Beatles: *Back in the USSR* 1968

I was born in 1954 – a important year for British policy and strained attitude towards the nuclear weapons that defined the Cold War. This was the year the United Kingdom (UK) committed itself to thermonuclear defence, and the one in which an anti-nuclear protest movement took popular root. However, for many of us the English world of the 1950s was defined by black and white British movies describing heroes from a war in which our fathers and mothers had fought against universally acknowledged tyranny. This was reinforced everywhere – from cheap comics to taught history in school, where we learned that Britain and its Empire had always stood for good against evil, abolishing slavery while forgetting our role as perpetrator and principal benefactor. We were told that we really were the most civilised nation on earth, whose values lived on through the post-colonial Commonwealth with our queen at its head. Popular TV shows and movies like the first James Bond titles, interchanged caricatured Soviet spies like Rosa Klebbs with international criminal masterminds; all were super-evil and deserved the attentions of our clever and determined secret services.

Near where I lived in the South of England were numerous army camps that had sprung up in the war, but which were still used; Britain at that time had maintained National Service conscription and there were still over half a million troops in the Army by the end of the decade. The Royal Navy, which my father left in 1955 having joined in 1941, still had 200 fighting ships and submarines in 1960. Our air force contained the nuclear armed V-Bomber fleet. Although depleted from their wartime heights, the armed forces still played a major role in society.

HMS *Vanguard* on Royal Tour in South Africa 1947 – an obsolete symbol of evaporating imperial power? (*Author's collection*)

The British worldview of empire and greatness had always been challenged on the left and progressive margins, but by the late 1960s, reaction against the status-quo had become popularised through the commercialisation of culture – especially that aimed at a young generation with money to spend. New ideas were expressed through music, art, movies and television, and for some the influence of New Left individuals and groups who rejected Western values as well as the Soviet Union's version of socialism. The world had become complicated and the stark and simple choices that characterised the 1930s – fascism or communism – seemed of marginal relevance.

The Cold War was always somewhere in the background throughout these years – the ongoing ideological battle that saw perpetual confrontation between the capitalist West and the Soviet-dominated East. It pervaded civilian life in Britain in ways that became taken for granted but could hardly be said to be obtrusive: the diminutive but universal presence across the land of the Royal Observer Corps and Civil Defence Corps, along with the well-known notion of the 'Four Minute Warning' being examples. The views and opinions of the other side were rarely heard; I do recall listening to Radio Tirana with its distinctive call sign, the voice of besieged (i.e. no friends) socialist Albania: while the commentary on world affairs given by the female presenter might well have been true, any credibility was lost in the caricatured language she used – peppered with references to 'running dogs' and 'imperialist lackies' quite apart from its description of Albania as a workers' paradise. Listening was a kind of radio Monty Python show. Later, in the mid-1970s, in true student 'left' style, I recall being involved in a rather uninformed debate about the relative merits of ZANU and ZAPU in the anti-apartheid civil war in far off Rhodesia, and have to admit in hindsight that the Soviet Union view was a lot clearer than was ours. We were all, naturally, opposed to nuclear weapons, and such views were shared across all spectres of left, progressive and religious opinion. This did not extend to most of our political representatives, tied as they were to the real establishment Cold War consensus dictated by our powerful allies, the USA.

There were other less obvious signs of the Cold War; my wife Diana grew up in Cheltenham and at her state Grammar School, Russian language was a rare option almost certainly associated with the secretive GCHQ Spy Centre located in the town where this language might be useful. In other communities where arms industry presence prevailed, technical skills were promoted in Secondary Modern Schools to generate engineers and technicians. The threat of Mutually Assured Destruction seemed to ensure that peace would prevail. British people could pride themselves on their own contribution – the white painted V-Bombers were followed in the 1960s by our very own (but not quite independent) mini-fleet of Polaris Missile equipped nuclear submarines. During my social work career towards the end of the Cold War, our office in the Firth of Clyde held secret instructions on actions required in the event of nuclear fallout effecting the community; this was due to the presence of 'Z Berths' just half a mile away, which would be used to moor submarines damaged in a nuclear accident. Our manager carried these in his briefcase wherever he went, 'just in case', although his advice to us was that we would all be pretty much doomed anyway should the worst happen. The Z Berths were removed in the early 1990s, but not the submarines, so perhaps some other even more remote community has the doubtful privilege of hosting them now. The Polaris (and later Trident) carrying submarines of both our own and US navies sailed by regularly to their bases further up the river – a sinister sight. Given the fact that U Boats had penetrated as far as the Firth in the Second World War, it seems likely that Soviet ones were lurking unseen, although it was one of 'ours', HMS *Trenchant*, that dragged the fishing boat *Antares* to the bottom of the sea, killing its crew, in deep water just off Arran's northeast coast one night in 1990.

Of course, the idea of global peace was never real to many; a series of wars in very poor countries that had (in most cases) been European colonies, were devastating and murderous, but far away from the immediate territories of the global superpowers. These went on throughout the post-war period until the Soviet Union crumbled into dust in 1991, but strangely have continued, suggesting they were never perhaps about the Cold War in the first place, but about the aspirations of local people versus global interest. However, if you believed in human progress in the 1960s and 1970s it seemed easy to reject both superpowers. In 1983 I made my own small contribution to trying to influence the course of the Cold War when I unsuccessfully moved an amendment at

RAF Vulcan Bombers 1957. (*Ministry of Defence via Wikimedia Commons*)

my trade union's national conference suggesting that our members (including local authority Emergency Planning Officers) should be instructed to boycott civil defence planning. This was at a time when new regulations were being introduced that reflected heightened tensions and which would in effect have introduced a military dictatorship in a post-nuclear attack situation. The union, however, stuck by its conscientious objection supporting policy, and I was left to fight another day.

Meanwhile, on the other side of the 'Iron Curtain' people lived their lives much as we did: going to school and growing up, working, having families, loving, laughing and crying just like us. The difference over there lay in their society's official idea

Civil defence duties matter of conscience

IN MANY WAYS the debate on civil defence at Conference was a re-run of last year's, but the threat of the new civil defence regulations brought a reaffirmation of NALGO's policy of support for members who refuse to take part in civil defence on the grounds of conscience or because their contract of employment has been unilaterally varied.

Anne Tapsell (Lambeth) proposed a composite resolution to this effect on behalf of the Metropolitan, West Midland and Scottish district councils.

An amendment by Strathclyde branch to dispense with a ballot and *instruct* all NALGO members to refuse to participate in civil defence planning was lost.

So was a clause from the original resolution asking for all branches to be supplied with publicity material on civil defence planning for nuclear war.

This was replaced by an NEC amendment calling for further publicity material and a campaign for support for NALGO's policies among other trade unions who had members concerned with any aspect of civil defence.

Terry Jowett (Derbyshire) warned Conference that civil defence would not go away and that if local authorities did not carry it out it would be privatised.

Anne Tapsell said that NALGO members were involved in the planning of an emergency service for use not only in the event of disasters but at times of what the law described as "civil commotion and unrest".

She told Conference she felt indebted to the men and women who sought to service the community in what was once the most honourable of organisations and that the proposers of the motion were not opposed to a real emergency service for natural disasters and accidents.

Colin Turbett (Strathclyde) said that his branch's amendment, instructing members not to take part, would effectively sabotage the Government's war plans for an authoritarian military dictatorship in the event of nuclear war. Only industrial action would defeat the war plans.

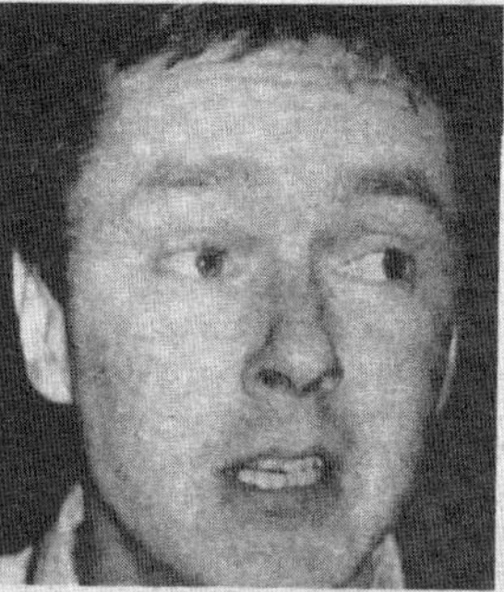

COLIN TURBETT

Graham Burgess (NEC) said the Council opposed the Strathclyde amendment on the basis of tactics. The publicity department was prepared to wage a major campaign to explain the case against civil defence to members, many of whom were not convinced. To issue an instruction would cause a massive reaction and undermine what the union was trying to do.

Maurice Chittock (Broxbourne), said it should be the job of members to lift the shroud of secrecy. He explained how he had attended a civil defence course in Hertfordshire and so found out about the plans to billet compulsorily half a million refugees from London in the county, and for rounding up "undesirable elements" in the event of war.

The final resolution, carried overwhelmingly by Conference was:

"Conference condemns the Government plans to increase the war planning duties of public authorities and the attempt to conscript unwilling workers into taking part in war-planning which is an insufferable limitation of the civil liberties of public employees. Conference believes that these plans are a sham, designed to mislead the public into thinking that a nuclear war could be survivable.

"Conference is opposed to any increased expenditure on so-called 'civil defence' by a nuclear weapons state, particularly when other public authority services are being slashed and lives are now being put at risk because of health service cuts. Conference instructs the NEC:

(1) strenuously to oppose any attempt to conscript workers into nuclear war preparations or any training of volunteers in emergency service roles which might enable them to be used as strike breakers;

(2) to inform union members that they will have the support of the union if they refuse to take part on the grounds of personal consciences or on the grounds that his/her contract of employment has been unilaterally varied, and to draw up such contingency plans as may be necessary to protect members if the proposals become law, such plans to include arrangements for the monitoring of any discrimination by employers against members who oppose this war planning and the central collation of evidence of such discrimination;

(3) to approach NALGO's parliamentary advisers urging them to support NALGO's declared policies with regard to this issue both inside and outside parliament;

(4) Conference reaffirms the policy adopted at the 1981 Conference instructing the NEC to take such action as may be necessary to protect any member who may be in any way prejudiced as a result of following his or her conscience in the matter. Conference also instructs the NEC to provide branches with further publicity material exposing the hypocrisy of civil defence planning for nuclear war.

(5) to campaign for support for these policies among other trade unions who have members concerned with any aspect of civil defence and to work together with 'nuclear free' councils and the peace movement on the issue.

(6) to initiate a campaign for increased public authority provision for dealing with civil emergencies in peace time."

The author, NALGO Conference 1983. (*NALGO News*)

of citizenship and collective endeavour. In the USSR and its satellite countries, an individual's responsibility for their fellows and the greater good came above personal accumulation and individual happiness. However, as the Soviet economy depended on discipline and inevitable curtailment of elements of individuality, the lure of the market and the freedoms enjoyed by people in the West began to make the apparent drabness of a more equal society pale by comparison. In the West, creeping individualism and consumerism emerged from similar post-war drabness and became endemic as neo-liberalism took a firm grip of government and economic thinking in the 1980s. The fruits of the marketplace, though, were not available to all, but enough people were able to own their own homes (the big sell in the UK), to convince them that they had in fact become middle-class, with a stake in capitalism. Dropping out and rejecting the values of consumerism was very much a luxury afforded through affluence, but it had resonance in the Soviet Bloc, where a youth culture based on emulation of contemporaries in the West, began to take hold alongside growing dissidence among intellectuals.

Thirty years on from the end of the Cold War, and a wealth of written history about a subject within memory for many of us, defines and redefines the period from 1945 to 1991. Just as most Western academic commentary during the Cold War reflected the views and values of the host protagonist, much written since has continued to represent events and their explanation in a very partisan fashion. In fact, this recent history has been the subject of serious and deliberate revision from both East and West, and the recovery of historical memory has become an imperative. Walk into any bookshop and the shelves are full of titles that characterise the Cold War as a battle against totalitarianism that was eventually won by 'our' side, which, whatever its failings, was infinitely better than that of the 'really existing' socialist states of the East. Books comparing Hitler and Stalin seem to be a popular genre of their own. The popular accounts of Russian and Eastern European history by writers as varied as Anne Applebaum, Antony Beevor and Simon Montefiore are deeply biased and assume Western entitlement and moral superiority. These authors are figures tied closely with the Western establishment, and whatever their merit and popularity, should be regarded as holding a bias (e.g., Applebaum's *Iron Curtain – the Crushing of Eastern Europe*, lavishly praised by all these authors). The problem with these histories is not in their account of the awfulness of Stalin's time, it is in their extension of such an underlying negative premise to the story of the USSR before and after his times. They generalise a dismissal of the values that enjoyed popular support among a people committed to collective action to make the world a better place. Just as Western propaganda portrayed the Cold War as a battle of freedom against tyranny, the Soviets – with justification in their worldview – characterised the US and their allies as imperialist and intent on grabbing the world's resources as their own. The contested definitions of what constitutes 'capitalism', 'communism', 'socialism' and 'imperialism' are important – most were used by both sets of powers to characterise both their own and the other side (a short summary of the most well used terms is provided).

Access to released official materials in recent years (especially formerly secret and extensive Soviet archives after 1991) by academic historians has not reduced the partisan narrative of the Cold War years and if anything has increased it; books like that of Haslam (2011) offer fascinating insights from well-researched sources but must be read carefully as they are laced with interpretation of events that carry the same heavy pro-Western bias as ones written during the Cold War years. Haslam frequently implies motives concerning territorial ambition beyond the Soviet Union's borders from the spoken statements of its leaders, because of the style of quasi-Marxist language they used. This would be familiar to anyone on the left who had read Marx, Lenin and their contemporaries, and almost certainly interpreted in a very different and less aggressively intended manner, the key question being popular support for communist ideas rather than the machinations of Kremlin leaders. Interpretation bias has always figured in political dialogue between contending parties, but is questionable when presented as academic objectivity.

In the 1960s and 70s a new left 'revisionist' school of Cold War interpreters who were critical of Western accounts blaming Stalin and the Soviets for the conflict emerged, and pointed to American imperialist designs for better explanation (Kolko 1990 is an example). The later post-Cold War historians (e.g. Kenez 2006) are critical of the revisionists, suggesting that their researches were ideologically driven by leftist views and, as they were unable to access Soviet archives at the time, lacking in rigour. However, these later historians might have revealed behind-the-scenes detail through their research, but their analyses offer little more than their Western-orientated Cold War era predecessors. The most widely read popular scholar of the Cold War, Gaddis, laces his meticulously referenced accounts of the period (e.g. *The Cold War,* 2005) with assumptions: Soviet intent through the Post-War Stalin period, to invade Western Europe if it had the opportunity, being the principle one. In the writer's view, no evidence is offered apart from the propagandist internationalism that characterised Bolshevism, but which was always played down by Stalin in favour of what he perceived were the interests of the USSR. Such narratives negate the significance of the popularity or otherwise of communism in the Western countries concerned (real in the case of France and Italy in the late 1940s) and assume that socialism could be brought about by the same Russian tanks that had rolled over Eastern Europe in the fight against the Nazis in 1944–45. There are, however, accounts written since the end of the Cold War that rise above the others; Mary Kaldor's 1990 attempt at achieving an understanding of the dynamics that lay behind the Cold War, is excellent and written from the perspective of a prominent activist in the Western European peace movement who was no slave to either side of the ideological divide.

The assumption of Soviet expansionist intent is central to most Western thinking, justifying the arms build-up, which as we will see, drove significant parts of the economy not only in the USA, but also in Great Britain and France. Western accounts also typically reduce the importance of the general economic interests that fuelled the actions of US governments and their allies. Politicians were bound to be influenced by the interests of the corporations that funded their parties, just as the people of their countries were influenced by their advertising and manipulation of popular fashion and culture. This is at least as significant as the value of the state propaganda put out by the Soviets and their satellite governments, but which are often emphasised unreasonably. The Soviet Union had abundant fossil fuel resources, including oil, and had less need for the thinly disguised imperial designs that accompanied the intrigues of their Cold War opponents (it did have other pressing needs).

In the countries that formerly had been under Soviet control in Europe, a new historical revisionism has reached dangerous proportions, with influence well beyond the extreme right-wing nationalist tendencies who emerged after 1991, from which it was spawned. The Prague Declaration of 2008, now the official position of the European Union, gives equal place to Soviet and Nazi war crimes and sees the peoples of Eastern Europe as victims of both, during and after the war and right up to the demise of the Soviet Union in 1991. This has led to the veneration in many countries, including Ukraine, the Baltic Countries and Bulgaria, of war criminals – individuals who fought with the Nazis and were involved in anti-partisan activity and the Holocaust (Ghodsee 2015 offers examples, but they are not hard to find). The redeeming feature of such individuals, it seems, is their patriotism and bolstering of nationalist sentiment, and more centrist politicians have allowed far-right elements to propagate their memories in a positive light in contrast to the way they were characterised under the former socialist regimes. The problem with this new narrative is not that it equates Hitler and Stalin as tyrants, it is that the Soviet role in defeating fascism is negated – a gross mistake with incalculable consequences if we are to properly examine the history of unity against a common enemy achieved in the Second World War (Turbett 2021a). It also very erroneously reads the brutality of Stalin and his accomplices into the characters and behaviours of ordinary Red Army soldiers and Soviet citizens. We stopped doing this with the German people in 1945 but it somehow persists in the popular imagination with Russians. Such revisionism also gives succour to those who would divide us further as we face common perils such as climate change and attendant global pandemics. Clearly the history of the Cold War and how we view it is significant – the accounts that simply convey the evils of the losing side are both distortions as well as betrayals of the profound idealism that accompanied the communist project of the twentieth century. There were, and still are, accounts of a different type, and some, from a vast array of literature, will be drawn upon in this book.

Open conflict in Eastern Europe broke out as Russia invaded Ukraine just after the first draft of this book went to the publisher. While there can be no justification for such an attack as far as this writer is concerned, it is interesting to note that reasons offered by the Russian leadership included the need to 'de-nazify' their victim. This is preposterous and a betrayal of the memory of the 5 million or so Ukrainian citizens who fought the Nazis as part of the Red Army in the Second World War. While some 250,000 Ukrainians for whatever reason did side with the Nazis, they were an obvious minority, as are those in Ukraine who celebrate their memory today. I would tend to agree with Valentina, my Kharkiv based researcher, that the real fascists are the invaders who have caused her to evacuate her home and laid waste her homeland.

A People's History of the Cold War – Stories from East and West is not another academic work on the subject. The archives have been well plundered now, thirty years after the end of the conflict. However, the experiences and views of ordinary people as the events took place, seen through the popular culture of the time as well as living memory, are less commonly presented and the words and images that follow will try and fill that gap. The writer is grateful for the contributions of the ethnographers Svetlana Alexievich and Kristen Ghodsee, whose work, in different ways, inspired this book. Lea Ypi's personal reflection on the changes in Albania are also instructive. The book also draws on the journalism and writings of the period as these both reflected views at the time and helped shape them. The almost forgotten Australian born journalist Wilfred Burchett (1911–1983) is regularly referenced as he commented on this period of history as it happened from locations on the other side (see Appendix for a short biography). Burchett's Cold War perspective was influenced by his direct witness of the horrors unleashed by the Western Allies with the coldly calculated explosion of a nuclear bomb above Hiroshima in 1945. A few months earlier, a young US Army soldier who was a prisoner of war in Dresden, Kurt Vonnegut, witnessed an Anglo-American bombing action that is often referred to as an atrocity and a war crime; his late and consequential sci-fi writings also offer an interesting contrast to mainstream views, reflecting his take on the Cold War and influencing a generation in the West – with ripples in the USSR where he was also popular.

The book also draws on other period historical accounts which have stood the test of time, including Fleming (1961), who was no fan of the Soviet Union, but whose factual account offers more objectivity than many. This book, though, offers a history from what Ghodsee (2015) calls 'the left side of history': a social and peoples' story with a focus on ordinary lives rather than the intrigues of the leaders. The book illustrates how each side characterised the other and how this affected the views and lives of their citizens. There are descriptions of how events were experienced at the time and their impact on the societies of both East and West. The format, with illustrations, follows that of my previous Pen

Wilfred Burchett and Ho Chi Minh. (*George Burchett*)

and Sword publications, *Red Star at War*, *The Anglo Soviet Alliance* and *Soviets in Space*. Although complementary, these books were not designed to be a series, so the reader will find some inevitable but minor duplication of material. This book does not reference every fact and opinion stated but (in the light of criticism of previous work) does so if these are considered controversial or contestable. A full list of materials accessed for the book's content is provided in the bibliography.

The book focuses on aspects of the period and does not provide a continuous timeline narrative; however, to aid the reader, the first chapter provides a summary of events as they occurred, many of which are referred to elsewhere in the text. While most of the book focuses on Cold War events from 1945 until 1991 (the generally accepted timeline), this summary starts earlier, in 1917, for reasons that are made clear.

In her 2015 book, Kristen Ghodsee interviews a former Bulgarian state employee whose job under the pre-1990 regime was to write propagandist articles criticising Western values and culture; this was apparently a job she undertook as her superiors expected, but all along she secretly held no real belief in what she was doing. In 2013, living in the reality of contemporary capitalist Bulgaria, she shared the view that what she had been asked to write was largely true – neoliberal values were shallow, worthless and fell far short of the expected promise as the communist world fell apart in 1990. This was something I did not recognise at the time despite an interest in the issues surrounding 'really existing socialism' (as it was described by its supporters). At last, felt many of us on the left, our beliefs could no longer be tarnished by the legacies of Stalinism and the undoubted repression associated with the Soviet and East European regimes. An array of socialist organisations from the far-left to the centre felt the same way: typified up by Callinicos (1991) who provided a very full account of the ills of the Soviet bureaucracy while ignoring the social benefits of life in the USSR. On reflection I can see that we might have got it wrong; what was lost with the end of the Soviet Union's seventy-year attempt to create socialism and then communism (a stage it never reached), was more significant than the freedoms and even the end of totalitarianism that the 1989–91 period represented. This is not to negate the horrors of Stalinism, or the repressive means used to quash dissent (real and sometimes imagined) during the Soviet era. That has been well recorded ever since Khrushchev made his secret speech admitting the murderous calamities of the Stalin period. History though is more complex when it comes to judging right from wrong, and simplistic attribution of blame when most of the main actors are long gone, seems more about pursuing current agendas than increasing knowledge of the period.

The communist project of the twentieth century was driven by a conscious and well-meaning desire to end human suffering and inequality, but was attacked and undermined by the powerful nations who controlled international trade and finance, so never had much opportunity to demonstrate its ideals in practice. It cannot be compared, as popular historians often do today, with fascism, the other ideology of change in the same period. Arguably a reaction to communism, fascism rested on racism and the exploitation of difference, and a cult of violence, holding appeal to the worst aspects of human nature. The ideal of communism, on the other hand, spurred self-sacrifice, and intense loyalty from its most ordinary adherents because of its promise for a humanity divided by class, nationality, race, war and oppression. This might have been eroded over time by the growing realisation of oppression in the USSR, and events like the suppression of the revolution in Hungary in 1956, but remained true until the end for many. This is a history that deserves recognition and even celebration, and its rescue and discovery through an examination of the Cold War that led to the communist project's end, is an aim of this book. It is one for which the author makes no apology. As Kristen Ghodsee has written, for those of us who believe that the world has outlived capitalism and needs a new system of sustainable trade, social justice and cooperation, such an exercise is crucial. This is not to return to the communist project, but to learn from its positive aspects while ensuring that its mistakes are not repeated in building a socialist world order for the future.

As these words were written, the headlines continued to offer up examples of new enemies, whether the Russian Federation in Ukraine or on the high seas, or China in the South China Sea; as ever in history, economic rivalry is underwritten with military shows of strength in what some were already describing as a new

Cold War (Niall Ferguson in the *New York Times* 2 December, 2019). History, we can only hope, will not repeat itself. So, do I feel safer today than I did as a child? Not really; competition over markets and resources still seems to drive the policies of the major powers just as it did in the Cold War (but with little emphasis on ideology); the threat of nuclear annihilation continues even though the Cold War justification for the existence of doomsday weapons ended decades ago; they really are not much use against enemies armed with rifles and hand-held rocket-launchers riding on pick-up trucks. The enemy today is climate change – within a generation of my own lifetime we have shifted from concern about deliberate destruction over which we thought we had control, to the unintentional and perhaps more inevitable means of slowly achieving the same end. While we all agree that urgent action is needed, it seems that, as in the Cold War, other interests are at work to prevent us doing what seems obviously necessary.

Navy Recruitment poster Paterson New Jersey 1950s. (*Author's collection*)

Chapter 1

The Cold War – a Timeline of Significant Events

October 1917 – the Bolshevik Party (later renamed the Communist Party) in Russia, an illegal underground organisation with a strong base among workers in the major cities, which had grown threefold to 350,000 members in the previous five months, leads an insurrection against the weak regime which had overthrown the Czarist autocracy the previous February. Tightly organised under the leadership of Lenin, it quickly consolidates control of the country, winning support from workers, peasants and soldiers with its simple programme of 'Land, Peace and Bread'. To the dismay of Russia's wartime allies, Britain, France and the USA, it makes peace with Germany and withdraws from the war, giving up territory in the process, but counting on revolution in Germany to resolve issues within the near future. The leaders of Europe's social democratic parties (in Britain, France and Germany) who had sided with conservative parties in support of the war also greet the formation of the world's first worker's state with alarm; the new Soviet State gives succour to their left critics and threatens their leadership of the socialist movement.

1919–1921 – a bitter and violently contested **Civil War in Russia,** led by disunited former Czarist generals operating separately across Russia's vast territories, lays the country to waste. Military assistance, including troops, are provided by the Western powers who fear the consequences of Bolshevik victory. By 1921 the revolutionary Red Army had won back control of the country. In 1919, with the aim of fomenting revolution across the world, the Comintern (Communist International) is formed in Moscow.

1922 – Joseph Stalin was elected First Secretary of the Communist Party of the USSR, a bureaucratic and administrative post that was part of a collective leadership. After Lenin's death in 1923, Stalin gradually replaces those around him with individuals loyal to him alone, and by the end of the decade has amassed dictatorial control over the Soviet Union, building a cult around his own personality.

1924 – the 'Zinoviev Letter' is published by the *Daily Mail* newspaper in Britain, just before a General Election, claiming that a Labour victory will enable seditious activity by British Communists. This ensures Labour lose at the polls and stokes anti-Soviet feeling. The letter later turns out to be a forgery created by the British Secret Services.

1928–1940 – land in the Soviet Union is put under common ownership (collectivised) in order to increase food production for the cities and their growing numbers of industrial workers. The policy is brutally applied between 1929 and 1931, worsening the impact of a food crisis caused naturally by a succession of poor harvests, causing the death of millions in 1932-33. Collectivisation was resisted in some areas, especially in Ukraine, and this was dealt with mercilessly. The episode continues to be debated and is often quoted as an example of the murderous failure of Soviet methods.

1929–40 – the era of Stalin's 'purges', whose victims numbered millions. Starting as an attempt to eradicate opposition within the Communist Party, and to deal with Kulaks (better-off peasants) and others regarded as the enemies of socialism. Trials and imprisonment became systematic tools of the state, creating a vast slave army – often worked to death in labour camps – whose purpose was to build the country's infrastructure. By 1936 denunciation of someone to the NKVD could win promotion and favours, requiring no real evidence of subversive activity. At its height judicious means were often dispensed with and victims were sent to the camps without any process apart from official recording of their crime and sentence, and many were executed. Stalin reduced the impact of the purges in 1938 with the replacement of the chief of the NKVD, but no one was freed, and the imprisonment of innocent people continued until Stalin's death in 1953. By 1940 and Trotsky's assassination at the hands of an NKVD agent in Mexico, all the principal leaders of the Bolsheviks in the period of revolution in 1917 had died, many through judicial murder in show trials where they were made to read out humiliating forced confessions of their criminal activities.

1929 – the Wall Street Crash brings about a collapse in share prices and causes financial ruin across the capitalist countries, creating unemployment and economic decay that would continue until the start of the Second World War. The Soviet Union alone seems to be untouched by the great depression of the 1930s, and for many communists, their supporters and admirers across the globe, it shines like a beacon of hope for humanity.

1933 – Partly due to miscalculation and divisive tactics by their rivals in the German Communist Party, **Hitler is elected to power in Germany**. He soon declares himself Fuehrer and dismantles democratic institutions on the basis that this is necessary to deal with crisis created by communists and Jews, and that only he and the Nazi Party can make the country great again. The aggressive shadows of Hitler and Mussolini hang over the rest of the decade until the inevitable war breaks out in 1939. The Soviet Union recognise the threat of fascism as the decade wears on and support efforts to fight it in Spain; its local parties are engaged in anti-fascist activity in France, Britain and elsewhere.

1938 – Britain and France sign the 'Munich Agreement' with Germany, agreeing to German (and later Polish and Hungarian) claims on territory in Czechoslovakia which resulted in its effective dismemberment as a nation state. European war, however, is averted. The USSR were not invited and regard it as a capitulation to Hitler that only encourages his further territorial ambitions, including those eastwards in their direction.

1939 (August) – Ribbentrop and Molotov sign a pact of non-aggression on behalf of Germany and the USSR. Prior to the secret negotiations between the two countries, the USSR had sought a triple anti-fascist alliance with Britain and France, but these were not taken seriously by the latter and got nowhere. Spurred by the Munich agreement of the previous year, the Soviets feel that they have no choice other than to seek agreement with Germany that will at least give them time to build up their forces. While this is naked and expansive aggression by the Nazis, the USSR see themselves recovering lands lost during the Civil War in Western Ukraine and ceded to the Baltic Republics at the same time; they view it as a move to secure their borders. The agreement also includes trade elements – German technology for Russian natural resources.

1939 (September) – The Second World War begins with Britain and France's declaration of war on Germany when their forces invade Poland. Soviet propaganda characterises the conflict as a war between imperialist nations in which ordinary workers have no interest – the same explanation (under quite different circumstances) given by Lenin and other left socialists for the First World War, and a change from their popular front anti-fascist policies that lent support to the Spanish Republicans in the 1936–38 period. This is a confusing and difficult period for Comintern supporters, especially in countries occupied and threatened by Nazi Germany.

1939 (November) – 'Winter War' with Finland. Another instance of the USSR using the pact with Germany (who have not agreed this action) to try to resolve border territory and security issues that had lurked since the Revolution and the Civil War. The existing border was close to the Soviet Union's second city Leningrad, and rendered it vulnerable to attack. The war aim is to push the border westwards, and came about after failed negotiations that would have seen territory swapped peacefully. The invading Red Army meets stiff resistance despite its overwhelming numbers and suffers great losses. A peace agreement is made in March 1940 that gives the USSR much of what it seeks. It is, however, thrown out of the League of Nations, and the episode sends a message to other world powers that demonstrates the USSR as aggressive in extending its territory, but that its Red Army is actually poor in quality – an observation not lost on Hitler.

1941 (June) – 'Operation Barbarossa' – the Nazi invasion of the USSR. The long prepared for invasion takes place over the shortest night of the year, taking advantage of the maximum daylight. Using Blitzkrieg tactics that had seen success in France and the low countries the previous year, Hitler's military planners are counting on quick success that will capture western Russia, including Moscow and Leningrad, and the oilfields of the Caucasus, by the Autumn. So confident are they of success that winter clothing is missing from the planning. German war aims range from the practical – the capture of the vast food producing areas of the western USSR and oil fields of the Caucasus – to the ideological. The latter involves reducing and enslaving the inferior Slav populations, repopulating their homelands with ethnic German settlers, ending communist ideology by murdering its leaders and principal adherents, and exterminating all Jewish inhabitants of the occupied regions. Bitter and costly war on the Eastern Front is continuous until Germany's defeat in May 1945, resulting in the deaths of an estimated 27 million Soviet citizens.

1941 (July) – the start of the 'Anglo-Soviet Alliance'. Instigated by Winston Churchill, the British Prime Minister, the alliance involves the continuous supply of weapons and other materials to the USSR for the duration of the war. Churchill, communism's implacable enemy, realises that the immediate threat to the nation comes from Hitler and resolves to ally with 'the devil himself if needs be' to seek his defeat. In August, Churchill and President Roosevelt of the USA sign an agreement that becomes known as the Atlantic Charter, setting out their vision of the post-war world order, although the Americans are not yet involved directly in the conflict. This changes in December 1941, after the Japanese bombing of the US Fleet at Pearl Harbor, leading to Hitler declaring war on the USA. President Roosevelt formally joins what is now a 'Grand Alliance' with Churchill and Stalin. The US and UK leaders realise that keeping the USSR fighting the Axis armies

British Ministry of Information booklet 1941. (*Author's collection*)

gives them the greatest chance of success on the fronts they control. Stalin and his supporters press from an early stage for a 'Second Front' to ease pressure on the Red Army. This is not forthcoming until late 1942. when an Anglo-American force invade Northwest Africa, a relatively inconsequential theatre of war. This is followed the next year by Allied landings across the Mediterranean to Sicily and then Italy. The Allied invasion of Northwest Europe does not take place until the Normandy Landings in June 1944. While this is welcomed by Stalin, and at last sees significant moves of German troops from Russia to France, his suspicion remains that this is a deliberate stall to save American and British lives at the expense of Soviet ones.

1942 (July) – Convoy PQ17 to Murmansk largely destroyed by enemy action. Amid unsubstantiated and incorrect reports that the German battleship *Tirpitz* is heading in the direction of this Russian-bound convoy, the First Lord of the Admiralty, Sir Dudley Pound, orders his Royal Navy escort fleet to abandon the convoy, which is then ordered to scatter. German aircraft and submarines pick off the merchant ships one by one – sinking twenty-four out of thirty-five, along with their valuable cargoes of war materials and much needed supplies. This is the Royal Navy's worst moment of the war and results in Soviet feelings of betrayal and abandonment, especially with the delays in the launch of a second front. After PQ17, convoys are largely restricted to winter sailing only, when the awful weather and darkness offer some protection from enemy attack, but substantially reduces convoy numbers.

1943 (February) – the German 6th Army Capitulates at Stalingrad. The bitterly contested four-month battle results in total defeat for the Germans and the capture of over 100,000 troops. After Stalingrad the Germans and their allies on the Eastern Front encounter no further easy victories and the Red Army gradually pushes them out of Soviet territory after a further two years of constant battle. This is the most significant turning point in the war in Europe.

1943 (November) – Tehran Conference. The Big Three: Stalin, Roosevelt and Churchill, meet in person together for the first time and agree on immediate strategy for winning the war. A commitment is given for the invasion of Northwest Europe (the long awaited second front) in May 1944 (D-Day takes place on 6 June 1944).

1944 (October) – Moscow Conference between Churchill and Stalin. Here an informal but recorded agreement about post-war 'spheres of influence' is reached between the two leaders, known as the 'percentages agreement', and based on a proposal drawn up by Churchill on a scrap of paper. Neither leader seeks the consent of the peoples concerned for their secret settlement.

1944 (December) – British Forces land in Greece to quell the threat of a communist influenced takeover of power. From the large areas they already control, the popular communist-influenced resistance sweep into the vacuum left in the wake of German withdrawal. In Athens they meet British troops tasked with ensuring the right-wing government-in-exile is restored. Stalin stands by his 'percentages agreement' and does not intervene. After some fighting, a hasty truce is arranged that leaves sufficient bitterness for civil war to erupt in 1946 in which the Americans back the government, and the communists, who are eventually defeated in 1948, are supplied by the Yugoslavs (acting as Soviet proxies).

1945 (February) – Yalta Conference. The 'Big Three' wartime leaders meet again to seek public agreement about the post-war settlement in Europe. Zones are agreed for the post-war occupation of Germany and a commitment given to restore original governments to the countries liberated from Nazi occupation, excepting Poland (where an administration sympathetic to the Soviets would be installed rather than the government-in-exile in London), Romania and Hungary (whose governments had been on the Axis side). It is also agreed that dislocated civilians will be returned to their countries of origin. A principle is accepted that national governments should be freely elected through the will of the people.

Red Army and US Army soldier meet in Torgau, Germany, April 1945. (*Wm Poulson via Wikimedia Commons*)

1945 (May) – the War ends within a week or so of the fall of Berlin to the Red Army. On the Allied side there is already fear and suspicion of the intentions of the Soviets, although the Red Army sticks to agreements and its forces meet the advancing armies from the West as previously agreed. In August the war with Japan ends after the explosion of two nuclear bombs by the USA over the cities of Hiroshima and Nagasaki. These atomic weapons were only made known to the Soviets at the Potsdam Conference (see next paragraph), but had been known to Stalin through his agents for some time.

1945 (July/August) – the Potsdam Conference of the Big Three. This finalises the division of Germany and Austria into zones occupied by the Soviets, the USA, Britain and France, including the moving westwards of its eastern border. The capitals Berlin and Vienna will also be broken up into four zones. It also agrees on the manner in which Germany will be de-nazified and de-militarised, and that war criminals will be put on trial either in a special court in Nuremberg (for the leaders), or in the countries of their crimes. It also agrees reparations to the devastated USSR from their occupied zone, and to the other Allies from the zones they occupy, and sets limits on German economic recovery. Potsdam is not a peace conference (it involves no representatives from defeated Germany) and none takes place to formally settle matters (such as borders) until 1990 after the fall of the Berlin Wall. Potsdam also offers temporary resolution to issues of control in French colonial Indo-China (Vietnam) after the defeat of the Japanese. The power vacuum allows the popular nationalist forces of the Viet-Minh to seize effective control in the North while the French are able to retain nominal control of the South.

1945 (August) – America explodes nuclear weapons in the skies above Hiroshima and Nagasaki. This marks the hasty first and only use to date of such bombs in war. This demonstration of American power is designed primarily to weigh decisions over the post-war world in favour of US interests, as the military significance by this stage of the war is questionable. This, however, is not how it turns out; there is now an imbalance between the greatest powers in the world that almost inevitably, leads to competition and the threat of war.

1945 (December) – Conference of Foreign Ministers in Moscow agrees an American proposal to divide Korea along the 38th parallel. Korea, a sovereign nation historically, has been subject to Japanese occupation since 1910. Their surrender sees the power vacuum being filled in the North by the Red Army, and in the South by the US Army. This temporary solution pending elections becomes semi-permanent as the two portions of the country head in different ideological directions; in the North Kim Il-Sung, a Manchurian-born Officer in the USSR's Red Army, is selected by Stalin to take power. In the South, the conservative Syngman Ree is chosen by the US to lead the country. Both are equally brutal in consolidating their control of their respective portions of Korea. Both have designs backed by their respective sponsors, to unite the country again along their respective ideological lines.

1947 (March) – Truman Doctrine. US President Harry S. Truman changes the non-interventionist post-war direction of US foreign policy to stem what is interpreted as Soviet expansion. This has immediate effect in Greece and Turkey where right-wing governments are aided economically to quell communist insurrection.

1947 (December) – the American and British occupiers of Germany unite their zones into a 'Bizone'. This follows failure to agree with the Soviets about uniting all of Germany; the Soviets favour a neutralised, united country, and resent the unilateral moves to create a new Germany along pro-capitalist western lines enacted in the US and UK controlled areas. A watershed moment is reached when a new currency (the Deutschmark) is created in the Bizone without Soviet agreement. In August 1948 the Soviets retaliate by blocking all land connections to the zones of Berlin controlled by the British, French and Americans. The blockade, however, is successfully broken by massive effort from the air, and surrounded Berliners are provided with food through the winter of 1949–49. The Soviets give up this tactic in May 1949; it has only served to unite pro-Western influence in the country, with France joining the Bizone to make it a Trizone. In May 1949 the Trizone is formally declared the self-governing Federal Republic of Germany (FDR or West Germany), with its capital in Bonn. The Western Allies agree to the creation of this new state but hold onto formal control of West Berlin. The German Democratic Republic (DDR or East Germany) is formally constituted in October 1949.

1948 (April) – Marshall Plan. This extends the Truman doctrine of the previous year, the US Congress agrees to a proposal, officially known as the *European Recovery Plan*, drawn up by General George Marshall, to bolster European economies and ward off communism through massive financial aid. The programme lasts until replacement in 1952.

1949 (April) – Formation of the North Atlantic Treaty Organisation. Originating with an Anglo-French mutual defence agreement against any future threat from the USSR and Germany, the alliance grows to include other European nations and is reformed in 1949 to incorporate twelve countries, including the USA and Canada on the other side of the Atlantic. In response, the Soviet Union create a military alliance with the European nations under their influence which becomes the formalised Warsaw Pact in 1955 in reaction to West Germany's admission to NATO.

1949 (August) – the USSR tests its first nuclear bomb. Equilibrium of destructive force is now restored between East and West, and the arms races begins in earnest.

1949 (October) – the proclamation of the People's Republic of China. China had never been a united country in recent history and had been further divided after Japanese invasion in 1937. The invasion resulted in the emergence of the Communist Party under Mao Zedong as a strong resistance force who controlled a large area of the country after the defeat of the Japanese in 1945. The Nationalist Kuomintang under Chiang Kai-Shek had nominally governed the country before 1937 and were supported by the victorious Allies to resume control in 1945. Civil war with the Communists ensued, resulting in victory for Mao's popular movement in 1949, this coming as a surprise to the Americans and British. The Chinese communists have achieved their victory with little support from the USSR, although Mao declares allegiance to Stalin as the prime leader of the world communist movement.

1950 (June) – start of the Korean War with the invasion of the South by the North. Stalin sanctions this action believing (after the acceptance of changes in China) that there will be no significant international reaction. However, the Americans, in the guise of the United Nations and with other foreign forces (including the UK), roll back initial Communist success after a seaborne landing. The Americans quickly advance into North Korea almost as far as the Chinese border, escalating the conflict to involve Chinese troops and covert Soviet forces. Consequent rapid American retreat ends in prolonged stalemate around the area of the 38th Parallel. Actual combat continues until an armistice is finally signed in June 1953.

1953 (August) – overthrow of Mohammed Mossadegh, Prime Minister of Iran. Organised by military forces directly backed by Britain and the USA, this sets back democracy and consolidates the absolute rule of the Shah who is friendly to Western interests. In particular it heads off planned nationalisation of the oil industry, owned by the Anglo-Iranian Oil Company (later known as BP) and any possibility of closer relations with the neighbouring USSR.

1954 (May) – Ho Chi Minh's nationalist Viet Minh forces defeat the French Army at Dien Bien Phu ending French rule in Indo-China. The subsequent Geneva peace conference divides the colonially controlled region into four self-governing countries: North and South Vietnam, Laos and Cambodia. The division of Vietnam is contentious from the outset as the Viet Minh had effectively controlled most of the countryside of South Vietnam, where the new government is heavily backed by the USA.

1955 (April). At a conference in Indonesia hosted by President Sukharno, 29 Asian and African countries agree a declaration known as the *Ten Principles of Bandung* which charts a course for non-alignment with either superpower, based on non-agression and peaceful co-existence.

1956 (February) – 20th Congress of the CPSU. Soviet Premier Khrushchev appears to mark out a new direction for world communism and the USSR, by telling delegates in detail about his predecessor Stalin's crimes and despotism. Although secret, the speech quickly finds its way into the worldwide public arena.

1956 (October) – Hungarian Revolution. Sparked by a liberalisation through the year that opened discussion and criticism, student demonstrations quickly explode into open armed revolt against what is viewed as Soviet inspired repression and control. After some apparent prevarication the uprising is brutally put down by Soviet troops in November. After some hope inspired by the 'Secret Speech' earlier in the year, the Hungarian events lead to widespread disillusion in the West with the policies of the USSR, and mass resignations from communist parties.

1956 (October) – Suez Crisis. Post-colonial regime change across North Africa comes to a head when the nationalist government of Egypt, led by Gamal Abdul Nasser, nationalises the Suez Canal, seen by the former colonial powers of Britain and France as a direct threat to their interests. Against the wishes of the USA (and the Soviet Union) they invade in alliance with Israel. Military victory by the three is quickly followed by political defeat on the world stage, humiliation and withdrawal. What Hungary did for illusions in the Soviet Union, Suez, simultaneously did for illusions in Britain and Empire.

Budapest, Hungary 1956 – decapitated Stalin. (*G. Racz via Wikimedia Commons*)

1957 (October) – Launch of Sputnik. The USSR surprises the world with its assertion of technical and scientific supremacy through the launch of the world's first satellite into space, leaving their US rivals behind by some distance.

1958 (January) – Eisenhower Doctrine. Designed explicitly to combat the threat of 'international communism' in the Middle East (as typified by Egypt's Nasser) military help is offered to any national government who feel threatened internally or externally.

1958 (July) – Lebanon Crisis. International tensions in the strategically important and oil rich Middle East increase when the weak and tainted pro-US government of Lebanon invokes assistance under the Eisenhower Doctrine. US military intervention, based on their massive 6th Fleet presence in the Mediterranean, is used to head off opposition thought to be promoting Soviet interests.

1961 (April) – Yuri Gagarin of the USSR becomes the first human to travel in space. This again confirms the Soviet lead in space technology and accelerates the US space programme in what has become a battleground for ideological as well as technical supremacy. As if to rub salt in the wounds of the USA, American spy plane pilot Gary Powers, whose U-2 plane was shot down over the USSR, is placed on very public trial.

Yuri Gagarin and Fidel Castro celebrate Communist progress, Cuba 1961. (*Unknown origin Wikimedia Commons*)

1961 (June) – Berlin Crisis. The USSR had for some time been pressing for an end to the shared governance of Berlin (the city lay well within the boundaries of East Germany – the DDR) and for the withdrawal of all Western forces. Failure in negotiations resulted in an ultimatum from Khrushchev that all American British and French forces had to vacate Berlin by 31 December, when the USSR would make a separate peace treaty with the DDR that would hand them back control of Berlin. Although US President Kennedy concedes the division of the city and the end of rights of entry of forces to one another's zones of control, he refuses to back down on rights in the Western controlled zones of the city. The Soviets respond by bringing forward plans to build a physical barrier around the Western zones that would isolate them from the Eastern sector and the DDR. A serious military standoff quickly develops during which Soviet and US tanks confront each other before Kennedy and Khrushchev agree to de-escalate and withdraw their tanks in November, leaving the wall dividing the city. Towards the end of the period of crisis, the CPSU holds its 22nd Congress, celebrating what, in hindsight, should be regarded as the zenith of Soviet post-war achievement.

1961 (September) – Founding of the *Non-Aligned Movement* (NAM). Initiated by Tito's Yugoslavia, the NAM is an attempt to formally bring together nations that did not want to be associated closely with either of the Cold War power blocs, but who wanted to exert global influence. This builds on the 1955 Bandung Conference. It initially involves twenty-five countries as diverse as Cuba, India and Saudi-Arabia. The US regard it as generally threatening to their global interests, even though some countries were much closer to them than the USSR. The latter welcomes the development as it provides opportunity for influence; throughout NAM's history during the Cold War, several countries such as Cuba were ostensibly non-aligned but clearly in the Soviet Camp with their active support of anti-Western popular liberation movements.

1962 (October) – Cuba Missile Crisis. A popular revolution in Cuba had overthrown the US backed dictatorship of Batista in 1959, installing a government regarded as hostile by the Americans. In 1961 President Kennedy authorises support for an attempt at military invasion by Cuban exiles based in the USA, which is easily defeated by Cuban government forces. This serves to further push the Cuban government into ideological, economic and military alliance with the USSR. As Cuba is only ninety miles from the US Coast this is seen by the US government as an overwhelming threat. In 1962 the USSR secretly moves strategic nuclear weapons to defend Cuba, mirroring similar US missile sites in Turkey on their own southern border. The Americans discover these plans and show the world photographs of constructions sites for missile launching, and place their forces on a war footing to prevent the further import

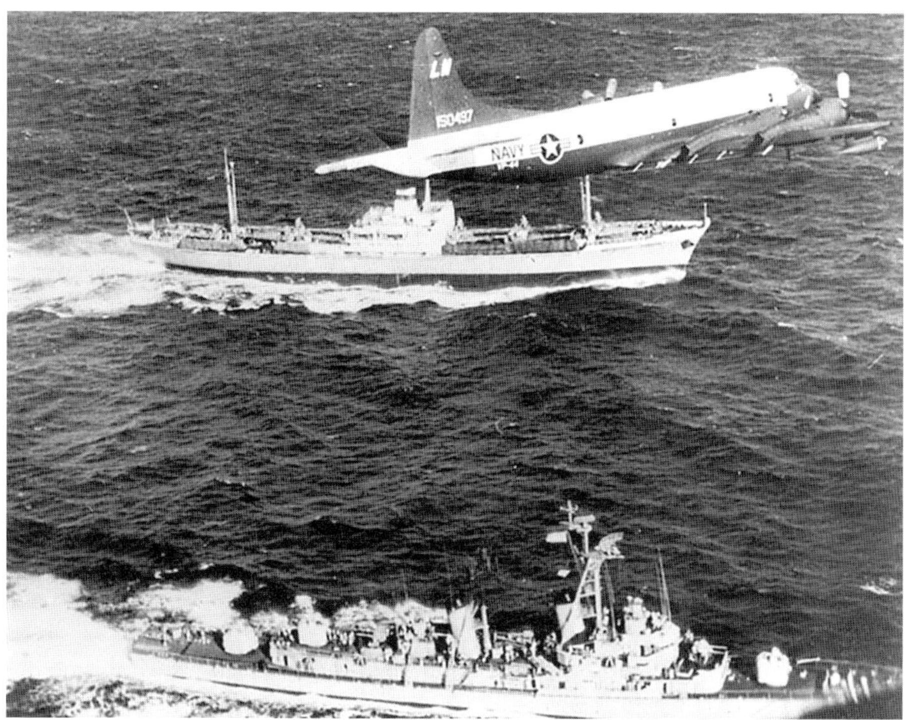

Soviet ship shadowed by US aircraft and warship carrying missiles en route to Cuba 1962. (*US Navy via Wikimedia Commons*)

of Soviet missiles to Cuba and force the removal of those already there. As the world teeters on the edge of nuclear war, secret agreement is reached between Kennedy and Khrushchev that de-escalates and ends the crisis.

1964 (October) – Leonid Brezhnev replaces Khrushchev as Soviet Leader. The tempestuous Khrushchev was seen as a liability by other Soviet leaders after the crises that almost led to world war in 1961 and 1962. He is replaced while on holiday, his successor being a quieter consensus-seeker internally. Brezhnev's rule for the next eighteen years is characterised by 'détente' in the nuclear arms race with the West, stability at home, the broadening of Soviet influence abroad, and the consolidation of power in Eastern Europe. It is also marked by stagnation – both economically and politically – an inheritance that bodes ill for his successors.

1968 (May) – Student protests and unrest in the Western World. Against a background of increased US military intervention and stalemate in South Vietnam, students across the Western world, led in many cases by 'new left' leaders not controlled by the USSR, revolt against Western decadence, war and capitalism. This is especially pronounced in France where workers (including

Soviet leaders Leonid Brezhnev. (*CIA via Wikimedia Commons*)

those led by the influential Communist Party) briefly take part in the events that culminate in a new government and some reforms, but no revolutionary change. The widespread dissent promotes the process of US military disengagement in Vietnam. It also leads to renewed protest around other long-standing social justice issues; from the oppression of Afro-Americans in the USA, to civil rights in Northern Ireland. In Czechoslovakia, Soviet domination is temporarily suspended, and reforms instituted, but, like Budapest in 1956, military intervention by the Warsaw Pact in August brings the nation back into line, ending the 'Prague Spring'.

1969 (November) – Strategic Arms Limitation Talks (SALT) commence in Helsinki, Finland, between the USA and USSR. This results in a 1972 agreement to limit numbers and types of weapons. Further talks led to SALT 2 in 1979 which seeks to actually reduce nuclear stockpiles, but it is never ratified due to the election of Ronald Reagan to US Presidency in 1980, and the Soviet invasion of Afghanistan.

1973 (November) – Military Coup in Chile. Secretly but heavily supported by the USA, fascist military leaders violently overthrow the elected Marxist government of Salvador Allende, murdering his active supporters, jailing and exiling others. Allende dies in an air raid by British-made Hawker Hunter fighter-bombers of the Chilean Air Force, some of which are later grounded because of boycott action taken by workers undertaking engine refurbishment in East Kilbride, Scotland. The revulsion in the USA at its government's actions in Chile lead to even more covert and illegal attempts to destabilise the popular left-wing Sandinista government in Nicaragua a few years later, and support for fascist thugs who ensure El Salvador remains a pro-US dictatorship. President Reagan later legalised US support for such forces in El Salvador and Guatemala.

1974 (April) – Portugal's 'Carnation' Revolution. Spurred by the pointless carnage of colonial wars to defend Portugal's empire in Angola and Mozambique, a group of young army officers inspire a coup that deposes the long-standing right-wing dictatorship. The popular revolution is heavily influenced by the country's Communist Party, but hesitancy on their part (and by their Soviet backers) in the face of international US-inspired reaction, results in compromise and the institution of a democracy that is not seen as threatening by Western interests.

1975 (April) the end of the war in Vietnam. US forces have effectively withdrawn as a result of the Paris Peace Agreement in 1973, leaving the beleaguered and

US Troops resting in Vietnam April 1968. (*D. Kurpius via Wikimedia Commons*)

unpopular government in South Vietnam to fight on alone. North Vietnamese troops eventually complete their victory on 30 April, forcing a humiliating evacuation of the last US representatives by helicopter from the roof of the US Embassy in Saigon. The pro-US regimes in Laos and Cambodia soon fall too, being replaced in the latter by Khmer Rouge revolutionaries almost unique in their brutality, who are themselves overthrown by the Vietnamese Army in 1979. The ignominious end to US attempts to retain hegemony in Southeast Asia spurs Soviet enthusiasm for supporting regime change elsewhere.

1979 (December) – Soviet invasion of Afghanistan. In an effort to support an unstable pro-Soviet government in Afghanistan the USSR sends large numbers of troops across the border and invades the country. The government however is unpopular, particularly outside the major cities, because of reforms that threaten long standing tribal and religious interests. A long and bloody war mounted by guerrillas easily able to hide among the population ensues, ending only when the Soviets withdraw in 1989. The various anti-Soviet guerrilla groups are armed by the West and their religious fundamentalism encouraged, especially by the USA; their weaponry is later used against their original suppliers in the subsequent wars that continue for years to come.

1980 (September) – Birth of the 'Solidarity' (*Solidarnosc*) trade union in Poland. Unrest over food prices bolstered by a combination of other factors, results in strikes among shipyard and other industrially powerful workers, leading to the emergence of Lech Walesa and a leadership who declare the formation of the free (i.e. not state controlled) trade union *Solidarnosc*. After initial toleration it is supressed, and its leaders interned, but re-emerges as a major opposition to the pro-Soviet regime.

1980 (November) – Election of Ronald Reagan to US Presidency. Former film star and fiercely anti-communist Reagan is elected on a promise of ending détente by confronting and beating down the threat from the Soviet Union. He finds a willing ally in Britain's Prime Minister Margaret Thatcher, and commences a risky, but ultimately successful strategy of outspending the USSR and taking advantage of its economic problems.

1983 (October) – US Invasion of Grenada. Ostensibly mounted against this tiny island republic to stabilise the country and protect US citizens working there, this is a contrived action whose purpose is to test Soviet resolve to defend a friendly government in the Central America/Caribbean region which the US regards as within its immediate sphere of influence. The gamble pays off and Reagan's hawkish advisers promote a policy of increasing pressure on the Soviet Union and end the Cold War on their terms.

1985 (March) – Mikhail Gorbachev becomes First Secretary of the CPSU. Charismatic and relatively young by the standards of his immediate predecessors, Gorbachev is faced with immense pressures from both within and beyond the USSR's borders to reform. His popularity helps him persuade his colleagues on the Central Committee to deal with the country's problems, and save the socialist project, through 'perestroika' (restructuring) and 'Glasnost' (openness). This includes arms reduction agreements beyond anything previously imagined and increasing freedoms for those whose aspirations were held in check by the tight controls of previous regimes. It also includes market reforms and the reduction of centralised control of the economy. All this begins an irreversible process that rapidly overtakes Gorbachev's plans and ideas to renew the Bolshevik ideal.

Mikhail Gorbachev's book *Glasnost* 1987. (*Author's collection*)

1989 (July) – Free elections in Poland. As a consequence of Gorbachev's abandonment of previous tight control of the governments of the Soviet satellite countries on its western and southern borders, the Polish United Worker's Party renounces its monopoly government in April 1989, leading to the first democratic elections in any of these countries since the 1940s. Solidarnosc, who have led massive strikes and demonstrations through 1988, and are now a recognised political party as well as a free trade union umbrella, win a mandate for change, heralding the end of really existing socialism in Poland.

Berlin Wall 1 December 1989. (*A. Van der Drift via Wikimedia Commons*)

1989 (November) – Fall of the Berlin Wall. Hungary's opening of its border with Austria in August 1989 effectively reduces the significance of the Berlin Wall and the tightly policed border between the DDR and West Germany. Popular agitation and a refusal by Gorbachev to back the East German government's initial wish to violently suppress demonstrations and attempts to breach the wall, ends with a confused message to border guards to allow free movement. Once the gates are open, there is no going back, and the border rapidly disappears as an obstacle to movement. The following year, the dream of post-war Western leaders is finally realised when the DDR effectively becomes absorbed by West Germany, uniting the country as a Western style capitalist democracy.

1991 (December) – the formal dissolution of the USSR. The years 1990 and 1991 see a number of the Soviet republics declaring a wish to secede. These include the Baltic Republics of Estonia, Latvia and Lithuania, the large republics of Ukraine, Byelorussia and Georgia, and several central Asian republics. This outbreak of nationalism results in civil war in certain areas where ethnic and religious divides had been supressed by communism, but a peaceful transition in others. A coup in August 1991 by some of the old guard who want to stop these changes is defeated through popular opposition and the loyalty of the majority of the armed forces. By December the USSR has in reality ceased to be an entity and is formally dissolved along with the CPSU. Gorbachev hands over to Boris Yeltsin who becomes the first leader of the new Russian Federation. The most valuable publicly owned assets of the USSR are grabbed by a new breed of Russian entrepreneur who rapidly become millionaire oligarchs. Other public services that had provided welfare support and social security disappear almost overnight. The free market is the dominant force in the new society and the seventy-year attempt to build world communism from a base in the Soviet Union comes to an end that surprises everyone, East and West.

The Red Army mass grave of 8,360 soldiers in Kazimierz Dolny Poland. (*Author*)

Chapter 2

Whose Victory? – The End of the Second World War and the Division of Germany

> A shadow has fallen upon the scenes so lately lighted by the Allied victory. Nobody knows what Soviet Russia and its Communist International organisation intends to do in the immediate future, or what are the limits to their expansive and proselytising tendencies.
>
> Winston Churchill, Fulton, Missouri, 5 March 1946

The Shadow of Bolshevism

The turning point in the struggle against fascism in Germany in the Second World War (or the Great patriotic War as it is tellingly called in Russia), was not Dunkirk, in 1940; El-Alamein in 1942; or even D-Day (the Normandy Invasion) in 1944; it was the outcome of the momentous Battle of Stalingrad at the start of 1943. This is accurately described as the bloodiest battle in history (see Craig, 1973, for a vivid account, and the two novels of Vasily Grossman which lend humanity to the experience of Stalingrad). Its five-month duration cost (estimates vary) almost 800,000 lives on the Soviet side (far more than combined British and American losses for the entire war) and slightly less on the Axis side. At the time this was well recognised in Britain, but within a few years of the war's end, had been replaced in the imagination of Western peoples by a different account of the conflict in which the other allies, particularly the USA, were the victors. The seeds of this were sewn while the war was underway, the subject of this chapter.

To trace why such a change occurred we need to go much further back – at least as far as 1917 and the revolution that changed Russia, and created a threat to the rest of the capitalist world that was to last for more than eighty years. The threat of insurrection from below had always preoccupied ruling classes in developing societies, from the time of the Spartacus slave rebellion in Ancient Rome and on throughout human history. From the mid-nineteenth century onwards revolutions were inspired by the ideas of socialism, developed, above all others, by Karl Marx. The danger of modern socialist revolution was dealt with in different ways – from accommodation and assimilation in the European democracies (and the USA) through to direct suppression and terror in the autocracies such as Imperial Russia. In all these instances the enemy was one that was within, and could be tackled internally by whatever means seemed appropriate. The Russian Revolution changed that – as the self-proclaimed beacon of world revolution the Soviet Union now became an external enemy state. It also represented a renewed and encouraged internal one, with committed idealists promoting its aims and values directed and guided by the organisation of world communists, the Communist International (or Comintern) formed in 1919. This terrified the capitalist states who combined to intervene militarily in the Russian Civil War that they fomented in support of the displaced ruling classes. That was always a half-hearted effort as it had little support at home from countries emerging from the carnage of the First World War. By 1921 the foreign armies had all withdrawn and the ravaged new state of the USSR triumphed through the determination of its people and their chosen ruling Communist Party.

Changes in the Soviet Union, unlike those that follow palace revolutions, impacted upon every area of society and every individual; private ownership was entirely replaced by state ownership and control, and private property was replaced by common ownership. Most of the small but previously powerful displaced ruling classes leaving their country by the end of the civil war. The head of the tiger was brutally cut off with the murder of the Czar and his family in 1918. Experiments immediately got underway to organise society more equitably and for the benefit of workers and peasants (the latter's needs and aspirations were soon given a distant second place). Education, science and the arts were all overhauled and responsibility for them handed over to state planners and idealists. It is hard to imagine the impact this had across the world; those who had preached socialism and the overthrow of the ruling classes now had an example to point to and follow.

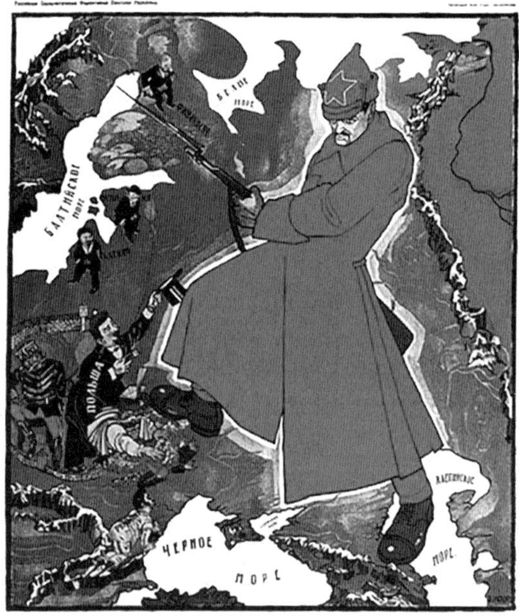

USSR poster from 1920 showing Trotsky towering over capitalist Europe. (*Dmitry Moor via Wikimedia Commons*)

The period after the First World War was unstable, and what happened in Russia was attempted elsewhere. Revolt and revolution were obvious reactions to the senseless slaughter to which the major powers had all subjected their people. In Germany serious armed revolt took place in 1919 and in cities from Barcelona to Glasgow, there were strikes of varying degrees that were often led by admirers of the Bolsheviks. None, however, were successful in overthrowing government and by the time the world situation settled (albeit temporarily due to the punitive terms of the Versailles Peace Treaty), the Soviet Union stood alone. Lenin, the political leader of the Bolsheviks, had always said that the revolution in Russia depended on successful communist uprisings in the more advanced capitalist countries. When this did not happen, he was forced to compromise to save what had been gained – state ownership was relaxed in the countryside to revive the economy, and economic assistance from outside happily accepted. His early death in 1923 after a period of incapacitation resulted in a power struggle won through cool calculation and vicious manoeuvring, by Joseph Stalin who had captured dictatorial control of the Soviet Union by the end of the decade. Stalin was to exercise absolute control over the lives and fortunes of his people until his death in 1953 when the Cold War was well underway.

Although he maintained a style of Marxist rhetoric that echoed Lenin, Stalin was ruthless in his abandonment of the principles of humanity and common good that had always governed the socialist movement. His policies at home created as many problems as they solved, and millions suffered through death and privation. His economic recovery programme designed to help the USSR catch up with the Western industrial nations in just a few years rested on slave labour recruited through the creation of a paranoid society where everyone was afraid, and jobs and favours were bestowed on those who turned in workmates, friends and neighbours. Arrest and imprisonment followed anyone considered to be acting against the interest of the state (protection against which was an ominous omission in an otherwise all-embracing new constitution published in 1936). By the end of the 1930s Stalin had judiciously (or in many cases without any process at all) murdered anyone who might offer serious or even potential opposition. This included many talented and committed communists, and seriously imperilled the military as well as industry and infrastructure such as the railways. The generation of idealists who had made the 1917 revolution were almost destroyed and, in their place, rapidly grew a new layer of technocrats and planners who owed everything to Stalin.

Britain's foreign policy towards the USSR regarded it as a threat for most of the 1920s and 1930s, trade deals were never lasting or especially significant. Covert activities took place from both sides, but after the late 1920s the Soviet Union were lukewarm about their commitment to international revolution. Foreign policy, which went through several dramatic turns, was driven by the internal requirement to build up the industrial and food self-sufficiency of the USSR. From the early 1930s the USSR recognised that the greatest threat to their existence lay in the rise of the Nazi Party in Germany, whose rhetoric was fiercely anti-communist and anti-Soviet. The USSR supported the Spanish government's doomed resistance to the Italian and German fascist uprising by Franco while the main democracies stood by, and as the 1930s ended, actively pursued an alliance with Britain and France against the threat from Germany. The Munich settlement of 1938, notorious for its appeasement of Hitler, effectively renounced the interest of Britain and other governments in Eastern Europe, apart from Poland (Fleming 1961). It confirmed rejection of Soviet attempts by the USSR to form an effective anti-fascist alliance right up until the eve of war in 1939. By, this time the USSR had little choice other than to reach an agreement about non-aggression that put off war in the East, at least for a while. The deal also allowed Stalin to deal with territorial and border security issues that had lurked in the background since the early 1920s. The Baltic States were taken back into Soviet control after a brief period of independence, but a military campaign to recover disputed territory in Finland was less successful. Territories in the Ukraine seized by Poland during the Civil War in 1921 were also retaken. To forestall future resistance to the latter, Stalin had thousands of members of the Polish Officer Corps, who had been swept up as his armies moved westwards into Polish Ukraine, murdered in the forests of Western Russia. This was a crime that was only admitted to in the present century.

By 1941 the pact between the USSR and Germany was looking shaky. The Red Army had not completed its recovery from the effects of the 1930s purges and was not ready for the inevitable war. Examples of mass-produced modern equipment that were later to play a crucial role in Germany's defeat were the Sturmovik Ground Attack aircraft, only a few dozen of which had been delivered by June 1941, and the T34 tank whose numbers were still only in the hundreds after deliveries started in 1940. The build-up of troops on Stalin's western border did not escape his attention, and neither did intelligence suggesting an invasion was imminent, but he remained determined to avoid provocation right up until the moment of Operation Barbarossa's launch on 22 June. You do not need to be a Stalin apologist to see that the histories which suggest he was taken completely by surprise by the invasion do not accurately portray what happened, even though this became a component of Khrushchev's devastating attack on his reputation in February 1956. Stalin was right in the sense that his defence forces were easily overcome despite the bravery of many of his troops and their leaders. Within a few weeks German armies had occupied Ukraine and Belorussia and were moving towards Moscow and Leningrad, and they captured hundreds of thousands of Red Army soldiers, including Stalin's own son. The Nazis were as cruel and murderous to them in capture as Stalin was in dismissing them as cowards who had failed to fight.

The Wartime Alliance

Churchill described the unity of purpose achieved between the USSR, Great Britain and the USA, after the Nazi invasion of the Soviet Union in 1941, as the 'Grand Alliance', quickly and pragmatically putting aside his long-established hatred of communism and the cause of workers. Nazism, Churchill recognised in a way that has been forgotten in recent years by many, represented a threat to humanity transcending that of communism, demanding mutual support and cooperation on a level that would have seemed unthinkable in the years following the Russian Revolution. This was particularly noticeable in Britain, whose anti-communism had been driven by a need to retain economic prominence achieved through its shakily held Empire. In contrast, the USA had followed a foreign policy characterised by isolationism since the end of the First War, so this change was perhaps not so dramatic.

The new spirit caught the imagination of ordinary people in the countries of the Alliance, with anti-Soviet rhetoric giving way to widespread understanding and acceptance of the USSR as a vital ally across society. Churchill's wife, Clementine, became in his words, 'thoroughly Sovietized', and raised millions of pounds to provide hospitals and medical aid in the beleaguered USSR through her *Red Cross for Russia* campaign. In the USA and the dominions of Canada, Australia and New Zealand, unity with the Soviet Union was also celebrated and the battles on the Eastern Front followed closely.

The Stalingrad victory in early 1943 was greeted with acclaim and no little amount of gratitude – after all, its calamitous nature had been born entirely by the Russian people with no direct casualties among Allied troops. In Britain, King George VI had a special jewel-encrusted sword struck that toured the country before being handed over to Stalin at the Tehran Conference in November. Soviet propaganda poured into the West, much of it in tune with the social democratic idea that the people being asked to make all the sacrifices needed a better world to fight for; the consequent ideas about a welfare state and social improvement had a particular impact in Britain where they contributed to a Labour election victory in the Summer of 1945. The drips of information that had reached the West about the Stalin terror of the 1930s were overlooked in favour of the image of a kindly 'Uncle Joe'. (I have covered this period in detail in *The Anglo-Soviet Alliance*).

Meanwhile, as the Western allies fought in North Africa and then across the Mediterranean to Italy, the Red Army was fighting continuously across a front of thousands of miles in battles of greater scale and brutality. Areas of conflict, such as that in the Rzhev where fighting continued for fourteen months between 1942 and 1943, were more reminiscent of the carnage of the previous world war and its trench warfare, than the modern mobile warfare normally associated with the Second World War. There was no time to bury bodies properly, and for years after the war they still littered the former battlefields, and many are still recovered to this day. Not for nothing was it given the horrific title of the 'Rzhev Meat-Grinder'. The siege of Leningrad that took a terrible toll on the civilian population in its first year started in September 1941, and was not lifted until January 1944, by which time an estimated 1.5 million Soviet citizens and soldiers had died, reducing the population from a previous 3.5 million to some 700,000. Nothing on this scale took place in any other theatre of the war in Europe. On 'Red Army Day', 23 February 1944, sincerely and popularly celebrated in the USA and UK as it had been in 1942 and 1943, the US Vice President Henry Wallace declared:

> We have seen a mighty people achieve a sacrificial singleness of purpose in this war which is unique in human history. From a defensive struggle against the horrors of aggression, the Russian armies have moved forward to a powerful offensive war for liberty.
>
> Quoted in Horrabin 1944 p.53

How such attitudes would change within the next year!

Calls for a Second Front to relieve the pressure on the Red Army started in mid-1941 and reached a crescendo in 1942, when mass rallies in the UK

Stalin, Churchill and Roosevelt 'the Big Three' Teheran 1943. (*US Army via Wikimedia Commons*)

made the call, led by popular figures such as Sir Stafford Cripps and Lord Beaverbrook. There is still debate about why the invasion of occupied Northern Europe from the West was delayed until mid-1944. Western historians echo Churchill's publicly stated view at the time that the necessary build-up of troops, aircraft and ships could not be achieved earlier, given the needs of other battle fronts and the lessons from the commando raids on the French coast of 1942; Soviet historians argued that the Western powers wanted to weaken the Red Army and save their own troops from battle losses. They point to the fact that even after the Normandy Invasion, the Allied forces (forty-three divisions) were facing sixty-five German divisions, while in the East, the Red Army continued to face some 235 Axis divisions (Zaitsev 1979). They do, however, acknowledge the importance of the Allied invasion of June 1944 and its contribution to final victory.

Post-war planning commenced within the respective leaderships at an early stage. Stalin wanted recognition of the USSR's 1941 borders, i.e., inclusion of eastern Poland within Ukraine with compensation by an expansion westward into German Pomerania, and some further territorial weakening of Germany, including the creation of a new Austrian state. Recent histories of the period (e.g. Gellately 2013), based on interpretation of material uncovered in former Soviet archives since 1991, make play of Stalin's 'secret' intentions to spread communist influence throughout Europe. This reinforces the Cold War narrative of Soviet expansionism and the continuation of the 1917 ideological pledge to create world communism. This became an obsession for Churchill and Western military leaders as the war reached its climax with Soviet victories spreading westwards. However, the evidence suggests that the Soviet intention was always to secure its western borders, just as it openly declared, and that any Marxist rhetoric about ending capitalism was just that – designed for the home and international audience who expected such verbal commitments. The Western leaders of course never ceased their own ideology of capitalism as the ideal for the entire world.

The Western Allies had laid out their post-war designs through the Atlantic Charter before the US had even joined the war but when, in August 1941, most of Europe was under Nazi occupation. This agreement about a set of principles for international relations and national self-determination was initially laid out by Roosevelt and Churchill, but was soon signed by twenty-six of the free nations of the world, including the Soviet Union, and the exiled governments of those under occupation like Poland. It went on to form the basis for the creation of the United Nations post-war, and made eventual decolonisation an inevitability. Prior to then, its principles were already being breached; in November 1944 Churchill and Stalin agreed spheres of influence in the nations of liberated Europe without consulting anyone in either, and this went on to largely become a reality. Until then their relationship had been marked by mutual suspicion and their cooperation at times limited in nature. The 'percentages' agreement caused particular feelings of betrayal in the case of Poland, for whose independence Britain had gone to war in the first place; its borders were not just shifted unilaterally in 1945, but Poland's exiled government was delegitimised by the liberating Soviets, and replaced with a handpicked one of their own creation.

By the end of the war Stalin's early objective of securing his borders had gained a certain moral legitimacy; the Soviet Union had been devastated in a Nazi-inspired racial war whose aim was not just occupation and economic exploitation, but contrived and systematic population reduction through murder and enslavement. Nothing like it was experienced in the Western European countries occupied by Hitler's armies – Western Russia, Ukraine and Belorussia lay in ruins and their populations either dead, dislocated or homeless living in holes in the ground. The soldiers of the triumphant Red Army found the opulence and prosperity of Germany almost unbelievable, and the reparations sought by their government seemed a natural and justifiable consequence. After repeated invasions in Russian history across the flat plains of Northern Europe through Poland, there seemed good reason to seek security for the USSR's borders. Much of this was accepted on the surface by Western leaders, but long-harboured suspicions of Soviet intentions soon surfaced. The Red Army advanced, as agreed with its allies, as far as the River Elbe in Germany, but Allied armies, with Wehrmacht collusion (in the sense that they made no effort to oppose them), broke through German lines to meet them on the Baltic Coast in April 1945 out of a genuine belief that they intended to advance into Denmark. This had indeed been discussed internally but had not even progressed as far as Churchill's own plan: 'Operation Unthinkable', to launch a surprise attack on Soviet forces to force an outcome over Poland's borders (Turbett 2021a).

The truth is that the Red Army was exhausted by four years of continual war and the ordinary soldier expected rapid demobilisation once the fascists had been beaten down. The term 'Iron Curtain' to describe the potential limit of Soviet advance into Germany was coined by Nazi propaganda minister Goebbels as part of a deliberate plan to sew dissent between the Western Allies, and play upon fears of Soviet territorial and ideological expansion. His plan did not set the Allies against each other and save Nazi Germany, but the seeds of its message found fertile ground. By 1946 Churchill himself had made this phrase famous enough to be used throughout the Cold War.

How the War Ended – The Place of Allied (and Enemy) Atrocities in Shaping the New World

The war in Europe ended in May 1945 a few days after Soviet forces won, at great cost, the battle for Berlin, the last redoubt of Hitler and his closest cronies. Prior to that, leaders in the West had considered a race to get to Germany's capital first, but eventually decided to leave this symbolic victory to the Red

Army who had done most of the fighting. They might have achieved this goal as fighting on the western front was considerably less ferocious than the continued carnage in the east; by the end of March 1945 the Germans had 170 divisions facing the Red Army, compared with twenty-six facing the British and Americans, most of which were defending the Baltic ports receiving evacuees from the east up until the end (Kolko 1990). Of course, the Allies realised that there might be a terrible battle for Berlin anyway, and so it was; again, Soviet casualties (over 80,000 killed or missing) saved the possibility of Western ones. This wish to avoid casualties is also used to explain Allied atrocities towards the war's end that would seem to outweigh, in their coldly calculated method, those committed quite unjustifiably by individual Red Army units and soldiers against civilians in Berlin and elsewhere.

In February 1945, when victory was assured, Allied bombers devastated the city of Dresden in Germany which was being rapidly approached by the Red Army from the east. The city was not especially strategically important, but had great cultural significance. It did have armament industries and was an important transport centre – although neither were particularly targeted in the indiscriminate attack. It was packed with refugees heading west, away from the advancing Red Army. The American and British raid, involving 1,250 bombers dropping 3,900 tons of high explosive and incendiary, took place over several days and killed an estimated 25,000 civilians, many of whom died in a firestorm that destroyed the city. Discussion among military leaders – including Churchill – prior to the raid, centred on whether it was more significant as a target than other more concentrated industrial areas from which aircraft would have to be diverted to this new target. It was, however, regarded as significant in terms of a continued attempt to unravel German morale at a time when a fight to the death by the Wehrmacht would increase Allied casualties. Such was the justification. Of course, it might have been, as since argued by some historians (e.g. McKee 1982), that the raid was intended to demonstrate to Stalin, whose forces would soon reach the city, how powerful were the bombing fleets of the Allies (at this time the Red Airforce had been developed to primarily aid attacking armies and had few high-altitude bombers). Pauwels (2002) offers evidence to back up this assertion, including the accounts of actors directly involved in the bombing. A witness on the ground was 23-year-old American prisoner of war Kurt Vonnegut, who sat out the raid in the concrete underground slaughterhouse in which he was working. Tasked with helping with the clear-up afterwards, his experiences made him a lifelong admirer (and member) of volunteer fire brigades whose members he considered to represent community spirit and mutual aid at its best. Vonnegut was appalled that the tactic of initial high-explosive bombing forced fire brigade members into shelters so they were unavailable to deal with the incendiaries that were dropped deliberately in their wake. Volunteer fire brigades featured in some of his best-known works, and the firebombing of

Allies bombing an already devastated Dresden February 1945. (*US Air Force via Wikimedia Commons*)

Dresden itself in his classic anti-war sci-fi novel *Slaughter House 5*, a book with a huge influence on the young Cold War generation of the 1960s and 1970s – and not just in the West.

This race to secure supremacy was also evident in the West's dealings with issues surrounding the surrender of German forces in May 1945. With memories of the awful atrocities they had committed in the Soviet Union, the remaining armies in the field were keen to surrender to American and British forces rather than these victims of their crimes. The Allies, driven by Churchill, were just as keen to negate the Soviet role, and their rapid advances into Northern Germany and towards Czechoslovakia in the face of little opposition made their territorial acquisitions seem important compared with the slow, fiercely contested progress of the Red Army. Eisenhower, the Supreme Allied Commander, received an official German surrender on 8 May in Rheims, Northern France, in the presence of relatively minor Soviet representation. Unsurprisingly, the Soviets were unhappy about this after all their sacrifices and insisted on a formal surrender involving all those involved in the alliance the next day in Berlin – the capital of the failed Nazi world domination project – on 9 May, led by Marshall Zhukov. Therefore the end of the war in Europe is celebrated (to this day) on consecutive days East and West.

At the Allied leaders' conference in Tehran in late 1943, Stalin had promised that the Soviet Union would enter the war on Japan three months after the end of the war in Europe. This would give the Red Army time to send forces

US and Red Army troops meet in Torgau, Germany April 1945. (*Bundesarchiv via Wikimedia Commons*)

to the Far East. He eventually held to this promise while his Western allies did all they could in 1945 to ensure this was unnecessary, fearing by this stage the consequences of Soviet involvement in victory in the Pacific (Kolko 1990). Their means of trying to achieve this end remain controversial – the use of the newly developed atomic bomb. This had been under top secret development for several years involving (at an early stage) British and Canadian scientists and engineers, but principally US effort at Los Alamos in New Mexico. This was to be an American weapon that would place them ahead of all their allies as well as their wartime enemies. The initial purpose was to use the new bomb against Hitler, but by May 1945 it had still not been tested. By this time the war in the Pacific – mainly undertaken by US forces, but also involving the British in Burma and Northeast India – was proceeding well, but slowly. This involved very bloody battles as the Japanese were committed to fighting to the death, and their resolve with dwindling forces seemed to harden as the fighting got closer to mainland Japan. The prospect of Allied losses in an invasion of Japan was daunting. However, there were signs in Japan that civilian leaders were beginning to challenge the military and that their realisation that the war was hopeless might result in surrender and avoidance of further bloodshed. By early 1945 Tokyo and other cities were being heavily bombed from the air using an early version of napalm, killing 125,000 inhabitants in one raid on Tokyo (Kolko 1990); the war had reached Japanese territory with the same methods of terror deployed against the civilian population that had been used on German cities including Dresden. Japanese war-crimes and fanatical resistance enabled the Americans to take the moral leap into the territory of 'the end justifying the means', just as had happened with the Allied bombing of civilians in Germany – but now on a new and horrifying basis, where the consequences were largely unknown to science.

The Allied leaders met in Potsdam in July 1945 and between discussions, President Truman (Roosevelt had died in April) advised Stalin that the US had just completed a successful test of the atomic bomb. The Soviets had known about the bomb for some time, details being obtained through several agents working on the project, so this was no surprise to Stalin. Its use on Hiroshima on 6 August was a political rather than a military decision, made to demonstrate American power; had that been the case it might have been used to bomb the very extensive Japanese army in China. Two days later the USSR declared war on Japan, just as promised (and as planned, although brought forward by two days), and engaged the Japanese heavily in Manchuria and Korea, inflicting rapid defeat on the powerful Kwantung Army. This surely meant the Japanese would surrender quickly, but before they had opportunity to consider, the Americans exploded a different type of nuclear bomb over Nagasaki, with again devastating and long-lasting consequences as a result of these experiments involving massive loss of human life. The message to the USSR though was clear, the USA now had the anti-power to call the shots in shaping the post-war world. Japan surrendered unilaterally on 18 August, with Soviet troops already in the Sakhalin islands and ready to invade mainland Japan.

The first ground witness from the West to the horror inflicted upon Hiroshima was the young Australian journalist Wilfred Burchett. He was certainly not anti-British or anti-American at this point, having spent the war frontline-reporting from various areas of the Far East war against Japan. By the spring of 1945 he was working for the London *Daily Express* newspaper; with Japan's capitulation on 14 August, he managed to get a place on one of the first American vessels to land troops there, and once in the bomb-ravaged city of Yokohama, was instructed by his editor to try for an exclusive from Hiroshima. With media attention focusing on the surrender ceremony aboard the US Battleship *Missouri*, Burchett's risky journey there by train on 2 September was in advance of any civilian or military presence, and his only authority was a letter of introduction (and food which was virtually unobtainable) to a Japanese pressman based there who had been transmitting messages by Morse Code. This was highly dangerous, and it was only many years later that a Japanese police officer he had met soon after his arrest on arrival (he was thought to be an escaped POW), told him that he had narrowly avoided being lynched by angry vengeful militiamen. Burchett surveyed acres of the flattened city but was only confronted with the true horror when he visited medical facilities overwhelmed with people, literally and mysteriously, burning up before the eyes of medical staff. In his shocking 'Warning to the World' bulletin published in London on 6 September 1945, he described an 'atomic plague' that was killing people in huge numbers a month after the explosion of the bomb. Initially he was disbelieved by US military leaders in Japan; his story was condemned as Japanese propaganda and an expulsion order was issued. This was withdrawn as the story of this inconvenient truth emerged from other sources, including colleagues who had visited Nagasaki. The confirmation of deaths from radiation sickness were only officially reported several months later, and by 1950 had risen to 300,000. (Information from Burchett 1980, and Burchett and Shimmin 2007 where the entire *Daily Express* report is reproduced).

The war engaged in by the Red Army against the Nazi invaders of their country was brutal but also conventional and involved no weapon-based acts of atrocity. Their war, however, ended with behaviours on the part of many soldiers often cited as barbarous and criminal, but also reflective of official attitudes in the USSR at the time – the mass rape of women as their troops entered German soil, and in Berlin as the war ended. While the numbers involved are indeed

The Palchkoff's neighborhood before the bombing.

The Palchikoff's neighborhood after the bombing.

Hiroshima before and after the atomic bomb explosion. (*Unknown origin Wikimedia Commons*)

horrifying (Beevor 2000 considers 2 million women and child victims a reasonable estimate), sexual violence is a weapon of war used by all armies almost without exception, although not necessarily with official sanction. Indeed, in the Second World War, all the Axis and Allied armies were culpable – sexual violence was not just about sexual gratification, but included a desire to emasculate the enemy by humiliating their women, and revenge for similar crimes committed at home (Burds 2009). In Berlin there seems to have been free reign for rape for the first two weeks after victory, until the stories that were emerging were so awful and widespread that the Red Army hierarchy reacted with harsh orders involving summary execution to end such attacks on civilians. The immediate physical effects were shocking enough (around 100,000 victims reported by the two main Berlin hospitals including 10,000 suicides), but the long-term psychological effects on the victims are incalculable as most shared a silence about their ordeal. The Austrian-born British soldier George Clare stationed in Berlin as an interpreter in 1946–7, discovered that this was such a common experience that the term 'Frau Komm' used by Red Army soldiers to summon their victims, was 'the most effective anti-Soviet and anti-communist slogan ever coined'. (Clare 1989 p.60). One unusual account, given by the Red Army sniper Rosa Shanina in her diaries, briefly and in coded form, describes the aftermath of a fierce battle in East Prussia in January 1945: 'found Frau there. Guys carried them away on tractors etc.'; that night she fended off an attempted rape by an officer who preferred her to 'an infected German girl' (Shanina undated). She was killed a few days later so her subsequent reflections are denied us, and what we do know only emerged with the publication of these diaries, which had been held by a journalist whom she knew, in 1964. There are few victim accounts of the rapes as German women were encouraged after the war to hide their victimhood and only began to talk about their experiences late in life (Anonymous 2005). Red Army soldiers had been fed constant propaganda as they fought westwards that dehumanised their enemy, and this was not unjustified given the scale of barbarity inflicted on their homeland. However, the official line as they conquered enemy territory was to treat their defeated enemy with magnanimity and generosity – partly to deal with the very real attempts by Goebbels and his Nazi propagandists to capitalise on vengeful behaviours and use them to try and divide the Allies (Burds 2009). The impact of the mass rapes is considered by many to have had a lasting significance for Germans (particularly women) that might have been overlooked at the time (Gaddis 1997). This factor frustrated Soviet and native German attempts to popularise communist ideals in the post-war period.

The Post-War Occupation of Germany

The question of how to deal with a defeated Germany had long occupied the minds of the Allied leaders East and West and was the subject of agreements between them when they met together through until the Potsdam Conference in July 1945. At Potsdam itself agreement was reached that the object of the conquering powers was 'not to destroy or enslave the people but to give them the opportunity to prepare for the eventual reconstruction of their life on a democratic and peaceful basis'. (quoted in Gelately 2013, p.290). This was to include disarmament, demilitarisation and denazification. As an initial step, 'Germany as a whole' (as per the pre-1937 borders) was divided into four zones of occupation and administration: the Americans in the south, the British in the northwest, the French in the southwest and the Soviets in the east (bounded by the new border with Poland along the Oder-Neisse line). Berlin was also divided into four zones, agreed to by the occupying Soviets in return for the provinces of Saxony and Thuringia being passed from the American to the Soviet sector. The initial plan was for a central administration that would assume authority for rebuilding the economy and eventually handing over control to an elected German government. This took the form of 'The Allied Control Council', whose aim was to steer Germany back towards self-government. However, from the outset its work was undermined through exploitation of occupied zones by the Soviets and French, who were understandably keen to extract reparations to help with the rebuilding of their war-damaged countries, and no agreement was ever reached about overall government. A Soviet objective also was the removal of shared control of Berlin, which lay well inside the Soviet zone.

'Denazification' was seen as a means to rid Germany and Austria of Nazi ideology by removing its adherents from positions of influence and power within society. The Allied Control Council set up in early 1946, based in Berlin, issued

Joint Allied policing operations, occupied Vienna Summer 1945. (*Author's collection*)

a series of directives on how these objectives would be realised, but interpretation and action varied widely, and not just between the zones of occupation. The problem (or danger) was not former Wehrmacht combatants – millions were being held in prisoner of war camps across Europe, Russia and Canada by that point, and their release was gradual; those held by the British American and Western allies were home by the end of 1948, but those held in the Soviet Union were held in some cases until the mid-1950s (Lowe 2013).

The main issue around denazification concerned the millions of German citizens (8.5 million of whom had been Nazi party members) who had been functionaries at various levels within Nazi Germany. The key part of this programme involved classifying all adults according to their previous history, with exoneration for those who had made no contribution to the Nazi regime. This soon turned out to be an overwhelming and almost impossible task given data analysis and investigatory systems available at the time; the British decided to investigate only those applying for occupations considered to have influence, issuing the exonerated with a certificate to that effect. The American administration, meanwhile, set about investigating everyone's background.

The Nuremberg International War Crime Trials concerned only those at the very top of the regime charged with 'crimes against humanity', while other notorious war criminals had been tried and sentenced at the place of their crimes. Punishing those responsible for the devastation of Europe had to be balanced against the need to help Germany recover so that it would not be a humanitarian and economic burden upon its conquerors, some of whom had reconstruction issues of their own. On this basis the Americans almost gave up from an early stage (the task as described above proved beyond their administrative capabilities) and the British and French adopted a lukewarm attitude from the outset. These governments were now more afraid of communist than fascist ideology, and bolstering Germany's economic stability to head off Soviet influence was of primary importance.

This had some surprising and shameful consequences; a major documentary film, *German Concentration Camps Factual Survey*, to be directed by Hollywood's Alfred Hitchcock, and using testament and film from Soviet footage as well as Western sources, would lay bare the truth and horror of the Nazi regime's vast network of slave and death camps. Work on the movie was stopped because of the anti-German passions it would invoke, and because of the demoralising and destabilising effect it might have on Germans themselves (Turbett 2021a). In another example, *All the Frequent Troubles of Our Days* (Donner 2021) tells the true story of how the Nazi prosecutor whose actions led to the deaths of German anti-fascist activists including the American citizen whose story the book concerns, escaped punishment because his US captors believed he could help them with their new crusade against communists (Donner 2021). Not unnaturally, this period has been picked over by historians ever since, often to highlight hypocrisy on both sides, such as the overlooking of Nazi connections in the case of scientists and engineers useful for weapons development – the case of Wernher von Braun who went on to become head of the US Space Programme being the best known. However, it was highlighted at the time; the American academic John Herz, himself a Jewish refugee from the Nazis, wrote a paper in 1948 titled *The Fiasco of De-Nazification in Germany*, which cited examples of senior Nazi officials escaping any kind of punishment in the US, British and French occupied sectors because it suited the administrative authorities to keep them in place. In the end, rebuilding German self-sufficiency and heading off the threat of communism took precedence over denazification.

Reassigned by the *Daily Express* to Berlin, Wilfred Burchett arrived in the city at the very end of 1945 and this remained his base until transfer to Budapest in 1949. His witness as a critical Western press correspondent to the unfurling division of Berlin and Germany are unique, and the opinions he formed are at variance with the interpretation of events that continue to prevail among British and US historians. Despite his eventual disillusion with Stalin, he continued to stand by his views thirty-five years later when he wrote his memoirs. He offers a contemporary account of one controversial example of disputed denazification (Burchett 1950) which is quite similar to that offered by a direct witness, British soldier and interpreter John Clare, writing many years later at the height of the Cold War (Clare 1989). Wilhelm Furtwangler, the famous conductor of the Berlin Philharmonic Orchestra, an iconic institution in Nazi times, was flown back to Berlin by the Soviets in March 1946. They were basing their desire to help revive German cultural life on the fact that he had been already cleared of close Nazi association in Vienna. His celebrity existence under the Nazis had included some small acts of defiance, and eventually, near the end of the war, he had fled to Switzerland to join his family when he learned from prominent friends in Nazi circles that arrest by the Gestapo was imminent. The Americans insisted that he was a prominent Nazi and used this as an excuse to take issue with the Soviets and withdraw from joint cultural activity (one of the few remaining areas of inter-Allied working) on the basis that the Soviets were using this for their own purposes. The British initially supported the American position until their own quite thorough investigations (of which Clare was part) agreed with the Soviets that Furtwangler had no significant Nazi association. Burchett goes further and remarks that the Americans had been initially enthusiastic about Furtwangler's return to Berlin, until learning that he had accepted the Soviet invitation to take over their new Berlin State Orchestra based in their sector. Once again anti-Soviet sentiment overcame agreement that could have been easily reached. Clare later describes in his book the extensive files discovered identifying Nazi Party members, and his and his colleagues' efforts to use these effectively to expose those with false exoneration certificates, despite claims of 'excessive zeal' by a senior British police officer in the Allied Control Council.

Burchett also witnessed the rampant crime and corruption evident in Berlin, where the black market ruled supreme among the ruins of the bombed-out city, and insinuates that American and British occupiers were complicit. His description matches that of the Vienna setting for the 1949 British movie, *The Third Man*. Vienna, like Berlin, was under joint occupation. He describes the efforts made by the Soviet-established city council in the first seventeen months of occupation to clean up the city, both physically and morally, and the lapse in such activity that followed, especially in the Western-controlled sectors. When four-power governance was in progress (much as characterised in *The Third Man*) the Soviet delegate at the Kommandatura managed to get agreement for a combined clamp down on crime, initially opposed by the American delegate. The operation was effectively nullified when the American broadcast news of it the night before. The Western Allies, for their part, would point out crime committed by men in Soviet uniforms and this became a propaganda issue. Burchett and others on the left in the UK (Montagu 1946) indicated at the time that there were many hushed-up examples of crime involving those in British uniform. While sympathy seemed to be growing among the British and American occupiers for the defeated Germans, hostility was now mounting against their former allies and new enemies in the Red Army.

In the Soviet controlled sectors of Germany, a strategy based on communist ideology was used in the denazification process among ordinary Germans. This recognised the deep penetration of Nazi ideas in German society and the need to create a state based on communist and socialist values of brotherhood and

Communist Mayday parade Berlin 1947. (*A.Pisarek via Wikimedia Commons*)

Tempelhof Airport during the Berlin Airlift 1948. (*USAF via Wikimedia Commons*)

international unity. This also took account of the notion that Germany had been the home of the largest communist party in the world outside the USSR until Hitler systematically destroyed it after his rise to power in 1933. It was considered that educating young people in the revolutionary traditions of their homeland would lay the foundations of the new society. This was alongside forgiveness and reconciliation for released POWs who would be induced to physically rebuild the new nation (Blessing 2006). When communism itself showed no signs of making a comeback, Stalin counselled German communist leaders like Walter Ulbricht, to be careful and to tread a democratic path in alliance with other social democratic and anti-fascist parties; the Communist Party (KPD) was renamed the Socialist Unity Party (SED) in an unsuccessful attempt to win alliance with the old Social Democratic Party (SPD).

Germany's Divided Return to Self-Government

The Soviet Union had long stood for a united post-war Germany and had argued against proposals by the Americans and British to divide the country into as many as five separate states and even reduce it to a purely agricultural economy. As the Red Army entered Berlin, posters were placed all over the city quoting a 1942 speech of Stalin: 'It would be ridiculous to identify the Hitler clique with the German people, with the German state. The experience of history teaches us that Hitlers come and go but the German people, the German state, remains.' On the day of Victory, 9 May 1945, Stalin declared that although Hitler had planned to break up the Soviet Union as part of his war plan, now that 'The Soviet Union is triumphant … it has no intention of either dismembering or destroying Germany.' (both quotes from Burchett 1950, p.233 & p.234). Stalin's pragmatic thinking was based on the notion that a divided Germany would create dissent and lend excuse to a resurgence of nationalism that could again threaten European security. At the July 1946 Allied Foreign Ministers' meeting in Paris, Soviet Foreign Minister Molotov argued for a neutralised but united Germany:

> I think our purpose is not to destroy Germany but to transform her into a democratic and peace-loving state which, alongside of agriculture, would have its own industry and foreign trade, but which would be deprived of the economic and military potentiality to rise again as an aggressive force.
> (Quoted in Burchett 1950 p.236)

Although Stalin's arguments won out at Potsdam, the American view was changing as Roosevelt's belief that the USA should withdraw from European involvement at the earliest opportunity was replaced, by his successor Truman, with policies based on growing anti-Soviet views. Their vision was driven by fear of communism and the need, at whatever cost, to create a barrier through a German state based on alliance with their interests. As they had no hope of achieving this in the Soviet occupied sector, division was deliberately pursued. This view was driven within the USA by anti-communist politicians whose rhetoric came close to insinuation that they had backed the wrong horse during the war, and that Soviet aggression had always been the real enemy (Fleming 1961).

George Kennan, US Diplomat. (*Library of Congress via Wikimedia Commons*)

The American view was shaped around the perception that the Soviet threat had to be contained. This was based on ideas put forward by a Berlin based US diplomat George Kennan in his 'Long Telegram' of 22 February 1946 (Gaddis 2005). Soviet hostility and expansionism, Kennan argued, were inevitable as a justification for the dictatorial and ideological nature of their state itself. The pursuance of containment resulted in a series of acts that consolidated the Cold War. Again, Soviet expressions of internationalism and communism as offering the salvation of mankind, were interpreted by the Western powers as signs of immediate aggressive intent, pushed on (as we shall see in Chapter 4) by the military industrial complex. It was easy to find evidence of this from routine Soviet propagandist rhetoric; in 1945 the Soviet newspaper *Pravda* republished a speech by Stalin made in 1927 to visiting American trade unionists laying out the ground for the future war between capitalism and communism, over which ideology would prevail in the world (quoted eagerly by US General James Gavin in his 1959 manifesto for arms escalation *War and Peace in the Space Age*). American policy was now to remain in Europe to bolster the defence line against communism, and this was confirmed with the Truman Doctrine announced in 1947, and the Marshall Plan of economic aid to European countries based around certain conditions, that commenced the following year.

By 1947 the regimes that were developing in the Soviet-controlled sectors and those occupied by the Western powers were moving in different directions, mirroring their respective hosts. While still pursuing the idea of a united Germany, the Soviets were not prepared to renounce their influence in return for a united but American-orientated Germany that could threaten them, given the escalation in tensions. Western determination to revive Germany's economy by making it market-dominated and westward-facing were consolidated when the American and British zones united administratively and economically into the 'Bizone' in December 1947. US business interests had been heavily involved in Nazi Germany from its inception and for some this was not interrupted by the war; as late as 1944 Standard Oil had transferred patents and technology to I.G. Farben which were used to replenish Germany's dwindling oil supplies through the production of synthetic oil from coal. This came in the wake of American giant ITT's direct but secretive involvement in supplying equipment and expertise to the German arms industry. This of course was being bombed by American aircraft produced en-masse by other branches of US Industry. These bombers used SKF ball bearings supplied to all sides in the conflict, some of which, also made in US subsidiary plants, found their way into the German fighter aircraft attacking them (all described in detail in Higham 1983). The scenario painted in Joseph Heller's novel *Catch-22*, of the war providing a business opportunity that could be conducted across the divides was no fiction! American post-war plans included increasing German involvement in government to enable the rebuilding of marketplaces as soon as possible. The road to a divided Germany, a central focus of Cold War tensions for the next forty-two years, was now confirmed and almost irreversible, although Lewkowicz (2020) argues that as the Soviet Union was not concerned with international capitalist market opportunity for their own ideological reasons, this laid the groundwork for peaceful co-existence rather than trade or actual war. However, quite direct and hard-hitting economic hostility towards the USSR and Eastern Europe was confirmed by the Coordinating Committee (CoCom) established by the US in 1949, which organised Western trade embargoes from then until 1954, cutting exports from these countries by 50 per cent (Kaldor 1990). While the Cold War would centre on ideology and influence across the world, trade did play a role and as time went on and Western economies boomed in terms of consumer goods, those from the East were typically, and not always reasonably, seen through Western eyes as primitive, faulty and comical (my own book on Soviet motorcycles of the period provides examples of this – Turbett 2018).

The need for currency reform in Germany had long been an issue as the Reichsmark had lost any value and currency took the form of banknote issues by each of the occupying powers. The Soviets made proposals but, according to Burchett, were clear about their wish to proceed jointly with the other allies. However, on the back of a fictitious story (still in circulation in many histories) that the Soviet Zone had printed banknotes and were about to release them, the Americans and British unilaterally released the Deutschmark on 18 June 1948. The German adviser to the Bizone, Ludwig Erhard, abolished the price fixing and production controls that had been put in place by the military administration, grossly – but successfully – exceeding his authority. All this enraged the Soviets who announced that they would implement their currency in Berlin and stop the land supply from the main American, British and French sectors of all goods, and the situation escalated quickly as the West retaliated with its own embargo. The Soviets had gambled on an early victory but instead found themselves on the wrong end of a propaganda war as the Americans and British began to airlift food and goods into their sectors of Berlin. Although Burchett (1950) offers evidence that the food shortage was largely a myth concocted by the Western Allies for their own ends, the Soviets were generally characterised as the aggressors, and the Western powers as the saviours of West Berlin's civilian population. The US and British provocations that had prompted the crisis were quickly side-lined and forgotten. The Soviets offered food to anyone crossing to their zones and registering their ration card there, but this was strongly discouraged by the Americans who dismissed anyone working for them who took up the offer. Despite this, 100,000 West Berliners were receiving food through Soviet sources by early 1949. The blockade and its consequent airlift operation, unimpeded by Soviet forces, continued until the Soviets lifted the blockade in May 1949. The airlift operation had succeeded in creating a divide across the city that confirmed a Western enclave within East Germany under overall military governance by the Americans, British and French, that would last until 1990. The inhabitants of West Berlin were transformed overnight from defeated enemies to stoical defenders of freedom against Soviet tyranny. Of course, those among them who were involved in the black market reaped substantial personal reward as well.

By 1949 the French-controlled sector of Germany had joined the Bizone, making it the 'Trizone'. The standoff with the Soviets offered space and opportunity for elections and the formation of a West German parliament in Bonn. This assumed total responsibility for government with the declaration of the Federal Republic of Germany (the FDR) in May. Given the attitudes by then towards denazification in West Germany, it was inevitable that there were many enjoying power who were associated in some way with the Nazis. The new chancellor, Adenauer, was no ex-Nazi, but neither were his actions between 1933 and 1945 demonstrably anti-fascist (Taylor 2011). He was tolerant of the end of denazification, arguing for an end to the division of society into two classes the 'politically flawless' and the 'politically flawed' (i.e. ex-Nazi Party members) so they joined the administration and newly created military forces in their thousands – by 1953, 60 per cent of departmental heads in the Bonn government were ex-Nazis (Taylor 2011). This involved whitewashing the wartime armed services as generally honourable but misled by the Nazis through loyalty to the homeland. This ignored the ample evidence of widespread war crimes by ordinary military personnel, but because most of this took place on the Eastern Front it no longer mattered as much. In 1957 the FDR passed a law that allowed the issuing of most German medals earned during the Second World War (albeit without the original swastika), which could again be worn proudly. Open reunions were arranged of former combatants and memoirs began to be published that described the writers and their comrades in the same complimentary and honourable terms as their Allied opponents. In English translation these have come to enjoy good sales among new generations of American and British military buffs. There had been almost unanimous resistance to German rearmament itself among the Allies when they were meeting to discuss the country's future prior to the ruptures of 1948. However, by 1949, with the formation of the FDR and its inclusion in the new NATO alliance (see Chapter 3), this was no longer of relevance to America and Britain – the new West Germany would have to be part of NATO's armoury.

By the end of the 1950s West Germany's armed forces were an important component of NATO's defence of Europe against Soviet aggression. Denazification had gradually turned into what Taylor (2011) describes as a 'sleep cure'. Burchett cites surveys of public opinion in the American sector which are revealing about the rapidly escalating erasure of inconvenient memory. In 1946, 60 per cent of those who had not been Nazi Party members thought that National Socialism (the doctrine of the Nazis) had been a 'bad idea'; this number dropped steadily until 1949, when only 36 per cent of those surveyed condemned Nazism (Burchett 1950, pp.248–9). It was not until the late 1960s that a new generation of West Germans, who had no direct memory of the Nazi period, began to question the Nazi associations that pervaded West German (and Austrian) society. The most extreme expression was through the actions of the anarchist urban guerrillas of the *Red Army Faction*, whose 'denazification' actions were violent and brutal.

In the Soviet occupied east of Germany things developed quickly after the formation of FDR. As this ruled out the possibility of a united Germany, the German Democratic Republic (DDR) was declared from 7 October 1949, functions having been transferred over the previous year. All this was against the better judgement of Stalin (Gaddis 1997). In the East, decisions about who might constitute the new leadership were made easier by the fact that the Communist Party leadership dated mostly from the pre-Hitler period; many had been in exile in the USSR through the Hitler years during which many of their less fortunate colleagues had disappeared in the Concentration Camps. However, the DDR did not enjoy the same status as an independent nation within the Soviet orbit (the Cominform) as did the other nations such as Hungary and Czechoslovakia. The question of German unification was not yet dead however; in March 1952 the USSR proposed to the Western powers that a conference take place to look again at the possibility of a united but neutral Germany established through free elections. This was rejected by the Americans, British and French, who were now committed to a NATO alliance within which the FDR was both a forward base and anti-Soviet force. With no alternative in sight, this paved the way for the confirmation by the Cominform (after Stalin's death) of full national status for the DDR. Germany was now divided and would remain so until 1990, with West Berlin, over 100 miles inside the DDR's borders, in an objectively illogical manner, remaining under joint rulership as a reminder of unfinished business, for that entire period.

As an interesting aside from the main narrative of this chapter it is interesting to note that the bogey of communism and the monstrous images it summed up in the American mind about their Cold War adversaries had strange manifestations. The ready acceptance of former Nazis into the administration of Western Germany has already been described. The incorporation of former Nazis into the military establishment of the USA also featured as a weapon against communism, the best-known example being the employment and elevation of Wernher von Braun, the SS officer and rocket scientist whose missiles had tried to turn the war in the Nazis' favour in 1944–5. American troops had not fought alongside the Red Army in any of the major battles of the Second World War and their generals had limited understanding of Soviet characteristics, organisation and strategy. For this they turned to captured German senior officers who had fought on the Eastern Front, commissioning several restricted manuals to help their understanding. As the US scribed introduction to *Russian Combat Methods in World War II* admits, they were laced with Nazi prejudice, but nonetheless regarded as valuable insights. Descriptions are given of matters that would have been alien to US Army commanders: the role of the commissar in providing ideological leadership and attending to matters of morale, and the determination, bravery and comradeship soldiers demonstrated to one another. They also described the role of women as respected and dedicated fighters. However, also discussed was the 'unintelligent' use of numerical superiority and 'disdain for human life' that meant that funeral rites were not observed. All this will have contributed to very false impressions of Soviet men and women as not human in the way Americans considered themselves, and served a purpose, regardless of source (Department of Army 1950).

Summary

This chapter has discussed the origins of the Cold War through an account of the generalised opposition by the world's capitalist powers to the threats presented by the October 1917 Revolution in Russia and its propagation of the idea of worldwide communism. Suspended to forge an alliance to counter the threat of fascism and roll back Nazi conquest during wartime, the end of the Second World War saw a rapid return to conflict because of resistance by the democracies to Soviet threats to Western Europe. While this represents the Western view, there is an alternative narrative that sees Soviet actions at the end of the war, and in the years following in the countries where it enjoyed influence, as defensive and pragmatic. Not only is the idea of revolutionary change founded on notions of popular support, but the Soviets under Stalin had long abandoned ideas about spreading revolution in favour of consolidating their power at home. They did though, want secure borders to ensure that the kind of suffering they had just emerged from never happened again. This view sees the use of the atomic bomb against Japan and the failures to come up with a one nation solution to Germany after the war, as the first acts of the Cold War, and

US Anti-Communist poster 1951. (*US National Archives via Wikimedia Commons*)

Soviet post-war poster depicting US military and financial influence in Europe. (*Author's collection*)

delivered deliberately by the US and its allies. The Marshall plan of economic aid was the US carrot, and sole ownership of nuclear weapons was the stick. The result split Germany physically and ideologically for the next forty years. The next chapter will examine how peace was maintained through a delicate but risk-laden balance of nuclear weapons ownership.

Chapter 3

Armageddon Beckoning – Mutually Assured Destruction and the Myth of Defence

> Hiroshima does not look like a bombed city. It looks as if a monster steamroller had passed over it and squashed it out of existence. I write these facts as dispassionately as possible in the hope that they will act as a warning to the world. In this first testing ground of the atomic bomb I have seen the most terrible and frightening desolation in four years of war. It makes a blitzed Pacific island seem like an Eden. The damage is far greater than photographs can show.
>
> Wilfred Burchett September 1945
> (Burchett & Shimmin 2007, p.2)

The Coming of the Bomb and its Subsequent Development

The Cold War is associated for most of us with the development and deployment of nuclear weapons – what was known colloquially and in the singular, by both proponents and detractors, as 'the Bomb'. This was a weapon that was so terrible it was never used but which cast a shadow over the planet for forty-five years, stockpiles still existing and no longer confined to two world superpowers. This chapter will focus on the phenomenon of the Bomb and its significance in the drama of Cold War. It will look at the myth of defence against nuclear attack and the near-misses that could have ended human life and civilisation as we know it.

'War', says the nineteenth-century military strategist Clausewitz, 'is the continuation of policy by other means … The political object is the goal and means can never be isolated from their purpose.' (2007, p.28–9). The onset of the age of nuclear war lent new meaning to this well-known dictum. If the effect of war was to be the destruction of one's own territory as well as that of the enemy, then war was no longer a viable means to achieve a policy goal. That is unless the policy was designed to serve the interests of only those who might survive and not, as in all previous wars between nations, a national goal behind which the population could unite and engage. These were the issues and dilemmas that surrounded the Cold War and its accompanying arms race. They involved competition, secrecy, and an ideological battle to convince populations that highly questionable motives and consequential actions were morally justified, desirable and virtuous.

Atomic Bomb explosion over Nagasaki 9 August 1945. (*C. Levy via Wikimedia Commons*)

The Bomb, as we saw in Chapter 2, was justified in the West as a necessary means to end the Second World War and save lives that might have been lost through conventional means of warfare. Its sub-text in 1945, and arguably the reason ultimately for its deployment, was to warn the Soviet allies of where real power and authority would lie in the post-war world. To the surprise of the USA this was not the effect it had on Stalin; it made him more determined to ensure that the USSR's security was consolidated by a rapid catch-up. Using knowledge gained through highly successful spying operations, the Soviets developed their own version of the Bomb, almost identical in power and specification to the American 'fatman' used in Nagasaki, which was first tested in August 1949. Rather than restore stability, this development increased American determination to stay ahead, leading to a race that lasted for the next forty years.

The idea of a terror weapon that would yield as much power psychologically as it might in taking lives was not new. Poison mustard gas had been used in the First World War by both sides with limited but terrible effect. In 1919 the British used chemical weapons based on arsenic dropped from aircraft against the Bolsheviks in the Murmansk and Archangel areas of Northern Russia, with the enthusiastic support of Winston Churchill (Jones 1999). According to some reports, they were used again by the British in Iraq against poorly armed tribesmen in 1920 (which puts the moral outrage about Saddam Hussein's later use of them in the 1980s into a certain context). In 1930 the Geneva Convention outlawed the use of toxic gas and bacteria in warfare, but not their development, which continued apace. Neither side used them in the Second World War for fear of retaliation, and damage at home to the popularised policies that supported their respective military campaigns (à la Clausewitz). However, we do know that the British seriously considered their use on several occasions and might well have done so had the Germans invaded Britain in 1940. Anthrax was later experimented with on Gruinard Island in the Northwest of Scotland,

and Churchill proposed dropping it on German cities in 1944 but was overruled by military chiefs (Harris & Paxman 1982). Although mustard gas production stopped in Britain in 1945, chemical and biological warfare development has never stopped – the Porton Down facility in Wiltshire remains active to this day. In the early 1950s the UK experimented with bubonic plague and other deadly diseases on animals quartered on a converted wartime landing ship moored off the coast of Lewes in the Outer Hebrides. Details of this highly dangerous and controversial activity were only released when whistleblower Clive Pointing wrote an article for the *Observer* newspaper in 1989 (Guardian 2020). Wilfred Burchett reported the American use of biological warfare in the Korean War and they also used chemical defoliants on a massive scale in Vietnam (both discussed in Chapter 5).

The Nazis used poison gases to murderous effect in their programme of mass extermination of Jews, Gypsies, and others, but never in open warfare. The advent of aerial bombing by the Nazis in Guernica, Spain, in 1938, involved naked terror, and its scale was dwarfed by the mass allied-bomber raids over Germany and Japan in 1944 and 1945, which killed more people than the atomic bomb deployments. In fact, a single raid on Tokyo in March 1945 killed an estimated 100,000 people, more immediate victims than either of the later atomic bomb raids. These 'conventional' operations involved high risk to the mission crews, whereas an atomic bomb, biological or chemical weapon with enough scale, could be dropped literally out of the blue, with none of the noisy fanfare of a mass bomber raid. The idea of a bomb whose silent killing effects would be felt long after its explosion was, as Wilfred Burchett reported from Hiroshima (Chapter 2), awful in its implications, but new only in terms of the scale of killing and devastation wreaked. The parallels between chemical/bacteriological and nuclear weapons must be considered in an account of the Cold War; the former involves low-level technology that might have catastrophic consequences in the event of deliberate use or accident, the latter high levels of technology with similarly awful possibilities. One only has to compare the consequences of the Chernobyl Reactor explosion in 1986, with the worldwide Covid-19 pandemic of 2020, to put this into some sort of perspective. However, the whole point about the Bomb was that it was out of reach to most countries (or terrorist groups) through both expense in development and technological know-how. That did not ultimately stop others (such as India and Israel) beyond the US, its immediate allies, and the Soviet Union, from developing their own. Surrounded therefore in mystique through its terribleness and finality, the Bomb had an aura that was not found in the equally destructive arsenals of biological and chemical weapons quietly assembled by both sides; it would be difficult to imagine a submarine on constant hidden deployment to serve as the ultimate deterrent, loaded with missiles containing anthrax or even Covid-19 particles. This, even though all the factors associated with risk to the crew, purpose in terms of containment of destructive effect, and morality, might apply as they do with Trident missile carrying Submarines and their equivalents.

The threat of Armageddon (or the Apocalypse for some) required the tangible quality of nuclear weaponry and so they were developed and refined continuously. In the beginning innovation was aimed at making nuclear weapons lighter but more powerful. The first major step at a time when size really mattered, was the entry into new territory of destructive potential with the Hydrogen Bomb (otherwise known as H-Bombs, thermo-nuclear bombs or fusion weapons). This technological breakthrough enabled a cheaper and smaller sized bomb that could deliver a much bigger blast, making it potentially more mobile and deliverable by self-propelled missile rather than by gravity from a large aircraft. As the whole nuclear strategy now depended on publicity so that the other side knew exactly what aggression might trigger in terms of retaliation, the talk now was of bombs that could deliver multiple 'Hiroshimas' or 'Nagasakis' in one detonation (450 times that of the latter in the first US test in 1952). The Soviets caught up quickly and in 1961 exploded an H-Bomb that dwarfed the original American version, and this remains the most explosive ever tested. Britain also successfully developed its own variant in the 1950s, as did France a few years later, and then China. The Soviets in the 1950s were the first to develop Inter-Continental Ballistic Missiles (ICBMs) – separate from but using the same technology as their successful space programme. The Americans (and British) were reliant in this period on large and fast bombers, but by the early 1960s the Americans had begun to depend on submarine-based ICBMs for their long-range capability. The British also developed a small fleet of US (but British made) missile-carrying submarines which remain the basis of its 'deterrent' over fifty years later.

UK V-Bomber Scramble 1958. (RAF Flying Review)

In the early 1950s the concern for the USA and its allies was that the USSR had much larger numbers of ground troops, tanks, and other conventional weapons (although, notably, not bomber aircraft). At this time military leaders were warning that attack was imminent and nuclear defence an absolute necessity; British Field Marshall Montgomery is on record as stating that nuclear weapons should be used in the event of any attack subject to political approval, although in his view that approval should be dispensed with if the worst happened (Ware 2016). The American response was to begin to talk of nuclear weapons not simply as doomsday threats, but as a 'family'. This would include smaller devices that could be used to support conventional warfare on the ground, in the air, and at sea. From an initial commitment to funding in 1953, such developments were rapid and alarming. By 1955, US forces had nuclear depth charges for use against submarines at sea, shells for use by the large guns carried on battleships, smaller ones for use by field artillery on land, short and medium range rockets for battlefield use, and an array of aircraft carried bombs and rockets for anti-aircraft and air to air use, and air dropped bombs (Noel-Baker 1958). The British committed themselves to such developments quickly, as did the Soviet Union in inevitable response. They were routinely carried on warships and aircraft, and not just stored for eventualities. After it became public knowledge, for example, the British admitted that several warships deployed in the South Atlantic for the short war against Argentina in 1982 to repossess the Falkland Islands, were armed with nuclear weapons because that was their 'normal practice' at the time, breaching international treaties and risking catastrophe. They were apparently rapidly returned to the UK after the sinking of HMS *Sheffield* and HMS *Coventry* (Ware 2016).

Possibly the ultimate development of such weaponry was the invention of the Neutron Bomb by the Americans in the late 1950s. This was a nuclear device designed so that the chemical reaction that causes the nuclear explosion was configured in such a way that the blast was limited, avoiding widespread physical destruction to buildings and infrastructure. The radiation effect was conversely heightened to maximise its effect over the immediate area. Not surprisingly, this was characterised by critics as a gift to Soviet opponents who were quick to describe it as a capitalist bomb which put property above human life. Khrushchev described it in 1961 as a bomb 'meant to kill people but preserve all riches … [embodying] the bestial ethics of the most aggressive exponents of imperialism.' (Quoted in the *Washington Post* 11 August 1981).

According to peace activist and historian E.P. Thompson, by 1980 stockpiles of nuclear weapons for potential use in a nuclear war amounted to enough to destroy humanity thirty times over (Thompson 1982). Peaks were reached in the USA in 1967, with 31,255 warheads, the Soviet Union in 1988 with approximately 45,000, and Britain in 1975 with 520 (although British capacity peak yield was in 1967 with 150 megatons worth of destructive power) (Ware

2016). Development proceeded steadily to make the warheads more accurate and smaller. By the end of the 1950s the fleets of heavy bombers employed by the US and Britain that could be used to obliterate the big population centres of the USSR were redundant due to improvements in early warning and anti-aircraft defences. In their place came long range missiles kept in static underground silos. From 1958 until 1963, fifty-nine US Thor missiles with 1.44 megaton warhead capability were sited in Britain, the only NATO country that would accept them. The British bases (all on RAF stations) were vital to their deployment because of their limited 1,600-mile range. It was only with the introduction of Minutemen missiles in the mid-1960s, with a range of 8,000 miles, that the siting of silos in remote areas of the USA itself became a possibility. Thousands had been produced by the time they too were overtaken by other developments in the late 1970s (with some 450 still in existence in 2016) (Ware 2016). Competition in terms of numbers became quite meaningless, although a strange logic of its own developed; US Secretary of State McNamara declared in 1962 that the 17–1 advantage that the US enjoyed at that time meant actual parity because the prospect of just a few nuclear bombs being dropped on US soil were enough to deter Washington from ever using them for fear of retaliation. This did not prevent the Soviets from probably achieving parity of nuclear capability within the next ten years (Gaddis 1997).

The MAD scenario really climaxed in terms of development with the advent of submarine-borne missiles in the late 1950s. By the 1980s they had effectively made all other forms of large-scale nuclear attack redundant. Lying beneath the waves, nuclear powered so that they could remain underwater for months on end, and with warheads that contained multiple missiles that could be separately targeted, they were undetectable and both sides had them on permanent readiness. The American Trident Submarine Launched Ballistic Missiles (SLBMs) introduced on US and British submarines from the 1980s, had a range of over 4,500 miles and each missile could carry fourteen warheads. Fifty-eight such missiles were leased to Britain, but their first patrols did not take place until 1994 after the end of the Cold War, lending to controversy about the continued necessity for such expense and risk. By 1980 Soviet SLBMs had the capability of destroying US cities from their USSR-located bases in the Northern Pacific and Arctic, although they were thought to lack accuracy to take out Minuteman underground silos (US Navy 1981).

With the idea of all-out nuclear war at an unthinkable stalemate by the end of the 1970s, military thought turned to how a limited war might be won with the use of tactical nuclear weapons that would not attract a MAD response. These had a lesser range but greater accuracy and could be deployed against the enemy's military installations and troop masses. These might be restricted to a particular theatre: Europe, the Middle East or elsewhere, and unlike an all-out conflict, wars under such mutual limitations were thought to be winnable.

USS Hunley depot ship removing Polaris missile from USS *Edison*, Dunoon Scotland 1967. (*USN via Wikimedia Commons*)

This featured both within US and Soviet circles and led to the development of a new generation of strategic weapons. Both sides developed small fast bomber aircraft that could fly below radar and launch missiles against targets without warning. Some of the Soviet developments were a shock to the Americans; the Backfire Bomber was a match for anything in the US armoury when introduced in the early 1970s, as Khrushchev had long before declared that the Soviets were so advanced in Intercontinental Ballistic Missile Development (ICBM) development that bombers were obsolete and they had no requirement to catch up with the Americans in this respect. The Soviets had very publicly demonstrated their lead here with the spectacular space successes of the 1950s and early 1960s (Turbett 2021b). Now, airborne dropped bombs and static rockets sat alongside mobile cruise missiles (developed from the primitive German V1 wartime devices) that could be launched from the ground, the air or from the sea. The Americans embarked on deliberate escalation in the early 1980s (see Chapter 10) with the siting of Pershing-2 Cruise missiles in Europe, including at two locations in Britain, from which they could be easily transported elsewhere and launched at will against precise military targets. As we shall see in later chapters, this increase in risk resulted in an emboldened and popular peace movement in Britain and elsewhere. Back in the late 1950s, General James Gavin, just retired from a post as US Army head of research and development, suggested that there was no need for missiles to be placed in the UK as there were more strategic sites in Southern Europe, the Middle East and Africa. Ultimately, political imperatives, including the roll-back of imperialist interests, determined such decisions; the bases needed to be on the safe and secure territory of closely tied-in allies.

The other late Cold War US strategy to outpace the USSR involved the development of Strategic Defence Initiative (SDI) 'Star Wars' capability in air defence; defence systems located in space, including lasers, that could target and take out ICBMs and other missiles before they reached their targets. Deliberately borrowed from the movies in order to capture the public imagination and blind the enemy with new science, Star Wars was mostly bluff, but nonetheless millions of dollars were thrown at it in order to prove that the USA could outspend the USSR (the background will be described in Chapter 10). At this time and throughout the Cold War an apparently contradictory game of proud and arrogant publicity within a framework of secrecy was played by both sides. The Americans were more public about their innovations and deployments, while the Soviets preferred to offer tantalising glimpses of new missiles at their annual parades through Moscow's Red Square, while prohibiting the photography by foreigners of not just military equipment, but just about every type of public building, structure and moving object within their borders (the fact is that by the end of the Cold War, Soviet infrastructure could be viewed at will from orbiting satellites in space). The publicity about new weaponry was important to impress audiences at home and abroad and served a purpose for both sides. In the absence of evidence from the battlefield (a scenario only the madder generals and politicians wanted), power lay in what you could convince your enemies you held rather than what you might actually have. The Soviets played this to great effect at the Tushino Airshow in 1955 when they fooled American observers into believing that their new Bison bombers were greater in number than they were, suggesting an offensive nuclear capability that did not actually exist (Turbett 2021b). They also reputedly flew single bombers round and round in circles near radar stations on the edge of foreign territory to make it look to the receiver that there were large numbers in the air.

NATO and the Warsaw Pact

The end of the wartime alliance between the USA, Britain, and the Soviet Union after 1945, and the onset of Cold War, meant realignment between nations. The Americans and their West European allies made the first move with the formation of the North Atlantic Treaty Organisation (NATO). Initially a pact between the British and French in 1947, it grew to include another ten western European countries and when the USA and Canada joined in April 1949, was reconstituted as NATO. NATO later expanded further and indeed continues to in response to perceived new challenges in the twenty-first century. The organisation's own history tells us that it was formed to ward off the threat of Soviet expansion, the possibility of any rise of militarism in Europe, encourage European integration, and ensure American involvement in Europe to guarantee these aims (NATO undated). The same document goes on to state that until the 1950s NATO was essentially defensive, and that it became, until the end of the Cold War, 'a political instrument for détente' (ibid). There is little doubt too that NATO offered guarantees that access to the resources its members needed would be defended, although this did not always bear fruit – as with the Suez debacle in 1956. For the Soviets, it signified Cold War realities and they only seriously responded in 1955 when a rearmed West Germany was invited to join NATO and place its troops alongside those of the 1945 Western occupiers (the USA, Britain and France) in confronting Soviet troops along the border that divided Germany. This was a step too far for the USSR. Only ten years after the end of the Great Patriotic War, an army staffed and led by many of their invaders was again facing them militarily.

According to information provided by the Communist Party in the UK, by 1960 the FDR's army had 104 generals who had served under Hitler (Gollan 1960). These included the Inspector General, Adolf Hausinger, who had planned the invasions of Belgium, Luxemburg and Holland in 1940, and later Yugoslavia, and who had colluded (according to his own testimony at Nuremburg) with the decimation of Jews. Heinrich Hax was a major general who had been staff chief of Hitler's 56th Army Corps and who had been sentenced to twenty-five years imprisonment for war crimes but amnestied in 1955. Hans Spiedel had been Chief of Staff of the Wehrmacht in occupied Paris and Chief of Staff of the 8th Army on the Eastern Front; he was now commander of NATO ground forces in central Europe. Friedrich Foertsch had been General Staff Chief of the 18th Army and also sentenced to twenty-five years for war crimes on the Eastern Front, amnestied in 1955 and now Deputy Chief of Planning Staff in NATO Headquarters. The FDR government included other prominent former Nazis.

The USSR's response to NATO developments that created fears of a rearmed and hostile Western Germany, was to form the Warsaw Pact, replacing looser alliances formed in the late 1940s, and alongside Comecon, the mutual aid pact formed to counter Marshall Aid in 1947. The formation of the Warsaw Pact was initially muted; the Soviets withdrew from Austria as previously agreed, and Khrushchev welcomed West German leader Adenauer on a visit to Moscow, both agreeing to reduce the dangers of nuclear war. Warsaw Pact forces reduced in numbers by some 2.5 million by 1958 and the USSR indeed offered to dismantle it if NATO was similarly wound up – an offer, like those of nuclear disarmament, never taken seriously. NATO and the Warsaw Pact mirrored one another: both involved single shared command structures (in theory anyway) and unity of purpose and action that signified a move away from historical notions of alliance between nations. Both bound allies together in a manner that would not have been possible had there not been a mutual adversary; in this sense the Cold War suited the powers on both sides as it enabled them to more easily implement policies that affected the spheres of the world they controlled or sought to control. In the case of the Soviet sphere this had more to do with the tight discipline of interparty relations between the respective communist leaderships than the military mechanisms, and in this respect was less effective than NATO (Kaldor 1990). The consolidation of Cold War ideological and military unity on both sides was evidenced in diverse ways from the brutal Soviet action to suppress a popular uprising in Hungary in 1956, to the terms of the Common Market and the European unity project.

The Bomb as Determinant in the Cold War

It is now universally accepted as fact that possession of the Bomb prevented all-out global war between the USA, its allies and the Soviet Union. This is not stated to justify such possession – on the contrary, the threat of nuclear war and the risk of accidentally starting one with consequent irreversible damage to the entire planet was a determining feature of the Cold War and its threat to us all. The Cold War was started, as described in Chapter 2, by the Americans in response to a perceived threat from the Soviets. This was done when they enjoyed sole possession of the nuclear weapons which gave them psychological as well as military advantage. This advantage was soon lost when the catch-up game started in earnest. Once balance had been achieved again, all-out global war on the scale of the two previous world wars became something both sides wanted to avoid very carefully, but proxy war (as we shall see in Chapter 5) assumed a new importance.

The possibility of a third world war between the Soviets and the Americans (involving their respective allies) was evaluated for a general readership in the late 1970s by a group of experts from military and academic backgrounds (Bidwell 1978). This was a well-grounded survey that was far sighted enough (almost uniquely) to correctly speculate that the Soviet Union might ultimately defeat itself through its economic problems and internal contradictions. The survey concluded that war was not just a possibility, but almost an inevitability given the proliferation of weaponry owned and supplied to others by the two big powers. It concluded with an invented scenario that a war in Northwest Europe might easily start through tensions arising from the emergence of a new far-right in West Germany and consequent easing of the NATO commitment to defend it against the Soviets. This in turn triggered FDR resolve to build their own Bomb for self-defence (this was really contemplated during the Cold War), and the launch of a Soviet conventional invasion to reunite Germany and head off such a threat. Rapid Soviet successes resulted in the use of tactical battlefield nuclear weapons, and this escalated rapidly into all out nuclear war with devastating consequences in Europe as well as the USSR and USA (contrary to the 'limited theatre' school of thought referred to earlier in this chapter). I have summarised this fiction, but the picture painted seems far from unreal. None of it happened, partly at least because of the enormous gamble taken by President Ronald Reagan in confronting the Soviets to end the arms race through overwhelming American might (discussed in Chapter 10).

Another alarming picture of how a war might start and progress was given in Cyril Joly's 1980 novel *Silent Night – the Defeat of NATO*. Joly was a retired British Army officer who had held several senior planning and policy posts, including adviser to the Secretary of State for War, and as a staff officer in the Supreme Headquarters Allied Powers in Europe (SHAPE). His scenario involved a rapid surprise invasion of Europe by the USSR involving fifth columnists and local communists. The stated motive was a labour shortage in the Soviet Union that was stifling its economy, and the need to exploit labour and productive resources in Western Europe. Although the events described were implausible (involving, for instance, the simultaneous docking of Soviet cruise ships in strategic locations throughout Europe with their special forces passengers disguised as tourists), its characterisation of the Soviets as cynical monsters bent on enslaving the people of Europe, is telling. Did this really reflect staff officer understanding of their adversaries? If so, it was remarkably naïve and misinformed; to interpret the massive loss of life in the USSR during the Second World War as anything other

General Jack D. Ripper *Dr Strangelove* movie 1964. (*Couse-Baker via Wikimedia Commons*)

than a motive for peace among both Soviet people and their leaders (certainly after Stalin) is crazy. It seems reminiscent of the mad motives of the character General Jack D. Ripper in the 1964 comedy satirical movie *Dr Strangelove*, who launched a nuclear attack because he thought the Soviets were trying to poison Americans through the water supply.

In fact, although the efforts by the Soviets to keep up with the US and its allies were ostensibly intended to maintain a balance of terror, even if many American people and their leaders chose to interpret it as aggressive in intent, a careful path was trodden to maintain what became known as 'peaceful co-existence'. This involved acceptance of difference despite constant sabre rattling, confrontation, and ideological and scientific competition. This was first spoken about openly in the post-war period as an aim of Soviet foreign policy. In a Soviet press article reprinted in Britain by the Soviet Embassy (Titarenko 1950), a speech of Stalin's from 1936 is quoted in which he states that 'we Marxists believe that a revolution will also take place in other countries. But it will take place only when the revolutionaries in those countries think it possible, or necessary. The export of revolution is nonsense.' The article went on to explain how the Soviet people wanted peace, that its maintenance was the policy of their leaders, and that peaceful competition between the two systems was preferable to war. This policy worked its way into Communist practice in capitalist countries – revolutionary theory gave way to acceptance that the conditions for insurrection did not exist and peaceful and democratic transitions to socialism were favoured. This doctrine outlived Stalin and became associated with the warmer foreign policy attitudes of Khrushchev, causing a split in the 1950s between the USSR and its most accomplished and largest ally, China, who could not accept such revisionism. Khrushchev, however, was always clear that peaceful co-existence referred to relations with capitalist governments and not with ideologies. The message of Peaceful Co-Existence and all the evidence that backed up its seriousness on the part of the Soviets was ignored by US administrations and every signal of aggressive intent seized upon eagerly. This included Khrushchev's outburst to Western ambassadors in Poland in 1956 that the USSR would 'bury' the enemies of revolution. The fact that he was referring to the old Marxist tenet that capitalism was its own gravedigger was totally lost in translation and interpretation, whether or not this was what had been intended by this impulsive character.

While 'deterrence' became the explanation for ongoing nuclear arms production in the West, it was only the peace movement (as will be discussed in more detail in Chapter 6) that suggested that with enough weapons to destroy all life several times over, this was unnecessary. In the Soviet Union the word deterrence was never used in this sense, and its translation as a Western term was 'intimidation'. They used the term 'сдерживание', which means holding back or restraining, to describe their own policy (Kaldor 1990). For Khrushchev this meant using nuclear weapons as a substitute for expensive conventional forces, and in fact Soviet military planners saw them as support mechanisms for conventional forces rather like the Red Army had made extensive use of artillery and ground attack aircraft in the Second World War. In later years his successors tried to keep up with and exceed NATO in both conventional and nuclear forces – all in the name of security, but by this time the arms build-up had gained a momentum of its own, as we shall explore in the next chapter. Conventional forces were important in the Soviet Bloc for the maintenance of control and were used in Hungary in 1956 and again in Czechoslovakia in 1968. The idea of the Soviet tank as the liberator (or invader depending on your point of view) of Eastern Europe in 1944–45, became an icon of Soviet strength just as much as the missiles displayed in Red Square in the November 7th Victory parades. On the left in the UK, enthusiastic supporters of the USSR (especially those who mourned Stalin) were known as 'tankies'.

Détente was a method used in the later years of the Cold War to defuse tensions and was promoted particularly by US President Nixon and the Soviet leader Brezhnev. The talks and summits resulted in the first efforts at arms limitation agreement (test ban treaties had been negotiated in earlier years), but détente began to wane when Nixon was deposed in 1974. It did achieve the SALT (Strategic Arms Limitation Talks) of 1972 (SALT 1) and the later SALT 2 talks that went on for the rest of that decade. Both reduced numbers of certain types of weapons and new developments, but SALT 2 was never ratified by the Americans after the Soviets invaded Afghanistan in 1979. Détente also resulted in the Helsinki 'Final Act' Agreement of 1975, which on paper at least agreed to status quo in Europe and a commitment to human and socio-economic rights. However, by 1980 the Cold War had returned in earnest, and this will be discussed in Chapter 10 when the final years of the Cold War are examined. The world at that time did not feel a safe place.

Despite all the checks and balances and wish by both sides to avoid nuclear war, there were several occasions when it was narrowly avoided – or so it seemed. How their use was seriously considered in Korea in 1950 will be touched upon in Chapter 5. Later, tensions erupted over the East-West German Border, especially as it divided the enclave of Berlin, in 1960–61. The DDR, suffered (its leaders argued) from an economy that lagged far behind its FDR counterparts because of continued Soviet reparations, which was haemorrhaging the very workers it most needed. They were crossing to the West in large numbers, in rejection of equality, for the consumer attractions and higher wages of an economy that was being bolstered by the American dollar. Negotiations to resolve the long-standing issue of West Berlin's continued joint occupancy had come to nothing and the East German leadership hinted that a tighter border control would be the inevitable outcome of failed negotiations to resolve the Berlin issue and reunite Germany. This only increased the flow of refugees to the West. In November the East Germans reacted, as everyone had expected, by erecting a barbed wire barrier that prevented the freedom of movement previously enjoyed across the city because of agreements over occupation made at the end of the Second World War. The immediate reaction involved a great deal of posturing by the Soviets and Americans whose tanks faced each other at the Brandenburg Gate on one notable day in October 1961. Nuclear weapons were placed on immediate alert amid talk of war. All this, however, was carefully choreographed and neither side made any move to provoke the other further. The East Germans, after all, had merely confirmed the status quo, albeit brutally, and had dragged a more conciliatory Soviet Union along with them. A few weeks later the Soviet space cosmonaut hero Titov, visited East Berlin as a visible symbol of Soviet glory and achievement – a rejoinder that East Germans should look east and not west. Many did, but others were frustrated at their new confinement, the reason for a massive and sophisticated network of neighbourhood spies and informers that characterised the DDR for all time in the popular Western imagination. The concrete wall that was erected in place of the wire became an accepted fact of life for the next three decades, and the cause of numerous heroic escape attempts and 136 lost lives (Hertle 2011).

In the 1950s, Cuba, only ninety miles from the US Coast and with a corrupt dictatorship, was the playground of American gangsters with an economy based on leisure, prostitution and gambling, where the poor and mostly rural people lived in abject poverty. Led by Fidel Castro and the Argentinian revolutionary Che Guevara, the country was subject of a popular revolution which was neither communist in inspiration nor ideology. After several years of rural guerrilla warfare and a gradual building of support, the revolutionaries swept into the cities and took power in 1959. In 1961 an American government-backed attempt by exiled Cubans to land in Cuba and restore the old regime failed miserably. The invading forces were easily repulsed at the Bay of Pigs, causing humiliation to the US – and a Cuban government to turn to the USSR for security. The Cubans took this to an unexpected length when they invited the Soviets to install nuclear missiles that they hoped would guarantee them safety from further invasion by their giant and powerful neighbour. This was done in secret and the Americans only discovered what was going on when their reconnaissance planes identified sites under construction. It should be noted that the US at this time had nuclear missile launching sites near the Soviet Union in Italy and Turkey (as well as in Britain). By late 1962 the USSR had begun to ferry missiles to Cuba and international tensions rose quickly. A US naval blockade was put in place and the Soviets were warned by President Kennedy that war might ensue unless the missiles were removed.

Although the squaring up of the respective leaders to each other was, as over the Berlin Wall the previous year, carefully staged, there was a very real danger of conflict starting through error and accident. The Soviets despatched

US President Kennedy and Secretary of Defense McNamara meet to discuss Cuba Crisis November 1962. (*C. Stoughton via Wikimedia Commons*)

a flotilla of four diesel-powered submarines to the Caribbean in support of their merchant vessels transporting the missiles and equipment. The flagship, B-59, was detected underwater by US Naval vessels enforcing the blockade. Having no other means of communication, the frigate USS *Beale* depth-charged B-59 with training bombs lacking the explosive power to bring it to the surface and find out its business. The Soviet commander was under orders to retaliate to any attack with his single nuclear torpedo, but was so deep in the ocean and out of radio communication that he had no idea what was happening and whether a war had broken out. He wanted to launch the torpedo but required the consent of two other senior officers aboard, and one, Captain Vasily Arkhipov, refused to give this, believing that it would trigger a conflict and that further orders from Moscow were required before any action was taken. The submarine surfaced, became aware of the real situation and then left the area without incident. On the same day an American U-2 spy plane, whose navigational systems were confused by the Aurora Borealis, accidentally strayed over the USSR from Alaska. The Soviets, fearing an attack, deployed jet fighters to intercept and destroy the plane, which in turn triggered the deployment of nuclear-armed American fighters. Thankfully, the U-2, which had now run out of fuel, was glided back into US air space before the two sides met, and conflict was very narrowly averted. The next day the two shaken leaders agreed to talks and a secret compromise agreement was eventually reached which saw the Soviets

US troops demobilise at end of the Cuba Crisis November 1962. (*USAF via Wikimedia Commons*)

abandon its Cuban missile bases in return for the withdrawal of nuclear missiles from US sites in Turkey and agreement not to back any further invasion attempt of Cuba. It is awful to contemplate sixty years later, but Britain's V Bombers were lined up on runways with engines running, fully armed and ready to fly at a moment's notice. Most people were at least vaguely aware of such preparations, and there was, for a short period in late 1962, a climate of panic and fear across the world.

By the late 1970s, with renewed tension created by a worldwide recession, the stand-off concerning MAD was reinforced by the development of systems by both sides that could provide effective (or so it was hoped) early warning of attack. This was problematic, it was open to error and on a notable three occasions, war almost resulted. The first such incident was in November 1979 when a technician in the North America Aerospace Defence Command (NORAD) accidentally set off a training programme simulating a Soviet missile attack. This was taken seriously – intercepting aircraft were mobilized and the president's Doomsday Plane, in which he would sit out a nuclear attack, was ordered to take off. However, further checks revealed the mistake and stand-down followed. The two sides exchanged terse correspondence after this but similar, if less dramatic, alerts took place at NORAD due to microchip failures in 1980. An erroneous warning at the USSR's equivalent site in Serpukhov mistook rays of sunlight over the US ICBM launch site in Montana as an attack by five missiles. The commanding officer, Colonel Petrov, was sceptical and held off alerting the high command of an attack for several tense minutes until confirmation was received that the alarm was false. Again, a nuclear holocaust was narrowly averted.

In November 1983, with tensions high (this will be discussed in detail in Chapter 10) Exercise Able Archer, a large-scale NATO exercise along the borders of the Eastern Bloc was mistakenly believed by the Soviets to be the start of an invasion of East Germany. Although an annual event, on this occasion it was made more realistic though the involvement of heads of government, new forms of communication and radio silences. Facing the well-publicised and imminent arrival of Pershing-2 Cruise missiles in Europe, Soviet generals were convinced that Able Archer was a deliberate ploy to cover a nuclear first strike on their forces in Eastern Europe. Soviet Nuclear bombers were prepared for an attack and Warsaw Pact forces generally readied for war. NATO generals became aware of the Soviet reaction to their own activity and ended the exercise. At the time, the US and their Western allies were unaware of how close they had been to war and as late as 2021 the declassification of US government documents suggests that – unknown to the public at large – this was the closest the world had come to global war since the Cuban crisis of 1962. It should be remembered that in 1983 the USSR, who were defending a border against the Chinese as well as being involved militarily in Afghanistan, only had some twenty divisions in Europe. They had deployed 400 to defeat the Nazis in 1945, so a nuclear defence option was a very real danger.

Saving Ourselves from the Bomb – the Myth of Civil Defence

The issue of Civil Defence in Britain had been a contentious one during the Second World War. In the early phase of the war shelters for the public in the cities that became targets for the Germans were woefully inadequate. It took a considerable shake-up of government attitude and management of resources to change this, including the simple expediency of opening London underground stations as organised and supplied bomb shelters (Calder 1992). Such matters were never an issue of magnitude in the USA, although an Organisation of Civil Defence was established that recruited millions of volunteers who were never called upon. In the USSR civil defence was highly organised; from July 1941, within days of the Nazi invasion, orders were issued that every citizen aged between 8 and 60 should be trained in basic skills. These included basic first aid, use of a gas mask, dousing incendiary bombs and clearing rubble from bombed buildings. By war's end some 98 million Soviet citizens had undergone basic civil defence training (Geist 2019). Such mass civilian involvement, in what became known as the Great Patriotic War, helped cement the identity of the mass of the population with a momentous war for survival that touched every family. No doubt countless lives were saved, although in places like Leningrad the civilian population was decimated by deliberate Nazi attempts to starve them to death.

The wartime experience was taken directly into Cold War planning on both sides of the divide. However, nuclear war required an entirely new approach; as Burchett observed in Hiroshima, while it might be possible to take shelter (although the populations of Nagasaki and Hiroshima received no warning to take to the shelters), the radiation sickness that followed was in the dust and very air that was breathed by blast survivors. It took a long-time for this factor to be fully understood, or at least officially recognised, and this was partly due to the deliberate blind-eye turned to the effects of radiation until the late 1950s. In the late 1940s both the Americans and Soviets shared the view that the reports of radiation sickness in Japan were inventions of the Japanese press (Geist 2019). The truth became very public when press reports appeared in March 1954 concerning radiation burns suffered by the crew of a Japanese fishing vessel, *Lucky Dragon*, that had been outside the safety exclusion zone surrounding Bikini Atoll in the Pacific where the Americans were secretly conducting thermonuclear tests. Between 1957 and 1958, the British undertook four similar tests on Christmas Island, exposing thousands of British and Commonwealth servicemen as well as indigenous islanders to damaging radiation, resulting in the early deaths of many in ensuing years. Recognition of the dangers of radiation, carried far from the area of the original explosion, failed to be properly considered until the 1963 Test Ban Treaty signed by the USA, the Soviet Union and Britain; from then on tests were only to be conducted underground where radioactive fallout could be more effectively controlled.

The *Lucky Dragon* incident brought the matter of what Civil Defence meant in the nuclear age directly into public imagination. In Britain, Coventry Council, representing a city that had been intensely bombed by the Germans in November 1940, announced that Civil Defence was pointless, sparking public debate in which those who were protesting nuclear weapons, were regularly characterised as communists and Soviet sympathisers (Barnett 2018). Britain's ownership of nuclear bombs and its agreement to site US Thor missiles on its soil in 1958 made it an obvious target, and being small and densely populated in comparison with the two main adversaries, brought the whole population into the front line in an unimaginably greater way than they had been in the darkest days of the Second World War. The revival of civil defence took place from 1950 and involved the spending of vast sums of money at a time of austerity and the persistence of wartime rationing. A Civil Defence Corps of 300,000 mainly part-time volunteers who would help the general population was put in place alongside an Auxiliary Fire Service and stocks of medical equipment and special vehicles (including some 3,000 'Green Goddess' fire engines). Bunkers were built for government and administration, but ordinary citizens were advised in a series of widely available publications on how to protect themselves in the event of a nuclear attack. This was barely any more sophisticated than had existed in the Second World War. The 'four-minute warning' of attack (sometimes quoted by experts as three or less) would give little time for people to do much other than get underneath the kitchen table. In fact a government White Paper in 1957 frankly admitted that the government were unable to protect the population. The first government pamphlet for citizens, *The Hydrogen Bomb*,

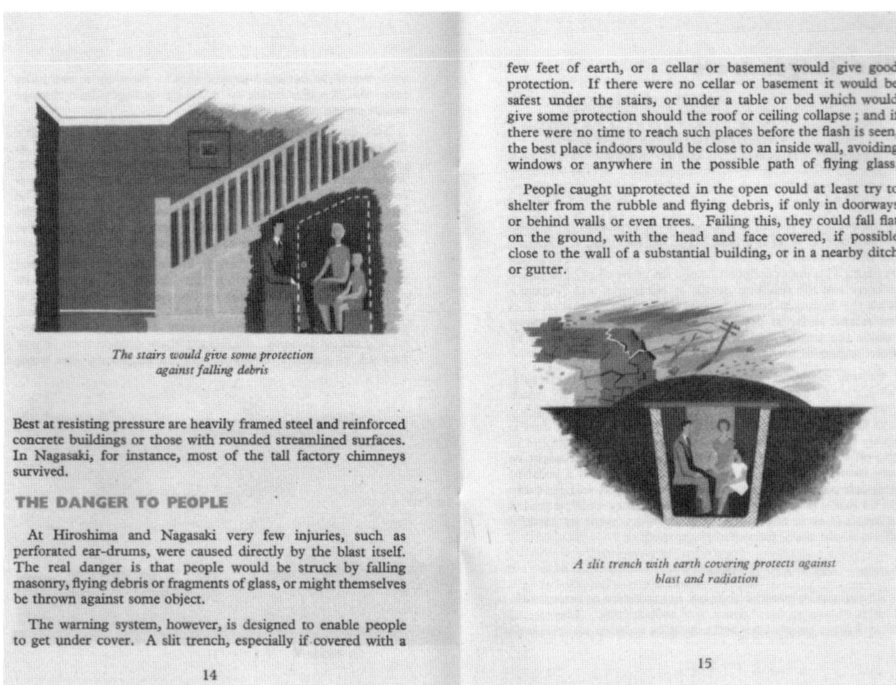

The stairs would give some protection against falling debris

Best at resisting pressure are heavily framed steel and reinforced concrete buildings or those with rounded streamlined surfaces. In Nagasaki, for instance, most of the tall factory chimneys survived.

THE DANGER TO PEOPLE

At Hiroshima and Nagasaki very few injuries, such as perforated ear-drums, were caused directly by the blast itself. The real danger is that people would be struck by falling masonry, flying debris or fragments of glass, or might themselves be thrown against some object.

The warning system, however, is designed to enable people to get under cover. A slit trench, especially if covered with a

14

few feet of earth, or a cellar or basement would give good protection. If there were no cellar or basement it would be safest under the stairs, or under a table or bed which would give some protection should the roof or ceiling collapse ; and if there were no time to reach such places before the flash is seen, the best place indoors would be close to an inside wall, avoiding windows or anywhere in the possible path of flying glass.

People caught unprotected in the open could at least try to shelter from the rubble and flying debris, if only in doorways or behind walls or even trees. Failing this, they could fall flat on the ground, with the head and face covered, if possible close to the wall of a substantial building, or in a nearby ditch or gutter.

A slit trench with earth covering protects against blast and radiation

15

Advice to UK citizens on protection from nuclear attack – *Hydrogen Bomb* pamphlet 1955. (*Author's collection*)

UK Civil Defence volunteers mid-1950s. (*Author's collection*)

published that year, placed a lot of emphasis on improvisation to counter the effects of all the horrors it listed: initial blast, heat and radioactivity. Its cartoon illustrations offered no idea of the actual horrors of nuclear war, even though photographs of the effects of the bombing of Hiroshima and Nagasaki were readily available. While giving no estimate of just how many might initially survive an extensive attack on the long list of potential targets known by then, the pamphlet did offer some reassurance that Civil Defence planning was in place with trained personnel who would provide help and organisation.

UK Civil Defence poster 1950s. (*Author's collection*)

However, all this was to change: the Civil Defence Corps was disbanded in 1965, and as the Cold War heated up again in the late 1970s and 1980s, emphasis was placed on early warning systems and extensive further development of deep bunkers for the military and administrative authorities. These involved the imposition of what amounted to military dictatorship in the regions. There were to be no shelters for the general population despite the proliferation of targets with the deployment of a new generation of American cruise missiles. A network of over 1,500 three person bunkers were built across the whole country that would be staffed by the Royal Observer Corps, whose purpose was to monitor and report on radiation levels to the central authorities. This was a total redefinition of role from their previous one (as in the Second World War) of plotting and identifying aircraft incursions – skills that had become redundant . The last publicly available Civil Defence guidance, *Protect and Survive*, all thirty pages, was published in 1980 and contained simple advice on how to build and equip a fallout room in an ordinary home. This would be distributed to every household in the event of possible conflict, but could be meantime purchased for 50p. It was easily ridiculed as entirely inadequate for its purpose by anyone who knew anything about the actual dangers (Campbell 1982). The main peace organisation, CND (Campaign for Nuclear Disarmament), produced a counter pamphlet titled *Protest and Survive*. The argument from the peace movement and expert critical analysts like investigative journalist Duncan Campbell was that the government were being dishonest to the point of deliberate deception. By contrast, neutral Switzerland built enough deep shelter with supply provision for 86 per cent of its population.

Abandoned Royal Observer Corps bunker, Appin Argyll 2021. (*Author's collection*)

During the early 1950s in the USA, initial official attitudes to civil defence were complacent and cost driven. However, politicians like the aspiring President John F. Kennedy used this to their advantage, stirring up public opinion with a view to changing policies. Public information followed to educate people

2. Use tables if they are large enough to provide you all with shelter. Surround them and cover them with heavy furniture filled with sand, earth, books or clothing.

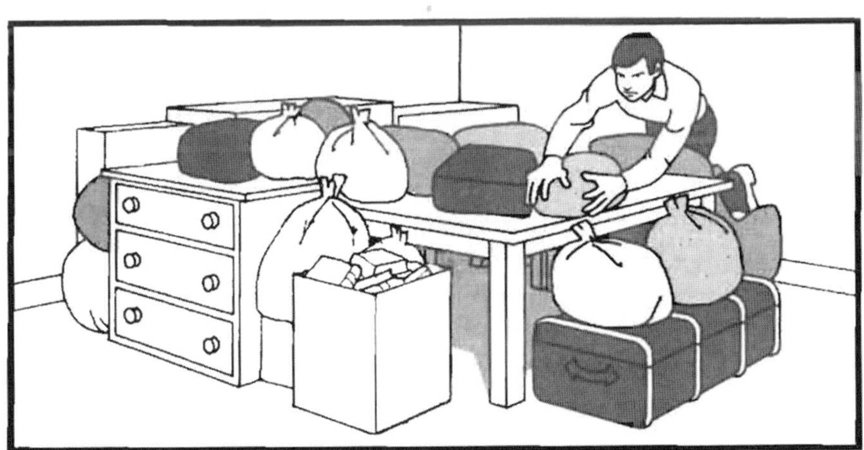

Home protection advice UK government. *Protect and Survive* 1980. (*Author's collection*)

and prepare them for the possibility of attack – this included a notorious 1951 education cartoon film for children, *Duck and Cover*, in which a turtle named Bert advised them to do what it said in the title to save themselves (Geist 2019). Shelter design and construction became an obvious business opportunity and after the Cuba crisis, spaces were provided in cities for at least some of the people (81.5 million by 1966 according to Geist). Stores of supplies to maintain such numbers underground for lengthy periods could not keep pace and the system was never completed. Later in the Cold War, US planning turned to mass evacuation from urban to rural areas, taking advantage of the size of America and widespread car ownership, encouraging highway development. Home fallout shelters were suggested, even though they would be of little value in urban areas subject to targeting by nuclear missiles and bombs. Meantime, the movie *Dr Strangelove* parodied the US state of mind with its depiction of the 'mineshaft gap' – worry that the other side had deeper shelters from which they might emerge after a nuclear holocaust to dominate the world. This was not far from the truth, as both sides focused on protecting government and administration rather than the general population – although the myth of effective civil defence became a component of the coercive pressure place on the USSR under Reagan's presidency in the 1980s. By this time many Americans had been erroneously led to believe that their government's SDI 'Star Wars' programme would provide a wrap-around shield for the USA preventing any missiles reaching their targets. Some Americans resorted to 'survivalism', which was encouraged by movies from *Panic in Year Zero* in 1962 and including *The Day After* in 1983, initiating a genre of novels and even lifestyle magazines. Survivalism became a cult for those who fatalistically saw war as inevitable, and survival dependent entirely

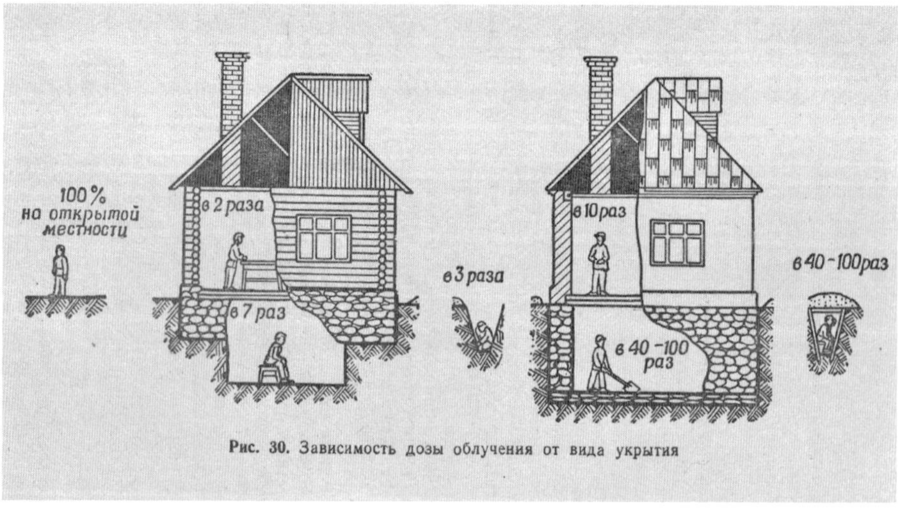

Advice to USSR householders in event of nuclear attack – *Everyone Should Know This.* (*Author's collection*)

on the efforts they made as heavily armed individuals to protect themselves and their families from not just the effects of attack, but also their fellow citizens in the aftermath.

In the USSR civil defence remained in the hands of those who had been responsible for its implementation during the war. It was an important facet of the voluntary mass youth organisation OSOAVIAKhIM (renamed DOSAAF in 1951), which organised paramilitary and associated sporting activity across the whole USSR. Specific shelter provision was ignored in the Stalin period, but deep shelters construction and mass evacuation plans from urban areas continued throughout the Cold War period. In Moscow alone some 5,000 shelters are thought to have been built (Ware 2016). As in the US and Britain, the general population were offered pamphlets that gave the same type of general advice – the best known and most widespread being called *Это должен знать каждый – Everyone Should Know This*. As in the West, the Soviets developed early warning systems and bunkers for the military and leaderships across the country, and in their satellite countries.

The Bomb as an Ideological and Religious Weapon

Although a very real war at times in Eastern Europe and the Third World, the Cold War was primarily an ideological one in which each side sought moral as well as military superiority over its adversary. The means of achieving this will be discussed in Chapter 6, but there are features that belong in this chapter about the primacy of the Bomb. Communism and capitalism were obvious foes if viewed as mutually exclusive, but in America, Christian belief was used to drive what was portrayed as an anti-communist crusade for freedom.

The Soviets were characterised by the West in the late 1940s as having overwhelming superiority in conventional forces. In fact, this was only true in terms of numbers of ground troops – Soviet demobilisation at the end of the war was rapid and only suspended when the Cold War became a threat to their security (Merridale 2006). America had a vastly superior Navy and as described in Chapter 2, air bomber fleets that simply didn't exist in the USSR's armoury. What is not often described in the usual Western narratives is the factor of popular support that might have installed left-wing and anti-American governments in Western Europe in the wake of the war – a more powerful side of the equation than Stalin's tank divisions. This did not happen due to several factors, including the success of the Marshall Plan of economic aid, and of course events in defeated Germany described in Chapter 2. But viewed from this perspective, the Cold War was as much about tackling the enemy at home as it was in defending against the threat of foreign Soviet invasion. Contemporary analysis of the Cold War took such matters into account, albeit as an aside from the general wargame mentality of comparing armed forces strengths (Bidwell 1978); the size and influence of Communist Parties in France and Italy was made to look like an issue even though neither showed any propensity for either revolution or putting out a welcome mat to invading Soviet forces. For much of the period the Italian Communist Party, as the first 'Eurocommunists', were in favour of NATO and the pro-capitalist European Union. So, a vital component of the Cold War were the efforts to convince home populations of the essential greatness of capitalism or communism, depending on where you happened to live (discussed in Chapter7). In this sense there was the good Bomb (on our side) and the bad Bomb (owned by the enemy) and much effort went into persuading home populations to support their own armed forces. Just as much effort went into dealing with dissident voices – and in the USSR and its satellites this involved varying degrees of brute force. In America, at times it also involved state oppression.

The Bomb, more than any other terror weapon, involved a vision of the 'Apocalypse' in popular imagination, especially in the USA where the Christian tradition was central to the good vs evil narrative of anti-communism (Barnett 2018). Rehill, quoted in Barnett, extends this analogy further to point to divergences in Western and Eastern thought that emerged from the split in the Christian faith a thousand years ago between the Catholic based churches (especially their later Protestant offspring) and the Orthodox church. The Book of Revelation, the final chapter of the New Testament, concerns the Apostle John's visions of the end of the world (the Apocalypse) and the final triumph of Christ's teachings. The Orthodox Church rejected much of Revelation and insisted on traditional teachings from the time of Christ himself, rejecting the various interpretations of the Apocalypse stories. The point here is that it explains perhaps how people in Russia and later in the Soviet Union, could hold a more fatalistic view of the future and therefore hold onto faith of sorts in their leaders – be they Czars, or Soviet Party Secretaries in the period under discussion here, when atheism was officially encouraged. Some of the Western church interpretations of Revelation, conversely, went to extreme and nonsensical lengths; late in the Cold War Robert Faid, a fundamental US Christian and prominent nuclear engineer, emboldened by President Ronald Reagan and his anti-communist crusade, explained the birthmark on Soviet Premier Gorbachev's forehead as the mark of the beast, and that the Soviet leader was the Antichrist. His book on the theme sold in large quantities, even though by the time of its publication Gorbachev had turned out to be the most pliable Soviet premier any US administration had ever dealt with.

Anti-communism was given forcible expression in the immediate post-war period. Right-wing politicians in the USA had never been comfortable with America's involvement with the USSR during the war, and as soon as it was over began to apply pressure to disengage and return to the enmities that had prevailed after the Russian Revolution of 1917. This was pursued based on communism's perceived antagonism to basic American values – it rejected capitalism, which was seen as intrinsic to the popular notion of the American way of life and integral to Christian belief; it favoured atheism, which was seen as an attack on the right to hold such beliefs, and it was synonymous with totalitarianism, which was anathema to those who saw the USA as having been founded on individual liberty.

> The ideology of communism, especially as it was incarnated in the USSR, was seen as a totality of social, economic, political, and religious falsehood that opposed everything the U.S. represented. Church people often referred to communism as a religion, noting the complete view of life it offered and the complete allegiance of its adherents.
>
> Nutt (2000) p.53

The Christian Right in America went to great lengths to prove their case; in 1946 the conservative *Human Events* newspaper printed the entire theses and programme (complete with index!) of the Comintern from their Second Congress in 1920 (Chamberlain 1946). This had been long forgotten within the mainstream communist movement, having been buried by Stalin in the 1920s, who, incidentally, had murdered almost all its authors. Stalin had also wound up the Comintern itself in 1943 as a gesture of goodwill towards his wartime Western allies. All this was turned on its head and presented in the short introduction as evidence of Soviet duplicity and dirty tricks.

Revelations that the US Manhattan Project, which had developed the first nuclear bomb, had been infiltrated by Soviet agents resulted in renewed emphasis on loyalty tests from 1947. Of course, such spying activity would not have been necessary had the US shared such science with their allies in the first place, lending credence to the idea that the Soviets were always intended as an eventual target of the Bomb. The spying drama contributed to the feverish atmosphere developing in occupied Germany in which every Soviet action or inaction was interpreted as aggressive. America became dominated by a 'Red Scare', despite having a tiny Communist Party who enjoyed little electoral support. Anti-communism in the USA reached its zenith with the rising influence of Senator Joe McCarthy between 1950 and the middle of the decade.

> Today we are engaged in a final all-out battle between communistic atheism and Christianity. The modern champions of communism have selected this as the time. And, ladies and gentlemen, the chips are down – they are truly down...... While I cannot take the time to name all the men in the State Department who have been named as members of the Communist Party and members of a spy ring, I have here in my hand a list of 205.
>
> Sen. Joe McCarthy speech in Wheeling Virginia
> 9 February 1950 (United States Senate archive)

The House Un-American Activities Committee (HUAC), which McCarthy dominated, held public hearings that mercilessly condemned communists and anyone associated with them to unemployment and pariah status and was especially aimed at anyone who might influence others, such as those in the entertainment industry (also discussed in Chapter 7). It was based on paranoia and intolerance and was eventually driven out in the mid-1950s by the successful marshalling of more liberal opinion. However, it helped embed a firm belief in the perceived evils of communism that persisted throughout the Cold War and lent justification to policies at home and overseas. Such ideas never went away but enjoyed a particular revival with the election of Ronald Reagan to the presidency in 1980.

Intelligence, Spying and the Murky Underbelly of the Cold War

The popular perception of the Cold War has been shaped by movies and novels that celebrate the world of espionage and counterespionage. This cultural aspect will be discussed further in Chapter 7, but it is worth passing comment here on the real worth of spying activity to the efforts of both sides to keep abreast of the other's technical progress. We have already seen that in the aftermath of Second World War, Soviet spy rings in the USA successfully passed details of the Atom Bomb to the Soviets. Soviet spies at this time were typically committed individuals with an ideological loyalty to communism and were found in Britain and the USA. The paranoia over spying in the USA in the late 1940s with the capture and execution of some real and not so real spies, made that difficult. Certainly the presence of Soviet spies at the heart of the British intelligence community in the form of the Cambridge Five (Burgess, Maclean, Philby, Cairncross and Blunt), led to the capture of agents sent to the Soviet Union. After 1956 and the suppression of the Hungarian uprising it would have been difficult to recruit such individuals, and traitors were either bought or blackmailed. On the other side notable spies include Oleg Gordievsky, a KGB officer who became disillusioned with the Soviet system after the Soviet invasion of Czechoslovakia in 1968. After being recruited by MI6 in 1972 when posted in Denmark, he became of great value when he was appointed resident-designate (KGB chief) in London from 1982. He passed on identification of Gorbachev as the next leader of the USSR, and also the USSR fear of a NATO first strike that almost led to war over Exercise Able Archer described earlier in this chapter. Gordievsky was returned to Moscow under suspicion in 1985 but MI6 effected a dramatic escape to the UK where he later became a writer and commentator on KGB matters (Macintyre 2018). Despite these and other Western coups, the belief of one intelligence insider is that the Soviets were the masters of this 'wilderness of mirrors' because of their absolute determination to defend their country from invasion by any and every means available, no matter how ruthless these might be (Magee 2021). Those who sold them information on a one-off basis were blackmailed into providing more and more.

The use of special forces to further covert nuclear war was also pursued by both sides. The Soviets are reported to have established caches of arms across the FDR (and possibly elsewhere) that could be accessed by special forces or agents already in place in the event of war. These are said to have included small 'suitcase' nuclear weapons that might have been used behind the lines. American special forces were also trained in the use of similar nuclear weapons that they might use when dropped by parachute behind Soviet lines (Magee 2021).

The most effective information-gathering about military activity was through surveillance, although only the US and its allies had the equipment to undertake this with any measure of success. Spy planes flown by US and British pilots were active over the USSR for most of the 1950s. In 1954 the RAF had flown several missions into Soviet airspace under the codename Operation Jiu Jitsu. This was to test Soviet radar and defensive reaction using American RB-45 Tornado aircraft in British markings. The aircraft were spotted and chased by MIG-15s, although all returned safely from this blatantly provocative mission. In 1961, an American U-2 high altitude spy aircraft was shot down and its pilot, Gary Powers, placed on public trial. This was a coup for the Soviets – especially as Powers was working under a code that suggested he should take his own life rather than suffer capture. By the time of his mission U-2 aircraft were being superseded by satellites in space which could operate with impunity and supply detailed photoreconnaissance of anywhere on the planet. Power's mission was supposed to be the last one – flying well over central Russia rather than the peripheral bases that were usually of interest. In a reversal of popular East/West perceptions, it seems that everyone knew about the U-2 incursions except the American public; the initial claim by the US authorities that Powers' mission was a weather flight that had crashed in Turkey was obviously ridiculous. Accurate intelligence could also prove embarrassing – as when the 'missile gap' of the late 1950s was shown by U-2 photographs to be a total fiction, undermining calls for more US ones to even-up a non-existent deficit (see Chapter 3). Soviet aircraft tested the boundaries of Western defences during the Cold War, and often overflew US and British warships in the open sea, but despite the way their missions were portrayed in the Western media, never engaged in the type of provocation undertaken by the Americans and British.

The other means of surveillance that was dominated by the Americans was the breaking of coded transmissions. This was undertaken largely by hand using technology that was not much further on in development than the equipment used in Bletchley Park in the Second World War to break German codes.

This took a huge leap in the 1970s with the development of fast computer technology. The Soviets were denied access to IBM computer equipment through trade embargos and never successfully developed their own at the rate achieved by the US. Some of this success was undermined by Geoffrey Prime, a Soviet spy who claimed to be ideologically motivated but who was a paedophile using techniques taught to identify and entrap children for sexual gratification. The Soviets recruited and trained Prime, who worked for the RAF and later GCHQ, the secret monitoring station in Cheltenham, and passed on information about British and US decoding through the 1970s, until caught in 1982. It was, however, this code-breaking and analytical advantage that allowed the US, according to Haslam (2011), to lure the Soviet Union into its own unwinnable and draining Vietnam: Afghanistan in 1979, a story that will be picked up in Chapter 5.

Less well known are the legally permitted Soviet and US Intelligence missions that were authorised by post-war agreement to range across Germany throughout the Cold War period. These involved intelligence officers openly driving about in vehicles gathering whatever information they could. Although these were not supposed to enter restricted areas on either side, a cat and mouse game often took place involving high speed chases, ambushes, contrived collisions with other vehicles and other attempts to divert and distract the other party's missions. Two American intelligence officers died through alleged accidents to US missions (Magee 2021).

One aspect of Cold War surveillance and spying was the use of civilian vessels engaged in peaceful activities to report on the activities of the Naval fleets of the other side, sometimes proactively. There are accounts of Soviet fishing vessels moored for long periods off the Northern Ireland coast that were clearly monitoring Polaris Submarine movements in and out of the Firth of Clyde. On the UK side there has long been speculation and controversy over the loss of the large Hull registered fish factory vessel, FV *Gaul*, in the Barents Sea in 1974. At that time some British fishing vessels were apparently tasked with reporting Soviet Naval movements in these, their home waters. The *Gaul* sunk mysteriously with all hands and evidence later revealed from inspection of the wreck, suggests she may have been in collision with a submarine, although no proof or official admission from either side has ever emerged.

In situ for most of the Cold War period (all replaced with satellites by 1982) were the weather ships provided by international agreement to aid transatlantic air navigation and aid search and rescue operations in the event of aircraft crashes in the ocean. Although their divisions of operation included (latterly) the USSR, according to anecdotal evidence passed to the author, there was suspicion among UK civilian crews (who had to sign the Official Secrets Act) that Services crew were involved in surveillance.

Conclusion

This chapter has explored the development of nuclear weapons (the Bomb) and their prime place in the history of an undeclared forty-five-year-old war that never broke out openly between its main protagonists. Such weapons were developed by both sides far beyond any practical use they might have in a real conflict, supporting Mary Kaldor's notion that this was an 'imaginary war'. They had a logic of their own that was condemned as madness by many, but nonetheless supported popular government policies of deterrence, restraint and peaceful co-existence in both similar and different ways by both sides. The good Bomb (ours) and the bad Bomb (theirs) also bolstered and justified ideological positions at home and in the respective areas of influence. Populations were asked to believe that a nuclear war was survivable despite the obvious fallacy of such ideas. On several occasions conflict involving nuclear weapon launches (either deliberately or accidentally) were narrowly avoided. While superficially this was an ideological conflict between capitalism and communism that had been conducted intermittently since 1917, there was a dynamic that went beyond such explanations: in the West it was about access to, and control of, resources, and in the East, security and bases for extending influence. The post-war arms build-up, especially with conventional weapons, will be discussed in the next chapter. Chapter 6 will examine how quite rational internal resistance to nuclear weapons was successfully made to be identified in the popular imagination with disloyalty and subversion.

Soviet 1970s poster depicting its armed forces protecting the nation against US nuclear aggression. (*Author's collection*)

Chapter 4

The Military Industrial Complex and the Profitable Race to Go Further and Faster

> The Second World War ended the depression by throwing America into a war economy. We are in a war economy still, and we are only slightly embarrassed by the difficulty of officially declaring a Third World War. But where there's a will, I hate to suggest, there's often a way.
>
> James Baldwin *Dark Days* (1980)

Introduction

It is an American, Bernard Baruch, who is generally credited for the term 'Cold War' to describe escalating East/West tensions in 1947 (although George Orwell had used it the year before); Baruch is described in the histories as a statesman, US government adviser, and, characteristically, as a multi-millionaire. It was the USA, driven by those with a financial interest like Baruch, who largely scripted the course of events over the next forty-three years. This chapter will describe the attempts by each side to gain the advantage over the other – in actual terms this always involved an American initiative based around some technological or scientific advance followed usually (but not always) by a Soviet attempt to catch up so that a balance of power could be maintained. Whether this was to ensure security or increase influence and power in the world remains a matter of historical debate, just as it did around the end of the Second World War as described in Chapter 2. Chapter 3 discussed some of the ideological reasons for the amassing of unnecessarily large amounts of destructive force by each side, this chapter will examine the economic reasons.

America and Britain in the 1930s were characterised by economic slump; closed factories, empty pockets, dole queues and soup kitchens were common experiences for working people. The war put an end to this; limitless credit was paid for enormous amounts of war materiel and created vast armed forces; relative prosperity was universal, even if life in wartime for many was precarious. In contrast, the Soviet Union in the 1930s saw economic progress and full employment, few outside realising the extent to which this workers' paradise was being built on the backs of slave labour provided by the Gulag system; millions suffering unreasonable lengths of imprisonment (by any standard!) and death so that the Soviet Union could advance its Five-Year Plans. The war changed things in the USSR too – millions more suffering as the Nazi armies swept eastward on a murderous course of genocidal destruction. However, it also united people in a common purpose to defeat the invader and save the motherland. Ordinary workers, many of them children, went to extraordinary lengths to maintain weapon and other supplies for the Red Army, while service men and women made enormous, heroic sacrifices to achieve final victory in 1945. By this time, Soviet industrial capacity, much of it moved eastwards beyond the Ural Mountains and out of reach of German guns, was massive. In 1945 the Big Three wartime allies had enormous armament production capacity; in the case of the Soviet Union a shift was needed to rebuild the shattered western regions which had hosted four years of ferocious war. The problems were enormous – the retreating Nazis had destroyed every vestige of productive capacity, resource extraction (especially the important coal mining capacity in Ukraine's Donetsk region), infrastructure including railways, and homes. This latter factor was significant in terms of human hardship – in the cities and larger communities, family life had broken down; people were living in holes in the ground and the ruined streets were full of the war-disabled and parentless children. For politicians and others in the USA, whose land was untouched by battle and where the war had created full employment and prosperity, to imagine that the Soviet people, with over 25 million dead, had the resources and energy to invade the rest of Europe, seems ridiculous. Reality, however, had little to do with the shaping of events.

The term used to describe the relationship between government, military and industry is the 'Military-Industrial Complex' (MIC) and the dynamic behind this known as the 'Permanent War Economy' (or 'Permanent Arms Economy'). Dwight Eisenhower first drew popular attention to the MIC phenomenon with his very last US Presidential speech in January 1961. In this he described the size and power of an industrial complex devoted entirely to defence production. This, he said, differed from pre- Second World War capacity that had been devoted to peaceful manufacturing, but which could convert to armaments: 'makers of ploughshares could, with time and as required, make swords as well' (Swanson 2013 p.10). Eisenhower went on to warn listeners of the dangers of 'unwarranted influence' and 'the disastrous rise of misplaced power', and that Americans 'should never let the weight of this combination endanger our liberties or democratic processes' (ibid). This was a stern warning about a situation that Eisenhower himself had contributed towards as a general turned politician of the early Cold War era – no one knew more about all this than he did…

The Growth of Power of the Military Industrial Complex in the USA

The origins of the MIC go back to the years of the First World War, but became embedded in American society in the Second World War. At the start of the war, the US Army had eighty tanks and forty-nine bomber aircraft; by August 1945 America had produced 88,000 tanks and self-propelled guns, and 97,000 bombers to give just two examples of the enormous development of defence manufacturing capacity. Much of this went abroad to allies, so export was an important component of the MIC. Unemployment consequently fell from over 14 per cent pre-war to just over 1 per cent through the spending of 36 per cent of US GDP on defence (Swanson 2013). Naturally, a proportion of wages was returned to government through taxation and increased spending power, benefiting other areas of the economy, particularly through the purchase of consumer items, and all-round prosperity resulted. This created dependency on defence spending between the owners of the factories that employed the workers (and their scientists involved in developing more and better weapons of war), and the military leaders and strategists who devised the plans for their use. They, with the politicians who voted through the funding, form what might be called a triangle of mutual reinforcement that spurred the self-interest driven Cold War.

This economic boom was threatened by war's end and so it was in everyone's domestic interests for it to continue, and reasons to do so inevitably followed. As described in Chapter 2, this started before the Summer of 1945 with manufactured fear of Soviet aggressive intent and open talk of a possible necessity to continue the war against this new enemy. The interests of the Christian Right (described in Chapter 3) and American capital were one and the same, and combined to present a scenario where defence production had to be maintained to meet the new (old) threat of communism. This process became an end in itself, and threats of communist aggression were continuously manufactured and reinvented throughout the Cold War. This achieved political and popular support for the continuous development of all types of weapons of war and high levels of military spending.

The first interest group in the triangular relationship were the corporations involved in manufacturing who had been involved in wartime on armaments development. They employed scientists drawn from the academic community due to the increasingly complicated nature of warfare. Politicians and military leaders were dependent on these scientists for explaining the use and potential of new weaponry and equipment and they soon became indispensable to both. Many scientists therefore did not go back to their universities on war's end, having themselves found rewards and well-funded possibilities to develop their projects in the defence industries (Garrison & Shivpuri 1983). During wartime, innovation was led by military requirement but in the post-war world of the Cold War, scientists were able to promote their ideas in anticipation of their audiences' wish to keep ahead of the Soviets. The Chief Scientific Advisor to the UK government, Lord Zuckerman, stated 'The nuclear world with all its hazards is the scientist's creation; it is certainly not a world that came about because of any external demand' (Garrison & Shivpuri p.250). The launch of the Sputnik satellite into space in 1957 caught the American establishment unawares and accelerated this trend. Even where there was no such real driver, scientists would collude with intelligence and military chiefs to exaggerate and even invent scare stories of Soviet plans to promote their agendas. US innovations in the 1960s and 1970s during the era of détente illustrate this: MIRVs (Multiple Targeted Re-entry Vehicles) and from them, more precise MARVs (Manoeuvring Re-entry Vehicles). These were promoted by the Lockheed Corporation who had sold it to Navy Chiefs, who in turn convinced politicians to authorise funding; this took US SLBM (Submarine Launched Ballistic Missile) capability far beyond any deterrence value, but vastly increased the possibility of a first strike against the Soviet Union to knock out their nuclear weapon bases. Profits meantime poured into Lockheed's shareholders' pockets, even though the SALT ABM (Anti-Ballistic Missile) treaty temporarily shelved development and production.

Lockheed was just one of the corporations involved in plucking this magic money tree (and more about them later in this chapter). In 1951 US military expenditure stood at $22 million, doubling to $50 million by 1953. What gave impetus to this was the top-secret review of national security published in 1950 just before the outbreak of the Korean War, 'NSC-68', which argued for a flexible response to the worldwide threat of communism, using whatever method and force necessary to contain and deal with local conflicts that the Kremlin might have an interest in promoting. This recognised that the methods used might not be acceptable at home but could be justified if deployed elsewhere. NSC-68 helped change American leaders into what Gaddis (2005) describes as 'Machiavellians', and its philosophy can be seen in numerous foreign interventions through the Cold War period (discussed in Chapter 5). This strategy would require an array of weaponry and equipment and there were plenty of enterprises queuing up to provide it.

Each branch of the armed services had its client manufacturers, close relations being enjoyed between scientists, corporate bosses and the generals or admirals concerned. Boeing Aerospace, General Dynamics and Rockwell International produced missiles and bombers for the air force; Grumman and Vought, fighter aircraft for the Navy; McDonnell-Douglas and General Dynamics fighter jets for the air force; Lockheed, heavy transports and SLBNs; Bell and Boeing Vertol produced helicopters; Electric Boat (a sub-division of General Dynamics) made submarines; Newport News Corporation, aircraft carriers and other naval warships. These are just a few examples (Garrison and Shivpuri 1983). Each of these concerns represented thousands of jobs spread across the USA, often in one industry towns or areas they dominated such as Boeing in Seattle, or McDonnell in St Louis, Missouri. Because these weapons were rarely, if ever, used, the focus was not, as in the Second World War, on replacing lost weapons and equipment, but in developing the next generation of improved equipment that would render what already existed obsolete. Aircraft were made to be faster, of longer range and as undetectable as possible; ships quieter and faster with better weapon-carrying facility. Strategic value was replaced by corporate and scientific competition (ibid). Justification in the 1960s was offered by reference to the 'Two and a Half Wars' concept – that the USA should be able to fight two major wars and one minor war in different theatres simultaneously; when that was seen to be unrealistic and more emphasis put on the contribution of NATO allies, this became a 'One and a Half Wars' idea (Deikin 1973). Some of these systems and units, despite their technological wizardry, would be largely ineffectual in actual conflict – what Mary Kaldor describes as part of a 'baroque arsenal' (Kaldor 1982). The F-111 jet bomber was designed to have a capability of short take-off from improvised landing strips, flying the Atlantic non-stop, combat at very low as well as very high altitudes, speeds more than 1,700 miles per hour, and a large bomb carrying capacity that could include nuclear weapons. The problem for this expensive icon was that once it had been detected by an enemy anti-aircraft missile system, it was probably doomed despite all its systems and capability. In 1980 the US government placed orders for $83 billion worth of contracts, nearly half of which went to the twenty-five largest defence manufacturers.

The next link in the triangle were the military generals, admirals, and strategists. Those with high military rank were often driven by inter-service rivalry and were keen to win investment and prestige for their own arm in taking the lead for the nation's defence. In the immediate post-war world, the air force with its bomber fleets were able to take on this mantle, replaced in the late 1950s by the Navy with its aircraft carriers that could take US power anywhere in the world, and its submarines that were the basis of the nuclear deterrent. NISC-68 also lent importance to the army in terms of conventional capability for engagement in limited wars to prevent the spread of communism in areas of

Nuclear aircraft carrier, the aptly named USS *Enterprise*, launched 1960. (*USN via Wikimedia Commons*)

the world where there was little risk of escalation to open superpower conflict. All this fed demand and kept the lucrative contracts rolling. As these military personnel made personal relationships with the scientists and corporation heads who they dealt with for their service, loyalties to them fed the competition between services and between the private companies who supplied them with what they were convinced they needed. So, even though warfare in the real world involves close cooperation between air, land and seaborne forces, the bureaucratic empires behind them were as involved in competition as were the corporations who wanted to win the lucrative contracts. The generals and admirals saw it as in their interests to talk up whatever Soviet threat they were the ones best placed to deal with. This resulted in conflicting claims, some of which were grossly exaggerated. In the 1950s a belief was expounded that the USA was in deficit over a 'bomber gap'. Evidence was produced which showed that the Soviets had outpaced the Americans; this included witness from the 1955 Tushino Air Show in Moscow where a handful of new 'Bison' Bombers were flown round in a large circle, their identification numbers obscured, to make it look like wave after wave of aircraft, when in fact it was the same ones. This deception suited USAF chiefs, especially the gung-ho wartime hero and heavy bombing fan, Curtis LeMay, who devised secret plans to increase his bomber fleets with enough capacity to attack the USSR and destroy 118 big

Boeing B-47 bombers of the 1950s. (*USAF via Wikimedia Commons*)

cities with a projected death toll of 60 million people. To achieve this, bomber numbers were increased to 1,800 B-47 and 850 B-52 aircraft. By the time this was underway the truth had emerged that the Soviets actually had 120 'Bison' jet and seventy 'Bear' turboprop bombers so the 'gap' was all in favour of the Americans (Garrison & Shivpuri 1983).

Fear of Soviet nuclear-bearing missiles pre-dated their actual existence; one US Air Force colonel during the Korean War, concerned at the lack of research and development in this field, took the matter into his own hands and concocted a Soviet design that he passed to an intelligence community friend who then included them in his next briefing to Air Force generals. His alarming description of this latest development of Soviet technology resulted in funds and resources (ibid).

Politicians also played pivotal roles in this triangle of deceit and financial interest. Talking up the Soviet threat and denigrating the record of your opponent was an easy way to gain popularity and election in conservative America throughout the Cold War, exemplified by Truman in the post-war period (see Chapter 2), and John F. Kennedy in the late 1950s and early 1960s. Kennedy used the 'missile gap', which had by then replaced the mythical 'bomber gap', in the 1960 presidential election. This was based not on evidence of arms build-up, but on the Soviet space firsts, primarily the Sputnik satellite which orbited the earth and was seen in the sky by millions of Americans on its passage. This and its follow-ups which took Soviet street dogs into space, were entirely peaceful even if the same rocket engineering might have military application, but they made a huge dent in American prestige (Turbett 2021b). Kennedy went onto to justify his arms spending based on what he knew to be false information about the 'missile gap', again resulting in massive imbalance in favour of the USA with its new generation of Polaris-carrying submarines and Minuteman missiles. All this was later revealed by Defense Secretary Robert McNamara who complained that the 'lack of accurate information … and (necessary) conservatism' had led to a secret Air Force first strike capability and a much larger nuclear arsenal than required for defence purposes (McNamara 1970 pp.56–7). All other US presidents played the same dangerous game until it reached a finale with the aggressive policies of Ronald Reagan which were designed to break the stalemate once the Soviets had caught up by the 1980s (discussed in Chapter 10).

US strategy was based on a series of reports, many secret, that provided estimates of Soviet capability. Kennan's 'Long Telegram' was mentioned in Chapter 2, and the influence of NISC-68 earlier in this chapter. In 1957 the Gaither Report lent justification to the spending escalation of that era, and the work that was required to win public support. The 1976 'Team B' report commissioned by President Gerald Ford reiterated belief in the commitment of the Soviets to world domination and suggested that previous CIA calculations of Soviet missile numbers were an underestimate – so increases in budgets followed. The information as always was highly dubious but was repeated so often that it became the new truth. More spending always followed the debates around these reports, feeding the consensus view of American conservatism that predominated throughout the Cold War, which more liberal opinion, such as that of President Jimmy Carter, was forced to appease. Such reports also encouraged demonstration of American commitment to anti-communism, the Vietnam War being the greatest example, and the post 1976 ending of détente, another.

The Reagan presidency brought the anti-communist crusade to new heights and justification was needed for the latest increases in military spending that could be viewed and understood in the public arena. The result was a series of annual reports from 1981 until 1991 titled *Soviet Military Power* which were widely distributed. These surveys from the US Defense Department were professionally produced and lavishly illustrated with clever graphics to prove their case (they can be viewed on the Wikimedia Commons website). With an introduction from Caspar Weinburger, Reagan's Secretary of Defense, they dealt with all aspects of the perceived threat to freedom and peace, from nuclear weapons to Soviet support for 'terrorism' worldwide. The latter included, by mention, the anti-apartheid ANC (African National Congress) fighters whose jailed leader Nelson Mandela was already being celebrated across the world as an icon of anti-oppression and freedom. The US brochure was followed by a NATO publication which laid out a set of simple graphics to make the same points as the American one (NATO 1982). The massaging of figures and misleading diagrams were central to these efforts, and it was only natural that the USSR would respond with its own version as a counter in this propaganda war; *Whence the Threat to Peace* was published at home and abroad, in English as well as Russian, in four editions from 1982 until 1987. The first was quite basic and included some diagrams and maps to illustrate US power across the world and the threat it posed to the Soviet Union and world peace. The quality improved and the last editions had colour photographs as well as graphics – a mirror version of the American titles, and for those who saw them, a frightening portrait of the Western threat to peace, as intended with the anti-Soviet originals. The Soviet also published a set of essays on peace and disarmament that went into their arguments in more detail, and with further information to challenge the picture drawn in the US and NATO publications (Shaposhnikov 1983). This points out the American overestimate by 200 of Soviet carriers of strategic nuclear missiles, but underestimate by 300 of the number of US equivalents. This publication also contains an interesting and forward-looking piece by Y. Fedorov reflecting the global environmental impact of nuclear and conventional weapons development. There was no doubt by this time that the Soviets had achieved a balance of destructive capability, but their version rationally explained their reasoning for doing so. Not that their

USSR Bomber Aircraft
METERS
60
45
30
15
0
Tu-95 BEAR
BACKFIRE
BLACKJACK
M-TYPE BISON
Tu-16 BADGER
Tu-22 BLINDER
UNREFUELED COMBAT RADIUS (KM)
8,300
4,000
7,300
5,600
3,100
2,900
MAX SPEED (MACH)
0.8
2.0
2.0
.85
.85
1.4

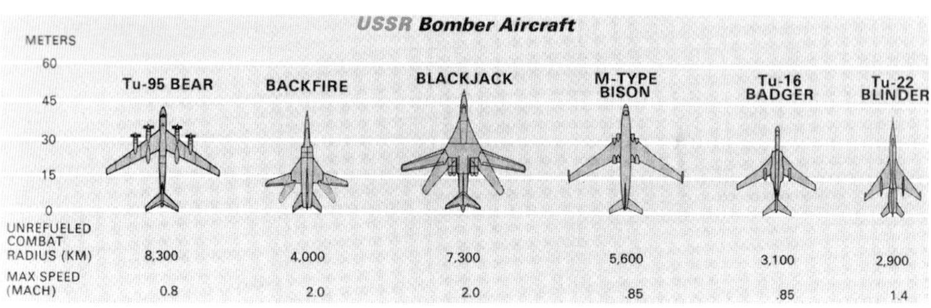

Soviet bombers from the US Govt. *Soviet Military Power* 1986. (*US government via Wikimedia Commons*)

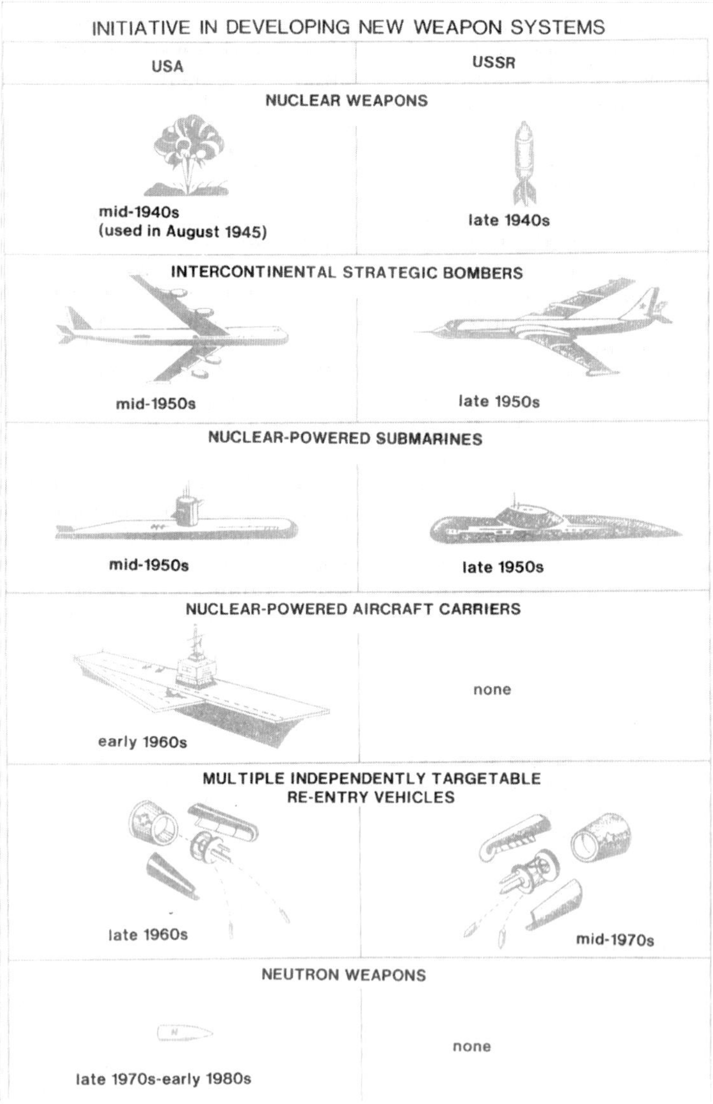

INITIATIVE IN DEVELOPING NEW WEAPON SYSTEMS
USA
USSR
NUCLEAR WEAPONS
mid-1940s
(used in August 1945)
late 1940s
INTERCONTINENTAL STRATEGIC BOMBERS
mid-1950s
late 1950s
NUCLEAR-POWERED SUBMARINES
mid-1950s
late 1950s
NUCLEAR-POWERED AIRCRAFT CARRIERS
early 1960s
none
MULTIPLE INDEPENDENTLY TARGETABLE
RE-ENTRY VEHICLES
late 1960s
mid-1970s
NEUTRON WEAPONS
late 1970s-early 1980s
none

USSR view of the arms race 1984 *Whence the Threat to Peace*. (*Author's collection*) arguments would have made any difference to the conservative and interest-driven forces that were driving matters from the US end.

The Soviets were not blind to the growth and nature of the MIC on the other side (their own MIC will be looked at later in this chapter) and featured it in other publications for both home and foreign audiences. In the decade of space successes from 1957, Soviet writers compared their efforts, achieved by people from working backgrounds like the cosmonauts themselves, with motives that were driving the American programme. Soviet success was built upon service to the people rather than the altar of profit; the racism of the American state characterised by the efforts to desegregate education in the Southern States, would always act as a brake on the journey towards peace and progress (Киселев, A., Ребров, M 1967). A speech by Brezhnev to the World Peace Congress in 1973 is worth quoting in part as its analysis of the MIC was close to that of US based critics:

> It should be clearly seen that the threat to peace is posed by quite concrete social groups, organisations and individuals. Thus, even on the testimony of the top-ranking leaders in the major Western countries, the sinister alliance of the professional militarists and the monopolies making fortunes out of weapons of war, usually known as the military industrial complex, has become something of a state within the state in these countries and has acquired self-sufficient power. Militarism cripples not only the society that produces it. The exhaust gas emitted by the war-preparation machine poisons the political atmosphere of the world with fumes of hatred, fear and violence. To justify its existence, myths are created about a 'Soviet menace' and the need to defend the so-called Western democracies. But the militarist robot fosters as its cherished progeny the most reactionary, tyrannical and fascist regimes, and devours the democratic freedoms.
>
> Quoted in Pyadshev 1977 p.186.

The Chilean Coup of September 1973 lent poignancy and truth to these words (described in more detail later in this chapter).

Britain's Post-War Aircraft Industry

A 1991 industry insider review of the British Defence Industry honestly admitted that the Cold War had lent 'remarkable stability' based on a 'successful policy of deterrence' (Kiely 1991 p.11). This was characterised by an established potential enemy in the Warsaw Pact, a guaranteed market in NATO, and steadily increasing investment based on the need for ever more sophisticated and advanced weapon systems. Defence procurement in the UK was big business, with £8 billion being spent annually on equipment for its own armed forces, and billions earned from exports (ibid). All this was based around the Cold War.

While focus so far has centred on the USA as the biggest and most powerful producer and user of weaponry on the Western side of the conflict, Britain too had its MIC, as did other NATO members. US armed forces were the principal consumer of American defence industry products and with a healthier economy, exports less important than they were in the much smaller manufacturing outputs of Britain and France. Here their value could help economies heavily in debt because of the Second World War and their loss of trading and power generally to the two superpowers of the USA and USSR. Exports also offset the costs of maintaining the nation's own defence.

In 1945 Britain had a vast manufacturing capacity for aircraft and really was a world leader. The list of manufacturers was long: Armstrong-Whitworth, Auster, Avro, Blackburn, Boulton-Paul, Bristol, de Havilland, English Electric, Fairey, Gloster, Handley-Page, Hawker, Percival, Roe, Saunders-Roe, Short, Vickers-Armstrong (including their Spitfire-producing Supermarine division) and Westland. The main manufacturers were supplied by a very large number of component factories and engine builders. Manufacturing plants of all sizes were spread across the UK, competition between them had not been an issue during the war and most were focused on areas of design and specialism concerned with different service requirements; for example, Avro produced large bombers, Blackburn specialised in aircraft for

OPPORTUNITIES

to work on

THE BRITISH LONG RANGE BALLISTIC MISSILE

BLUE STREAK

Following the recent Government White Paper, the Blue Streak development programme is demanding men with initiative and drive who are seeking an assured future. Immediate vacancies exist in the following categories:—

ELECTRICAL FITTERS

Applicants must have experience of assembling and wiring electronic equipment of a wide and varied nature, coupled with the ability to work to electronic circuit diagrams.

ELECTRONIC WIREMAN

Experience of assembly work and wiring to point to point diagrams is essential.

INSTRUMENT MAKERS (ELECTRICAL)

Applicants must be capable of calibrating, adjusting and repairing electrical measuring instruments, and also have the ability to check, build and calibrate electronic test gear.

TRANSFORMER AND ARMATURE WINDERS

Preference will be given to applicants who have experience of windings of a small nature consistent with the radio trade.

TECHNICAL CLERKS

Must have the technical knowledge to enable him to appreciate electrical schedules, and be able to work on own initiative in progressing the work of the Department.

PROGRESS CHASERS

Applicants should have an electrical background.

Single accommodation can easily be arranged by us. Please write, call, or telephone Hatfield 2300, Ext. 338.

THE PERSONNEL MANAGER (REF. 418),

DE HAVILLAND PROPELLERS LIMITED

HATFIELD, HERTS.

Skilled jobs in the UK arms industry – jobs advert 1958. (*RAF Flying Review*)

the Royal Navy. Competition and takeovers reduced this number, and the need for government intervention eventually resulted in the creation of state-owned British Aerospace (Bae) in 1977, which was privatised as a single entity in 1980.

Britain was ahead of all the wartime Allies in terms of jet engine innovation; it developed and flew not just the first operational Allied jet aircraft of the Second World War, the Gloster Meteor, but designed and developed a supersonic aircraft that was cancelled after its plans were passed to the USA. From this developed the Bell X-1, the first aircraft to break the sound barrier in level flight in 1947, not the first or last example of the handing over of advanced technology and expertise to others. As it had used American made transport aircraft in wartime, the UK was poorly placed to develop civil aviation, and the industry was in a precarious position. By August 1945 employment had fallen from a high of 1.7 million a year earlier to just under 1 million. Orders at that time amounted to 10,300 aircraft compared to 43,300 in August 1944 (Hansard October 1945). Production throughout all types of industry was geared towards exports to improve the economic deficit, and at home consumption was controlled through rationing and scarcity. Despite all the difficulties the aircraft industry in Britain maintained prominence into the 1950s; this was a result of the Cold War and the continued development of Britain's own MIC, but with an emphasis on exports. In 1952 the aircraft industry became the third largest employer in the UK as the result of increases in defence spending with the Korean War and the heightening of international tensions. Britain at that time still had a substantial military presence in bases across the Mediterranean and the Far-East. Although the UK's overseas assets reduced to almost nothing over the course of the Cold War period, its defence manufacturing sector remained buoyant and production of military hardware of all types maintained skilled jobs, earnings and exports; in 2020 Britain's aerospace industry was second only to that of the USA. The triangular links between British manufacturers, military leaders and politicians serviced an MIC every bit as embedded as that in the USA.

The Society of British Aircraft Constructors was formed in 1932, and from 1948 began holding annual air shows at Farnborough airfield, near London. These were put on to showcase the British aero industry, aircraft were put through their paces by test pilots (some, like Neville Duke, became household names). Air displays and demonstrations of new technology impressed home audiences, and foreign buyers. Export was welcomed with allies and indeed any country able to get a licence from the Board of Trade for purchases of civilian and military aircraft and their associated weapons. The Farnborough shows would have been observed closely by Soviet guests, just as their Tushino air show and Moscow Parades were by the Americans and British – the intention by both sides being to display might and power, but for the British, also to sell for much needed national income.

Post-war austerity affected RAF orders from the British aircraft Industry just as it did much else. While it had kept up with other combat aircraft, British bomber design had fallen behind and to make up for this deficit eighty-eight wartime American B-29 aircraft were brought out of mothballed retirement, refurbished, and supplied to the RAF in 1950 with the benefit of the American Military Aid programme. This was a Cold War replacement for the wartime lend-lease arrangement through which large numbers of US built aircraft (and other equipment) had been supplied to Britain and the USSR, but now to NATO allies. By the mid-1950s the B-29s had been largely replaced with the British built and designed Canberra bombers, which had nuclear weapon carrying capability.

The drive for exports started as soon as the war was over, and the latest designs were not excluded. Rolls Royce had developed a jet engine from the first wartime model of the early 1940s, known as the Nene. In 1946, the then Labour government sanctioned the sale of ten to the USSR on the proviso that they would not be used for military purposes. At the same time, they sold a licence to the USA where Pratt and Whitney manufactured rebranded Nene engines for the Grumman Panther carrier-based jet fighter. The USSR were eventually supplied by Rolls Royce with fifty-five Nene engines, which the British arrogantly believed could not be copied. Not so; as tensions developed over Germany and the consolidation of Soviet power in Eastern Europe, the Soviet military felt they could ignore previous agreements and reverse-engineer the Nene engine. This was done very successfully, and the resulting Klimov VK-1 engine installed in the new and secret MiG-15 jet fighter (NATO codename 'Fagot'). An *RAF Flying Review* article on the Soviet Air Force at the time of the Berlin Airlift in October 1948 referred to their inferior aircraft compared to Britain and the USA, and the matter of the Nene engines was overlooked entirely. American pilots were to get a surprise when they entered combat over Korea after the outbreak of war in 1950, where the MiG-15 proved itself to be the best in the world, maintaining this position until US Airforce Sabre fighters were introduced with their better firepower. In well-trained hands the Soviet aircraft were still the better aircraft. The MIG-15 was produced in very large numbers (13,000 in the USSR and several thousand more under licence) before being succeeded, as with all hardware in the Cold War, by inevitably better designs.

So concerned were the USAF in Korea with the success of the MiG-15, that they launched 'Operation Moolah', a concerted attempt in the spring of 1953 to woo defection of a pilot and complete aircraft in operational combat condition. Fifty thousand dollars (plus political asylum and resettling if desired) was offered to any pilot landing in the South, and a further $50,000 to the first to do so. In April and May, B-29 bombers dropped 1.5 million leaflets explaining the offer onto bases in the North. Between then and the signing of

Soviet MiG-15 Jet Fighters 1950s. (*USAF via Wikimedia Commons*)

the armistice on 27 July no defections occurred in Korea, but in September a North Korean pilot flew his MiG-15 to a base in the South, from where it was taken to the USA for full evaluation. The idea of offering bribes to encourage defection with equipment was to be tried again, first in Iraq by Mossad (the Israeli secret service) in conjunction with the US in 1963 to gain knowledge of the Soviet supplied MIG-21 aircraft; in 1966 the US launched 'Operation Fast Buck', a replica of the Korean venture, to capture for evaluation the Mil Mi-6 'Hook' helicopter.

The Hawker Hunter and Fascism in Chile

One of the most notable British aircraft export success stories of the Cold War period was the Hawker Hunter jet fighter bomber. This was rushed through its early development stage when Soviet MIG-15 aircraft appeared in Korea, too quickly as its appearance in RAF service was not to happen until 1954. It was adaptable, very functional and became a mainstay of front-line squadrons until replacement by the supersonic English Electric Lightning in 1960. In all, 1,972 were made until new production ceased in 1960: 959 in Kingston (Surrey), 299 in Blackpool and 269 in Coventry; in addition, 256 were built under licence in the Netherlands, and 189 in Belgium. Orders for the RAF were reduced in 1957 when the Defence White Paper suggested more emphasis on ground launched missiles – on this occasion, mirroring developments in the USA, the air force lobby within the UK MIC had lost out to others with detriment to the aircraft industry. Air Forces supplied with new aircraft were allies, even if not in NATO: Netherlands, Sweden, Belgium, India and Switzerland. To prevent the aircraft falling into the wrong (pro-Soviet) hands, Hawker (on instruction from the government) made it a contractual obligation that any buyer who no longer required their aircraft would have to re-sell to them. This resulted in a new life for the Hunter; from 1962 until 1975, 400 aircraft in various forms for front line and training purposes, were refurbished and exported again to Rhodesia,

RAF Hawker Hunter jets in Amman Jordan, August 1958. (*IWM via Wikimedia Commons*)

Peru, India, Kuwait, Switzerland, Iraq, Saudi Arabia, Jordan, Lebanon, Chile, Singapore, Abu Dhabi, Qatar and Kenya – all countries under Western influence (Wilson 1995).

Among the foreign sales were those to Chile, an interesting Cold War story. Having established a naval base in Chile, one of the richest, democratically pluralist, and stable countries in South America, the USA set about increasing its influence post-war to aid its mission to head off Soviet influence there and elsewhere on the continent. This became especially important after the Cuban Revolution in 1959 and the growth (or at least threat) of similar movements for change elsewhere across South America. A focus was made on the military, which – through subsidised hardware supply, training and advisory influence – became (by formal agreement) a virtual arm of US forces abroad, with loyalties by its leaders to the USA rather than the Chilean government (Francois 2018). In the mid-1960s the growing air force, equipped with obsolete US and British aircraft, needed to update. The refurbished versatile Hawker Hunters fitted the bill perfectly and a total of forty-one were sold in various specifications between 1966 and 1974, and again at the time of the Falklands War in 1982. In 1970 Salvadore Allende, a left-wing Marxist (but not a member of Chile's Communist Party) was elected president. This happened despite corporate interference from US interests determined to force a different outcome; the communications company ITT alone donated $350,000 to fund right-wing candidates. Allende's social reforms were consistently opposed by the organised middle classes with covert US CIA support, and despite his efforts to appease and win over the leaders of the country's military, social tensions mounted. Although military coups were not uncommon in South America this was alien to traditions in Chile, and when this happened in September 1973 it was particularly brutal and shocking. Hawker Hunters were used to bomb the Presidential Palace in the capital Santiago, where Allende died defending Chilean democracy. His place was taken by the leader of the armed forces, General Pinochet, whose Junta proceeded to rule by fascist dictatorship, influenced by neoliberal free-market views shared with Pinochet's friend, UK Prime Minister Margaret Thatcher, until 1988. American complicity in the coup was proven beyond doubt. The then Labour government in the UK responded to human rights violations in Chile with an embargo on further arms sales in 1974, but work was meantime going ahead on refurbishment of previously supplied Chilean Air Force Hunter engines in the Rolls Royce plant in East Kilbride, Scotland. There, inspired by shop stewards whose anti-fascism was shaped by their various backgrounds in the Communist Party, the church and direct experience from soldiering in the Second World War, the workers took things into their own hands and boycotted the engines, which were left outside in the damp Scottish climate. They were eventually removed in a secretive middle-of-the-night military-style operation in 1978 and returned to Chile, but whether they were still serviceable was another matter. The story of the boycott is told in the 2018 movie *Nae Paseran*.

The Centurion Tank

While the aircraft industry was very important to Britain's economy, the production of conventional weapons for the army was also significant. During the Second World War, tank warfare became important in all theatres, but particularly on the Eastern Front, where the largest tank battle in history took place in Kursk in 1943. Until the advent of the Soviet T-34 tank and its volume production as the war progressed, the Germans were producing tanks that were superior in terms of armour, firepower and speed. The fact is that had Kursk been fought with British and American tanks, its precarious outcome as a Soviet victory might have been very different. Recognising this deficit, design work on a tank that would replace the series of light, medium and heavy types then in production began in 1943, culminating with the first production models of the Centurion Tank in the Summer of 1945, too late for the Second World War, but in time for the Cold War in which it played a significant role. Stripped of its turret side boxes and skirting over the drive wheels, the Centurion resembled a T-34, also featuring sloping armour which gave it added protection, and also a large gun that could be increased in power as the years went by. Indeed, one of the virtues of the Centurion was its adaptability and convertibility. The Centurion was built in the Leyland Factory in Lancashire, Woolwich Arsenal, the Royal Ordnance Factory Leeds and at the Vickers factory in Elswick, Newcastle, and was in production until 1962. An export success, it was sold to the armies of

Australia, Canada, Denmark, Egypt, India, Iraq, Israel, Netherlands, South Africa, Sweden and Switzerland, accounting for more than £200 million worth of overseas sales. In all, 4,400 were built, with 2,500 going abroad (Norman 1967).

Many Centurion tanks saw combat in the side-conflicts and wars of the Cold War era; Korea, Vietnam and the Middle East, as well as in the India-Pakistan wars of 1965 and 1971. They were deployed by the NATO forces they were supplied to in large numbers in Northern Europe as a mainstay of the forces that would oppose the Soviets in the event of attack. The Centurion sales to Israel from 1958 caused some internal UK government debate when they were used in the Six Day war against Egypt, Syria and Jordan in June 1967. The UK were at pains not to upset their Middle East oil suppliers and announced an embargo on arms sales to Israel, who had been an ally in the Suez episode a decade earlier, this after maintaining supplies prior to and during the conflict itself. The Israelis wanted more tanks, spares and ammunition and new Chieftain tanks (the successors to the Centurion). The British quietly relented and supplied several new Centurions in July 1967, suggesting that this was balanced out by their sales of Hawker Hunter jets to Jordan. Over the next few years there was more debate over whether to sell Chieftains to the Israelis; arguments within the Labour government against such a deal prevailed despite the blow to exports along with the possibility of encouragement of further sales. In the end, economic realities prevailed; income from trade relations with the Arab world was much greater than that with Israel, and the threat to oil supplies needed to be minimised. In the event the 1973 Yom Kippur War between Israel and its neighbours resulted in massive increases in oil prices internationally and consequent widespread economic impact (Smith 2014).

British Naval Construction

British Naval shipbuilding did not fare well in the post-war period. Britain's massive Navy in the late nineteenth and early twentieth centuries was based on defending her trading routes to her colonies and overseas assets. The end of Empire reduced the requirement, with the American contribution to NATO filling any consequent defence void. The great shipyards of the Clyde, Tyne and elsewhere went into decline, with vastly reduced Royal Navy orders focused on smaller but more sophisticated ships, although the steady supply kept things going (Kiely 1991). No longer were the world's Navies turning to the UK for their requirements, although sales of redundant and obsolete vessels to friendly but less wealthy nations continued. There were exports, but usually of identical submarine and frigate designs to those for the Royal Navy, to those considered Cold War allies. An example were the Oberon Class diesel submarines built in various yards between 1957 and 1978: six to Australia, two to Chile, and three each to Brazil and Canada, along with thirteen for the Royal Navy. An exception in innovative export were the operations of the small shipyards of

Centurion tanks being unloaded in New Zealand 1953. (*Archives New Zealand via Wikimedia Commons*)

Vosper-Thorneycroft on the South Coast, who specialised in small fast vessels that were popular with smaller Navies – the sinking of an Israeli destroyer the *Eileat* (an ex-Royal Navy WWII-era vessel) by missile carrying gunboats in 1967 had proved their worth. From 1966 these yards produced 140 vessels for twenty-seven countries, most of these were small vessels that the Royal Navy saw no need for but included a series of ten uniquely designed frigates for Brazil in the 1970s.

Characteristically, as with the MIC everywhere, a minor war might come along just at the right time to change direction and secure new contracts. This was certainly the case with the Falklands War of 1982, a short, sharp and bloody conflict confined to the UK and Argentina over a sparsely inhabited and remote UK possession in the South Atlantic. It had once been an important coaling station but now had little strategic value. It was, however, populated with very patriotic British-orientated islanders who had no wish to be absorbed by their near neighbour, whose right-wing dictatorship had whipped up the conflict to bolster its popularity at home. Although beaten militarily, the Argentinian forces and their French-built aircraft and missiles succeeded in sinking several British warships and proved the need for aircraft carriers, which the Nott Review of 1981 had been about to make redundant so that future operations would be

Chilean Navy flagship *Blanco Encalada* (ex-HMS *Fife*) and UK built submarine *O'Brien* late 1980s. (*USN via Wikimedia Commons*)

restricted to the immediate NATO area. Not only were the carriers, and other forces needed for global rapid deployment, saved, but orders were placed to replace the vessels lost.

Lockheed: the F-104 Starfighter and C-5a Galaxy

Just as the British were keen to export their military products to friendly nations, so was American industry. In their case the imperative was to win influence and maintain global power, so supplies were often heavily subsidised as demonstrated in Chile. The F-104 Starfighter produced by Lockheed is an example of the MIC at its worst – a design soon considered redundant by the USAF but exported through the extensive use of bribes to other allied air forces, where it amassed a record for fatal crashes and earned the nickname 'Widowmaker'.

Like the Hawker Hunter, the F-104's story starts in Korea with an identified combat requirement for a high-altitude, fast-climbing supersonic fighter of simple design and construction. The first flight took place in 1954 and the deliveries to the USAF began in 1958, the designated role being as an interceptor to face the (largely fictitious) threat from Soviet Heavy Bombers. That year it gained simultaneous world records for altitude and speed – 1,404 mph and over 100,000ft. The F-104 was, however, limited in both weapon-carrying capacity and range, as well as the subject of several accidents, and other designs were considered more suitable for the interceptor role. Only 296 were placed in American squadrons, far fewer than originally envisaged, and by 1960 all had been withdrawn from their intended front-line role, and from US service entirely by 1969. However, the F-104 was a futuristic and impressive piece of kit – 'a missile with a man in it', according to Lockheed publicity, and undaunted, Lockheed executive led sales teams set out across the world to sell it to America's allies. They took with them enormous amounts of cash to dish out to politicians and others of influence. According to the US Congressional Committee chaired by Senator Church, many years later in 1975 when details began to emerge, Lockheed employed influential 'consultants' who knew little about aircraft but had friends in high places; $1 million dollars was handed over to Prince Bernhard of the Netherlands (husband of the queen), whose air force subsequently bought 135 F-104s, forty-three of which were lost in accidents (Sampson 1976). In West Germany it was much the same story; more than $10 million was allegedly handed over to the political party of the Minister of Defence Franz Joseph Strauss, and 916 aircraft purchased, 292 crashing with the loss of 116 pilots. The West German deal saved Lockheed from bankruptcy as it was large and encouraged purchase by others. Japanese politicians also accepted Lockheed bribes for the F-104 and other aircraft, consultant here being former war criminal Yoshio Kodama who was paid $7 million. They purchased three F-104s and licence to produce a further 227 in their Mitsubishi factory. Other countries fell

USAF F-104 Starfighter used to train German Luftwaffe pilots in Arizona. (*USAF via Wikimedia Commons*)

victim to the same corruptive practice and F-104 production soared: 2,578 were produced worldwide and sold to fourteen nations. Much embarrassment to purchasing governments arose when details of the bribes emerged in the 1970s leading to change of government in West Germany in 1976, and the near collapse of Lockheed itself (Hartung 2011).

Memorial in Germany to a crashed and killed F-104 pilot. (*G. Freihalter via Wikimedia Commons*)

Lockheed's exposure in the Church Committee Hearings also concerned the development and procurement by the USAF of the C-5a Galaxy transport aircraft. Development began in the 1960s of a transport aircraft capable of massive cargo lift and fulfilling other specifications such as simultaneous loading and unloading through doors at each end. Based on cost and through a process of intensive lobbying, Lockheed beat Boeing and Douglas even though the military preferred the Boeing design (based on their proven experience developing the 747 Jumbo Jet). This aircraft, it was said, could transport troops and materials at 600 mph across the world at a moment's notice, landing on almost any airstrip, anywhere, with no requirement for ground crew, and with a load twice that of the nearest aircraft; just twelve would have handled that of the 224 planes used in the Berlin Airlift of 1948. The trade advertisements stated the C-5a was 'like having a military base in nearly every strategic spot on the globe' (quoted in Rice 1971 p.4). From the outset there were establishment critics, including William Fulbright, chairman of the Senate Foreign Relations Committee, who pointed out in 1969 that military capability which aimed to police the world amounted to a form of modern gunboat diplomacy and could have serious consequences for international peace (ibid). The US at this time was bogged down in Vietnam, and while this was a great destination for MIC innovations and products, opposition at home and abroad was mounting and the president had committed to no more 'Vietnams'. The C-5a would lend opportunity for US engagement in 'brushfire wars' that could easily spread into more serious conflict at a time of détente.

The first C-5a appeared in 1969 but there were problems from the outset: wings cracked, wheels and even engines fell off, and the costs rose astronomically. However, such was the promise of capability and performance that the politicians, persuaded by Air Force chiefs who were in far too close a relationship with Lockheed, were prepared to overlook this and bless its continuation. Such collusion involved the silencing of whistle-blowers, including notably Ernest Fitzgerald, a cost estimator with the USAF (Hartung 2011). By 1971 the price had risen to $5 billion for the eventual supply of eighty-one aircraft – twice the cost of the Federal Programme for public schools and three times the budget for all Federal Poverty Programmes (Rice 1971). Cost increases arose from technical problems that beset initial production to the extent that the aircraft met few of the required specifications in terms of performance, flexibility and payload. Lockheed were able to bear the cost of fixing technical faults based on additional orders beyond the first batch, but appalling levels of inefficiency and waste in production were endemic to the project; fixes sometimes caused new problems further down the line. A record $2 billion overrun led to Congressional scrutiny on production, some of which was based on information from a company insider, Henry Durham, a supervisor in the Marietta, Georgia, plant. He was threatened by both management and fellow workers who both saw it as in their interests to hush up production issues. Despite this he gave testimony and offered examples of how public money was being wasted: $65 for a bolt, $19 dollars charged for a piece of sheet metal worth 67 cents, and others that totalled many millions of dollars. Durham also raised safety issues – rushed production leaving last minute installation of vital components as C-5a planes were being prepared for test flights and completed aircraft lacking specified parts (ibid).

Although the original order was reduced from 120 to eighty-one, bailouts ensured production would continue despite doubts about the C-5a's purpose for

Lockheed C-5 Galaxy transport planes. (*USAF via Wikimedia Commons*)

national security. As with so much else within the MIC, the excuse of keeping ahead of the Soviets was sufficient fuel for the profitable self-interest that drove the machine on, so Lockheed was saved from bankruptcy and the C-5a appeared in service through the course of the 1970s. It was later modified and upgraded with further orders and continues in use to this day with a service life expected to last until 2040. The 1975 Congressional Hearings did not end corruption and scandal within Lockheed in relation to various contracts for aircraft and missiles, and during the 1980s the C-5a again featured in relation to spare parts supply. Two items achieved public notoriety: the $600 dollar toilet seat and the $7,662 coffee maker, both at a time of controversially huge increases under Reagan in defence spending with assurances by Defense Secretary Weinberger that there was not 'an ounce of waste' (ibid p.136)!

The USSR's Military Industrial Complex

With a centrally organised and planned command and control system focused on projected need for production, the Soviet Union's socialist economy was not based on profit and competition. There was a ruling class of sorts in the Soviet Union – a group at the top of society known as the 'nomenklatura' who often acted out of self-interest in collusion with one another, just as did their adversaries within the MIC in the West. Officially, the nomenklatura was a list of CPSU and state appointments that required higher Party approval. Those on the list ultimately constituted a secure and self-perpetuating social class within the USSR whose numbers were estimated to total 2 million during the Brezhnev years (1965–85). The relationship between politicians, industry and the military mirrored that in the West, with the difference being that profit was not a driver, and neither were markets and exports important as measures of success or failure. The products of the Soviet MIC were consumed by its own armed forces and those of its allies. Exports to others did take place, but these usually involved subsidies and immediate loss to the Soviet economy in the hope of ideological and trading gain in the longer term. Some of these relationships, as with Cuba, were almost all one way, the import of Cuban sugar offering only a paltry return on investment. The USSR was self-sufficient in terms of fuel, and indeed a net exporter of oil and gas; it did, however, rely on grain imports to fulfil its most basic nutritional needs, despite failed efforts over the years to improve agricultural output – as a landmass the USSR was simply too far north, with short summers and long winters, to avoid the cycle of poor harvests. Humiliatingly, grain supplies often came from the USA.

As MIG-15s with British-designed engines ruled the skies over Korea in 1950, an existing US embargo on the trade of engineering and other products was reinforced and made obligatory for its allies, and this lasted in various forms until the end of the Cold War. The Soviets had to resort to ingenious industrial espionage and reverse engineering to try and keep up but fell behind in areas such as micro-computing – a gap by the mid-1980s estimated to amount to between two and seven years (Garrison & Shivpuri 1983). As the years went by all this had a negative impact on the Soviet economy, which was not helped by its focus on defence.

By the end of the Cold War the Soviet Union's MIC (an official structure known as the VPK – the Military-Industrial Commission of the USSR, formed in 1957) had become a means to its own ends and almost beyond political control. This is typified by an anecdotal comment of the defence minister Dmitri Ustinov who effectively ran this sector from 1965 until his death in 1984. He advised at one point that no more nuclear weapons were needed; the response of a weapons production head was to suggest that a dozen more be ordered anyway as the workers had to be fed, so Ustinov went ahead with the order (Swanson 2013). As American defence spending increased, the Soviets were forced to keep up. From the early years of the Soviet state military production was favoured – the best materials and personnel at all levels were reserved for such output with the result that only military products were really deemed of quality; only Khrushchev, and finally Gorbachev, made any serious challenge to this orthodoxy and shifted emphasis to consumer production. By the late 1980s defence spending was estimated, according to an American study (no one at the time really knew), as amounting to a quarter of gross economic output, and one in five adults across the USSR were working within the MIC, with half the workforce employed in defence plants in some regions (Curtis 1998).

Chelyabinsk, a city just east of the Ural Mountains in Western Siberia illustrates the development and trajectory of the Soviet arms-based economy. Between 1917 and 1990 its population grew from 70,000 to over a million. This growth was accelerated with the wartime relocation of the Leningrad S.M. Kirov Factory No. 85, which produced tanks. The existing high-volume tractor factory, established as part of the first Five Year Plan in 1933, was also converted to tank production and the city became known as 'Tankograd'. During the war these plants, fed by the region's metallurgy industry and coal mines, turned out 18,000 tanks, many of the 10,000 Katyusha Rocket Launchers, over 48,000 diesel engines and 17 million shells and gun cartridges. Post-war, despite some return to tractor production, the city and surrounding region continued to be heavily dependent on arms manufacturing, including nuclear weapons at Ozyorsk, fifty-five miles from the city, and its neighbouring plutonium producing plant at Kyshtym. The two cities Chelyabinsk (Tankograd) and Ozyorsk (Atomgrad) have been described as 'a kaleidoscopic representation of post-war [defence] development' (Samuelson 2011). Their location in the Southern Urals was no accident – they had been moved there in wartime to protect them from direct German attack, and post-war the location could continue to be used for conventional weapon production – and was well placed for secretive nuclear weapons development. Chelyabinsk was also large enough to educate to university level the technicians, scientists and research institutes needed to support all this. The Polytechnic was directly linked to the military industries. It was in Ozyorsk (known by its postcode 'Chelyabinsk-40') that the first Soviet Bomb was constructed in great secrecy from stolen American plans. The self-contained town was closed to unauthorised Soviet citizens and had its own schools, social and cultural activities, all of high quality, and was regarded in late Soviet times as a safe, secure and well-resourced community. In 1957, buried nuclear waste at the Mayak plant at Kyshtym exploded causing contamination over a wide area, leading to the evacuation of 10,000 and the deaths of hundreds of people, a disaster only exceeded by Chernobyl and Fukushima, but on this occasion in a plant devoted to weapons manufacture. This was not revealed publicly until 1976 (Medvedev 1980), and the secrecy that surrounded this closed area prevented it getting into the public domain. Interestingly, there was a fire at the UK's weapon plutonium plant at Windscale Cumbria the same year which also resulted in three-figure fatalities.

Udmurtia in central Russia, and also remote from areas of possible conflict, was an autonomous Soviet Republic heavily dependent upon weapons production, with two thirds of the adult population so employed, many of them in the city of

LURD child soldier from Liberia armed with an AK-47 rifle. (*US Army via Wikimedia Commons*)

Izhevsk. This is the location of the giant Izhmash plant that developed through the first Five Year Plans of the 1930s, and in wartime turned out 11 million rifles, surpassing the entire output of Nazi Germany. In 1949 it became the centre for manufacture of the AK-47 Kalashnikov automatic rifle, which continues to this day. The AK-47 was invented by a wartime soldier, Mikhail Kalashnikov, his design being simple in construction and operation, reliable (it did not jam) and capable of immense firepower for its size and weight. It required no detailed manual or training and was as effective in the hands of a fighter who could neither read nor write (as was often the case in the Red Army) as an educated and trained soldier. The AK-47 became the mainstay infantry rifle of not just the armies of the Soviets and their allies, but that of rebel armies across the world. Millions were produced in the USSR and elsewhere with and without licences. The USSR, concerned less with export trade than with spreading influence, supplied them free and in large quantities to insurgent movements in Africa and to other allies fighting 'imperialism'. Many finished up in the hands of arms dealers and private armies whose aims and aspirations were far from the Soviet ideal, including those who used and exploited children. So symbolic was the AK-47 that it was embedded on the flag of Mozambique and Burkina Faso, and became an icon of anti-American and Western paramilitary struggle (Kahaner 2007).

Conclusion

This chapter has discussed the triangular relationships of the Military Industrial Complex monster, how it became self-perpetuating and self-serving, fed the Cold War and drove it forward. The seriously weird 1960s American rock singer Frank Zappa wrote in his autobiography that 'politics is the entertainment division of industry', a throwaway but profound comment that sums up corporate influence on government in the Western democracies, and the MIC (Zappa 1990). Its power and influence were not confined to the capitalist countries of the West, but mirrored in the USSR where the MIC played an even more significant role in the economy (Chapter 10 will describe the Soviet MIC's contribution to the system's collapse at the end of the 1980s). The effects of the MIC were to flood the world with weapons of all varieties, many of which were never used, and which were always bound to be rendered redundant and be replaced by the wealthiest of the adversaries with something faster, more powerful or more useful tactically. Reason and human progress had little place in this equation unless you either believed that the ideology of your adversary was so evil it was worth dying to defeat, or alternatively that armed might kept the peace (the argument for 'deterrence'). The latter was certainly the prevailing view of government on both sides for most of the period. The next chapter will challenge this assumption by examining the areas of the

Soviet Ground-Air missile. (*Author's collection*)

US Army Davy Crockett theatre nuclear weapon. (*US government via Wikimedia Commons*)

world where the Cold War became real and where the conventional products of the MICs were unhappily consumed. While this did not impact violently on the civilian populations of the main protagonists, it certainly did on many of their servicemen and women.

Chapter 5

Proxy Wars or Chimes of Freedom Flashing? – Decolonisation and National Liberation, from Korea to Afghanistan

> 'It became necessary to destroy the town to save it', a US Major said Wednesday…
>
> Associated Press reporter Peter Arnett, Mekong Delta, South Vietnam, 8 February 1968

Introduction

This chapter attempts to cover the world's conflicts that were of interest to both sides in the Cold War. All the chapters cover themes that have themselves filled whole books and indeed volumes, but probably none more than this one. The purpose here is not to describe each conflict in detail with their battles, sequences of events and complexities, but to complement the rest of the book's account of the meaning of events for ordinary citizens and how they illuminate background, motives, and actions. References are given to literature that the reader might want to examine further for more information than space allows here. Many of these wars were connected to decolonisation and as such are unlikely to reoccur now that the world has largely moved beyond that phase of the history of the European nineteenth-century powers. Others, such as those in Central and South America, and Afghanistan, were very much about regime change and were not necessarily ended with the Cold War; the external influences and support to one or other side that characterised these wars in faraway places have changed, but certainly not gone away.

The Big Powers Converge on Korea

Korea, a nation of 25 million people, was a Japanese imperial possession through occupation and direct rule from 1910 until war's end in 1945. At that point it was liberated by the Red Army when the USSR joined the war against Japan in August. Although it had no army in Korea, the US proposed division of the country along the 38th Parallel, with them occupying the South, and the Soviets occupying the North. A US Army move into the South of the country was hastily arranged in late August to create a barrier that had been on no one's agenda when the Red Army had first been invited to plan its attack on Japanese-held territory only months previously. Stalin agreed to this division, which was a surprise to some given the general Western consensus by then of Soviet expansive intent. The arrangement, drawn up by two US Army colonels in Washington who referenced a *National Geographic Magazine* map, was meant to be temporary pending agreement about the democratic reunification of the country, and left most of the population in the South (Pembroke 2018). Events mirrored that in Germany: the Soviets proposed a plan of unification that was initially agreed by most parties – but not the South Korean leadership or the US military generals in charge of occupation forces, who effectively torpedoed the idea. Elections were held under UN scrutiny but only in the South. The respective superpowers moved on within a few years, leaving their planted and imported dictators sympathetic to their respective ideologies. Outcomes consolidated the country's separation along the entirely artificial 38th Parallel. The Republic of Korea (the South) was declared in August 1947, and almost simultaneously the North proclaimed itself as the Democratic People's Republic of Korea under Kim Il Sung, the founder of a dynasty that exists to this day.

Kim Il Sung, a former Red Army officer, was keen to reunite the country through invasion, end the anti-communist repression in the South, and the frequent border clashes. This required Stalin's permission as guarantor of security against Western reaction (and de facto leader of world communism). By 1950, the neighbouring Chinese revolution under Mao Zedong was in complete control and the USA had done nothing to save its erstwhile allies the Kuomintang, who were now confined to the island of Taiwan. The USSR had also exploded its first nuclear device and felt more secure now a military balance had been achieved again. Germany seemed permanently divided due, in Soviet eyes, to the machinations of the Western occupiers (see Chapter 2) and if this was to be avoided in Korea, action had to be taken and the circumstances now looked favourable. Stalin was clear that the Red Army would not be directly involved but would supply the North Korean army and the Chinese People's Liberation Army, who could be called upon for direct military help if required.

In his extensively researched book *This Monstrous* War, written prior to the eventual peace agreement in July 1953, Wilfred Burchett maintains that the war started in 1949 when the army of South Korea, urged on by the USA, began attacks on North Korean forces along the border. These clashes led to 100,000 casualties before the officially recognised start of the war. Eventually, in June 1950, an incursion aimed at invasion into North Korea was repelled and chased back into the South and so commenced the conflict. Kim Il Sung's forces were immediately successful and within weeks the capital, Seoul, was in their hands. The United Nations reacted swiftly and in two resolutions called first for the withdrawal of the invading forces, and then for assistance to South Korea to repel the attack. Meanwhile in Washington, President Truman and his advisors and generals at last had the definitive proof they needed of Soviet intentions to spread communism through military invasion. Resolve to lead the UN forces defending South Korea followed with twenty-two nations committing forces and assistance, 90 per cent of whom were Americans. Although initially overrun, the US presence turned the tide; the southern port of Busan was successfully defended and an American landing much further north in the rear of the invading army at Incheon, succeeded in dividing the North's forces and eventually pushing them back towards the 38th Parallel. Up until this point the prevailing Western view was that whatever the background and failed diplomacy, the invasion of the South was an aggressive act that there was at least some justification in opposing. This was about to change from a defensive war to a more aggressive anti-communist crusade.

The American popular political will to at last challenge communism was now to combine with a forceful anti-communist commander, General Douglas McArthur, who had a reputation, gained during the war against the Japanese, for taking risks and carrying the fight to the enemy. Allies, including the British Labour government, were concerned that political control of the conflict had been handed over to McArthur and were alarmed when his forces pursued the North Koreans over the 38th Parallel and into their own territory. McArthur had gambled, with Truman's consent, that the Chinese would not react and hoped that the Soviets (who he feared more) would stay clear of direct involvement. The Chinese People's Liberation Army did, as agreed, come to the aid of the North Koreans who were being pushed back towards their mutual border. The tide again turned and by early 1951 it was clear that McArthur's plan to create a short sharp victory over North Korea and send a message to communists everywhere, was in disarray. His troops were now in rapid retreat against a large Chinese army and with the war in the air dominated by Soviet supplied (and often piloted) MiG-15 aircraft. The Chinese were successfully practicing Mao's well practiced techniques of irregular warfare – 'Enemy advances, we retreat; enemy halts, we attack; enemy tires, we attack; enemy retreats, we pursue' (Pembroke p.106).

At the time, McArthur contemplated using radioactive poison on enemy troops and nuclear weapons in a deliberate effort to broaden the war to take on both China and, if necessary, the USSR. Ultimately McArthur was denied devolved authority over nuclear weapon use. His troops, however, engaged in a deliberate scorched earth policy as they retreated, razing villages to the ground and destroying food sources. This was assisted by shellfire during the final evacuation from the port of Hungnam in December 1950, from the battleship Missouri, using a force of destructive malevolence that spoke more of impotent fury than strategy (ibid). Not surprisingly, given the devastation wreaked by the Americans and the starvation they faced, thousands of civilians demanded

Refugees from the fighting, Korea July 1951. (*US Army via Wikimedia Commons*)

passage on fleeing ships, adding to the myth of communist persecution. This is perpetuated into modern times; the chapter devoted to Korea in the oral history book based on the 2016 BBC Radio series *Stories from the Big Freeze*, focuses entirely on pro-Western refugee stories from that episode (Kendall 2017). By early 1951 Truman was becoming increasingly impatient with his out-of-control commander, and dismissed him in April, a move that cost him immediate popularity but perhaps saved the world from nuclear war. Attempts to begin peace negotiations bore fruit and began in June 1951. In August 1950 the UN forces were ordered to end offensive operations and from then on, the ground war became bogged down around the 38th Parallel. Moving beyond this point was considered after that but ruled out as provocative.

In 1953 Burchett produced hotly disputed but sound evidence, based on his own eyewitness investigations, that the US Air Force had engaged in germ warfare to spread disease among civilians north of the 38th Parallel. One of the reasons his findings were questioned was that he had crossed into North Korean territory from China (along with a British *Daily Worker* journalist, Alan Winngton) and was considered to be reporting the war from 'the other side'. Their findings suggested that aircraft had dropped bacteria-laden insects that had spread cholera and bubonic plague, diseases that had not been experienced before in Korea, apart from one incident of cholera in 1946 that was rapidly isolated. The occurrences were in widely located places that were not connected. Burchett's findings were eventually examined by an international commission led by a Cambridge University professor, which concluded that the allegations were correct. The Americans continue to deny them, and 300 copies of Burchett's 1953 book in which they were outlined were confiscated upon arrival in the USA.

One of Burchett's sources about bacteriological warfare was the testament of an American prisoner of war in the North who had been sickened by his own involvement. Burchett's interviews with UN prisoners in the North and exposure of murder and abuse of North Korean and Chinese prisoners in the South (see below) provoked outrage because of the challenge they made to prevailing Western narratives that offered an opposite view. He was accused of interrogation of prisoners and dubbed a traitor in Australia; when Burchett later lost his passport, he was denied a replacement (see Appendix).

The ground war stalemate was accompanied by a renewed war from the air that was purposefully aimed at destroying the will of the people of North Korea and force a peace on Western terms. While Truman was concerned that his commander, General McArthur, was prepared to make the conflict a global one, he was happy to escalate locally. On 16 December 1950, in the wake of Chinese and North Korean victories, he made a proclamation of national emergency designed to fire up the American public in this anti-communist crusade. The cigar chewing USAF General Curtis LeMay (see Chapter 4) was given free licence to bomb North Korean population centres, which he proceeded to do enthusiastically. In July 1951 an almost deserted Pyongyang was subjected to a raid by 370 aircraft but with minimal publicity about the scale of force involved. LeMay's bombers went on over the next two years to destroy as much infrastructure as they possibly could – making deliberate war on civilians through the erasure of every community of any size in which they lived. LeMay himself admitted that his forces probably killed over a million civilians, none of whom, in his view, were innocent because of the nature of their government (Pembroke 2018).

Commonwealth forces from the UK, Australia, Canada, New Zealand, and South Africa, became engaged in Korea in August 1950. The British contribution was by far the largest – with over 14,000 troops involved over the three years of the war. Many of these were National Servicemen, involuntary male conscripts aged 17–21 years, serving a two-year period followed by four years in the reserves. The Korean conflict was viewed in the West as a war of international defence of freedom, about principle rather than immediate national interest, and accounts from later years by former officers, reflect this (e.g. Carew 1967). They suggest that morale was good and anti-communist feeling universal. It is doubtful that such memoirs would reflect alternative views, but it seems unlikely that regiments that included conscripts would not

US B-29 bomber (later shot down) over Korea July 1952. (*USAF via Wikimedia Commons*)

include critics of the war and the manner of its conduct. Carew's comprehensive book on the Commonwealth contribution certainly makes no mention of such matters as the American intensive bombing of the North. The UK suffered over 3,700 casualties, including 1,078 killed, and when the survivors got home their sacrifice in a faraway land in a war that nobody won, was soon forgotten.

The peace negotiations dragged on for two years, conducted on a three-way basis by Chinese, North Korean and UN Teams. On the US-dominated UN side there was a belief that communists should not be bargained with as they were inherently evil, and to this was added a derision of the Chinese and North Koreans by some Americans, who considered them racially inferior (Pembroke 2018). The main reason for delay were failures to agree the process of repatriation of prisoners; this effectively prolonged the war on the battlefields leading to further casualties through deliberate obstinance on the part of US negotiators doing the bidding of their political masters. The 1949 Geneva Convention on Prisoners of War (POWs) had determined that repatriation to the country of origin should quickly follow the cessation of hostilities. Both the USA and the USSR had agreed this despite some concern from the International Red Cross and others that this did not take account of those who sought their freedom elsewhere. Arguments over this were to dominate the peace talks from the end of 1951 until the middle of 1953. The root of this was not, as most Western narratives suggest, a wish by the civilised UN combatants to make repatriation voluntary, but about the involuntary indoctrination of very poorly treated Chinese and North Korean prisoners held by the US in the South. There, what have been described as the 'dregs' of the US and South Korean Armies, mistreated POWs and (according to Burchett's findings) engaged in murder and sadistic practices. POWs were then subjected to systematic psychological brainwashing to replace any communist illusions they might have with a belief in the market freedoms of the West. Some of the more reluctant North Korean and Chinese POWs were more susceptible to this than other ideological communists, so clashes ensued between them. The Psy-Ops exercise was led enthusiastically by the US Intelligence community in the hope that defections would confirm belief in the values of capitalism and lend justification to the war for a home audience (Pembroke 2018). The Chinese delegation was aware of what was going on but their attempts to raise issues and seek repatriation along the lines of the Geneva Convention were stonewalled by US negotiators imbued with the righteousness of the American way of life. They maintained a formal position that such was the punishment facing those who wanted to defect to the South that this must not happen for humane reasons. When agreement was finally reached and repatriation took place based on a Chinese backed proposal that those who did not want to go home should be

Black US POWs in Chinese captivity North Korea, March 1951. (*Chinese Govt via Wikimedia Commons*)

relocated under the protection of a neutral authority, the US did everything they could to subvert the process so that few who wanted to go home, ever got there.

The propaganda victory this secured was bolstered by stories of ill-treatment by repatriated UN POWs (particularly US and UK ones). Long after the war was over the British Ministry of Defence felt the need to actively promote this alternative narrative, in a pamphlet which, they said, was based on the testimonies of returned British POWs (Ministry of Defence 1955). This went as far as questioning, on political grounds, the reports from Burchett and Winnington, and the visits to the POW Camps of others sympathetic to the communist cause. Facts that have since emerged suggest that this was far from true and that the treatment of POWs in the North, particularly those held by the Chinese, had been reasonable (as reported by Burchett at the time). The Chinese did make efforts at indoctrination, but these were more subtle and voluntary than the crude methods used by their American counterparts (Pembroke 2018).

A deal to end the conflict was finally signed by the Chinese and UN negotiators on 27 July 1953. The war ended but no final peace settlement had been reached because the South Koreans refused to recognise the agreement to split the country along the 38th Parallel. Both sides claimed victory and proceeded to build vastly different countries. As subsequent events demonstrated, the USA establishment learned little from the conflict and soon moved on to oppose communism with their military might elsewhere, as to a lesser extent did the British in their attempts to prevent their decolonisation process ending in communist takeover. The war was terrible in terms of human casualties, taking more lives than any other Cold War conflict: over 2.5 million civilian deaths – most through US bombing after the commencement of peace talks. The lives of 170,000 soldiers on the UN side were lost, including over 36,000 Americans; on the North Korean and Chinese side the figures can only be estimated but could be over a million dead and missing. Legacies of the Korean conflict remain with us – especially in the intransigent, belligerent and paranoid nature of the North Korean regime.

The UK's Decolonisation and Resistance to Communism

The post-war period saw an acceleration of decolonisation as Britain sought to end the expense of far-flung direct rule. This was both a matter of acceptance that its role in the world had reduced and that resistance to British rule was growing and unstoppable. The aim of British propagation of conflicts of that era was never to prevent decolonisation, but to ensure as far as possible that it took place on terms that protected British financial interests. As a result of this general strategy, UK armed forces became involved in a series of bloody anti-insurgent conflicts in Malaya, Borneo, Kenya, and South Yemen. These have Cold War associations because their opponents were often directly supported by the USSR and its proxies. These wars were anti-imperialist in nature and therefore of ideological importance to the communist movement worldwide, justifying policies of opposition to the West and its economically driven designs.

Almost unchallenged until recent times was the story that the UK's role in rolling back the communist advance in Malaya was a textbook example of how to win a war against a guerrilla-based insurgency. If only, the narrative goes, the Americans had followed the same tactics more effectively in Vietnam, the outcome might have been different (for example, Jackson 1991). As we have already seen in this book, the accepted versions of events in the West are often far from objective truth and that was certainly the case here. British tactics, learned over many years of preserving colonial power, were brutal, and nothing to feel proud about. Methods were used that would never have been deployed against peoples not considered racially 'inferior'. Indeed, when they were tried in Northern Ireland in the early 1970s, despite adaptation, this was exactly the feeling of the Nationalist population. The reality was that the British never really succeeded in 'winning hearts and minds' as they convinced themselves had happened, but divide and rule, backed by coercive military occupation over a long period, created very difficult conditions for insurgents (Burleigh 2013).

The roots of the conflict in Malaya go back to the Second World War when the British were happy to train and arm resistance fighters from the Malayan Communist Party (MCP) against the Japanese occupation. The MCP had been involved in an armed revolt in the 1930s that had been crushed quite mercilessly. The Malayan People's Anti-Japanese Army, as it became known, was only moderately successful in its operations and the crucial role it would have played in supporting a British invasion, never realised as the war ended before this might have taken place. The main reason for its limited success as a popular movement uniting the population against their occupiers was the fact that the MCP was based on the Chinese Malay community. They were an oppressed but significant minority originally imported as cheap labour to staff the British owned and managed rubber plantations (Newsinger 2015). In true colonial style, they had always been successfully played off against the indigenous Malay peasants, and this factor was to prove crucial to what later occurred in the 1950s. When the war ended the MCP could have taken advantage and moved to take power as the British had not yet returned and were overcommitted militarily in the region. However, various factors – including their lack of support among Malays – drove the MCP back to trade union building and a constitutional road to power. By 1948 the British had announced the formation of the Federation of Malaya, in which the power of the Malay Sultans was consolidated, and ethnic minorities denied any place. This dashed any hopes of addressing the aspirations of Chinese Malays through the constitutional reforms promised by the British in wartime, and forced them down the road of armed insurrection. Contrary to the usual Western narrative, this was not ordered by the Kremlin as an instrument of the Cold War but determined purely by local circumstances and the local MCP leadership. Violent suppression by British controlled police against strikers (in mid-1948, eight strikers on one estate were beaten to death) also provoked a violent response. The British then banned the trade union federation after the shooting of three estate managers. At this time Malaya played an important role in Britain's fragile post-war economy; its rubber output was worth more than the UK's own total export of manufactured goods.

Lee Meng, Leading Communist Woman Fighter, Malaya March 1951. (*Australian War Memorial via Wikimedia Commons*)

With an economic imperative driving its desire to hold onto Malaya, the British declared a state of emergency on 19 June 1948, even though the MCPs plans for an armed uprising were still in the planning stages. This use of the word 'emergency' to describe the conflict over its nine-year duration, was apparently at the behest of British planters, whose London based insurers would not have paid for losses if this was considered a civil war (Burleigh 2014). Within weeks thousands had been arrested, taking the MCP by surprise and crippling their response. Those that avoided arrest took to the jungle and in uncoordinated fashion began attacks on British officials and property with the aim of creating communist-controlled zones in the country's interior. This tactic effectively handed control of the cities, where a large proportion of potential supporters lived, to the British, reducing their campaign to remote rural areas largely inhabited by unsympathetic Malays. Despite the poor start that had been forced upon them, the MCP army, relaunched as the Malayan Races Liberation Army (MRLA), were mounting small scale but successful operations by the end of 1949. The British responded with brutal methods of coercion and control, involving torture, internment without trial, trials, execution, long prison sentences and other methods of terror in what was a police state. Villages thought to be sympathetic to the guerrillas were razed to the ground, and atrocities committed. When the British Communist *Daily Worker* printed a picture in 1952 of a Royal Marine holding up the severed head of an MRLA fighter there was little reaction and no other newspaper took up the story – the Cold War anti-communist consensus between Labour (under whom the British terror in Malaya had begun) and the Conservatives, was embedded in British society. However, terror methods were only consolidating support for the MRLA, so the British rolled out the *Briggs Plan* that forcibly removed over 400,000 villagers and resettled them in areas secured by the British and their native Malay forces. This period also saw the use of herbicides and defoliants dropped by the RAF and sprayed by hand to deny the MRLA food and cover, but mainly affecting innocent civilians and often the servicemen who handled them. The British also used saturation bombing from the air but even sympathetic historians admit that this had little effect and resulted in pointless civilian deaths (Jackson 1991). British tactics of isolating the guerrillas were further developed and the country cut in half to prevent supplies getting to the insurgents from their supporters. The war rolled on with atrocities on both sides but with British tactics successfully confining the MRLA. In 1957 Malaya was granted independence under a regime opposed to the communists and protecting British-owned interests, effectively ending the anti-colonial campaign of the MRLA. It is estimated that the conflict cost nearly 7,000 lives of MRLA fighters, about 5,000 civilians and 2,500 pro-British servicemen, including 519 British.

The creation by the British of the Federation of Malaya led directly to further confrontation with the neighbouring emergent post-colonial state of Indonesia. The British plan involved creating a Federation of Malaysia that would include Malaya, North Borneo, Sarawak, Brunei and Singapore, which was enacted in September 1963. This was opposed by Indonesia, whose government – led by the nationalist Sukarno – was backed by the USSR in their opposition to the creation of a more powerful Western orientated state in the region. He also favoured the creation of a larger Indonesian controlled federation. Indonesian troops in what was now East Malaysia (the island of Borneo, which also contained Indonesian territory) began military operations along the border after the creation of the new state and were opposed by Commonwealth forces including thousands of British troops. The war was between opposing ground forces and limited in scope, although incursions were made by both sides onto foreign territory; Indonesian troops landed on the Malayan peninsula but were quickly rounded up, and a secret operation involving Commonwealth special forces took the war into Indonesian territory. In 1965 Sukarno was deposed and the appetite for conflict dissipated, with a peace agreement recognising the Federation of Malaysia in August 1966 (Burleigh 2013).

The conflict in Kenya in East Africa from 1953 to 1960 involved the same level of brutality as seen in Malaya, with deliberate use of similar tactics to isolate the Mau Mau (Freedom Army) insurgents and frighten away their potential supporters. This was an anti-colonial war where British forces were deployed in strength to defend and protect British owned assets and fiercely racist white settlers. The conflict arose through the dispossession of land by British settlers from the Kikuyu; by 1948, 1.25 million people were confined to 2,000 square miles of tribal lands, while 30,000 colonists occupied 12,000 square miles of the best of them. This process accelerated in the next few years, forcing Kikuyu into poverty and migration to the growing city of Nairobi. When they demanded better representation in government in 1951, the visiting Labour government Colonial Secretary, James Griffiths, offered them five seats (for their 5 million people), as against six for the 100,000 Asian Indians, and fourteen for the 30,000 white settlers (Newsinger 2015). The native black population, so the argument went, were primitive people who were not ready for responsibility and needed to be looked after by the British white minority.

Lack of democracy and rising poverty resulted in growing dissent among the organised trade union movement and the Kikuyu majority, and the panicked British rulers declared a state of emergency in October 1953. This prompted an organised armed rebellion by the secretive Mau Mau led among others, by Jomo Kenyatta. As in Malaya, armed conflict was pre-empted by British repression. Now the emboldened white minority saw the state of emergency as an opportunity to eradicate Kikuyu culture and identity through Police-led summary executions, torture, and a belief among the Kikuyu that their destruction was imminent. Before serious organised armed opposition had even begun, the police had shot 430 individuals 'trying to escape' (Newsinger 2015). Led by the Kikuyu but involving other black tribal peoples, the Mau Mau set up camps in remote areas of the country and enjoyed massive support among the population. As with all such wars of national liberation their attentions were focused not just on the white settlers but on their supporters among the native and Asian populations (the notorious Lari Massacre in March 1953 being the most horrific example), which gave justification to the British authorities for their increasingly repressive methods. As in Malaya great efforts were made to cut off the Mau Mau fighters from their supporters – over a million villagers were moved into special camps and treated to anti-Mau Mau propaganda which, in the absence of any counter information, became increasingly effective (Osborne 2015). As in Malaya vast quantities of bombs were dropped on jungle areas by the RAF in the hope of hitting some rebels – whether this made any impact is arguable (Newsinger 2015). One innovative British officer, Captain Frank Kitson, established gangs of defected rebels who returned to the Mau Mau-held areas and succeeded in penetrating and breaking up the real fighters. In October 1956 one of these units captured the principal leader, Dedan Kamati, who was subsequently hanged. After this the movement went into decline until the emergency was officially declared over in 1960.

The Mau Mau were anti-colonial but had no communist ideology or affiliation, despite their characterisation as communists by white settler communities across Africa. The USSR used the conflict in Kenya for propaganda purposes; after the

Kikuyu anti-Mau Mau fighters employed by the British in Kenya. (*IWM via Wikimedia Commons*)

establishment of Moscow Radio African broadcasts in 1958, the struggle in Kenya featured regularly alongside other efforts to draw national liberation aspirations across the continent into their own Cold War alignment (ibid). Kenyatta had joined the Communist Party when studying in England in the 1930s, but by the time he was leading the Kikuyu agitation around land ownership in the early 1950s he was a nationalist. After his arrest and trial in early 1953 he was effectively isolated through a long detention. During his trial he had denied links between his Kenya National Union and the Mau Mau, and maintained the separation after his release in 1961. Kenya was finally granted independence in 1962, by which time the British were confident that the new rulers would respect property rights. The British had effectively beaten off the Mau Mau challenge, but their methods, long covered up and obscured by discussion of the primitive barbarities of the Mau Mau, were shocking and unworthy of a nation who regarded itself as civilised. Kitson is on record as stating that the British fought in Kenya with one arm tied behind their back because of adherence to human rights concern. This seems at variance with the truth.

Deaths of those considered to have any type of association with the rebels (many of them young children) are estimated to be as high as 50,000 – out of all proportion to the actual numbers of Mau Mau fighters who were probably never more than low thousands in number. In contrast the actual numbers of white soldiers, police officers and settlers killed barely reached three figures over the whole eight years of the emergency. The scale of British repression has only come to light in recent years resulting in apologies and substantial awards of compensation (£20 million according to a 2013 BBC News report) to the torture victims of British terror.

The final anti-colonial anti-British insurgency that will be described here because of Cold War association, is the one that took place in what is now South Yemen in the Arabian Gulf from 1963 until 1967. Aden was an important British military base and naval coaling station on the sea route to India and the Far East, but declined in importance after India and Pakistan gained independence in 1947. In the early 1960s its importance increased when it replaced Cyprus as the headquarters for Britain's presence in the Middle East, now defending oil interests rather than sea routes. Arab nationalism had already proved problematic in Egypt and, with active as well as tacit Soviet support, was spreading. Aden was part of a series of protectorates that bordered on each other, self-governing but autocratic states whose foreign policy and defence were determined by the British. Nationalism had spread to these in the 1950s leading to armed risings and the usual British methods of suppression: bombing and overwhelming ground force action. The British forced all these protectorates into a federation in 1959, including Aden, with no reference to the wishes of its population but with the intention of retaining the important base there with the help of the surrounding ruling sultans. British plans were threatened in 1960 by a coup of nationalist army officers in Yemen, and mounting labour and anti-British unrest in Aden itself. Tensions escalated with a bomb attack on the British High Commissioner at Aden airport and a State of Emergency was declared. The National Liberation Front (NLF), whose aims concerned the entire region, was formed in the Republic of Yemen (YAR) and began a guerrilla war against the British and its puppet regimes within the federation. NLF and Radfan tribe guerrilla attacks met with a forceful British response: the depopulation of areas where the rebels were operating, aerial bombardment, the destruction of crops and other food sources, and brutal methods against insurgents and their supporters.

While the rural rebellion in the Radfan mountains had been crushed, British military might had not defeated the NLF whose focus was now on targeted attacks on British security forces and staff in Aden itself. This involved a change of tactics and those developed were later used in Northern Ireland; small squads (including special forces) targeting individuals known to be associated with the NLF, and the use of basic and sophisticated torture techniques on suspects including standing for long periods, sensory deprivation and the slapping of eardrums simultaneously to burst them. A Federation Army mutiny and concerted action by the NLF and allied forces in the Crater district of Aden in 1967 was brutally supressed by the British Argyll and Sutherland Highlanders. Their toughness was celebrated at the time but later, when they came to use the same methods in Northern Ireland, the Argylls unacceptable methods were brought to light and condemned. While these methods might have contained the NLF, it did not end their activity; eventually the British pulled out in 1967 as the whole campaign seemed hardly worth the effort, despite the protestations of the British military and right-wing establishment. The NLF formed the new government and within a few years declared themselves a socialist state aligned with the USSR.

The Aden emergency marked the last British military action in defence of empire against an insurgent population, but the tactics used there and in the other conflicts discussed in this section were regarded as holding important lessons in counterinsurgency when the situation in Northern Ireland headed into crisis in 1968. Frank Kitson, now a colonel, was seconded by the Ministry of Defence to write up British counterinsurgency experience, much of which he had experienced first-hand. His *Low Intensity Operations: Subversion, Insurgency and Peacekeeping* (published in 1971) was regarded as a classic, containing experience already shared with the Americans in Vietnam. However, when it was applied to Northern Ireland it was less than successful and, if anything, drove the Nationalist population to seek protection from the Provisional IRA. Kitson held operational command there at the time of Internment and Bloody Sunday, controversial moments in that long conflict (Hughes 2014).

The Long War in Vietnam

In 1968, the year of the Tet Offensive that proved to the world that the Vietcong in South Vietnam were ubiquitous and powerful, the American government commissioned the publication of a 'survey' into the motives and morale of North Korean and Chinese soldiers captured drawing the Korean War (Meyers & Biderman 1968). This proved to a home audience, faced with evidence on their TV sets every day that suggested the contrary, that the other side were brainwashed ideologically, inherently weak, and proof of the malevolence of communism. Some of these conclusions were based around a proposition that only twenty-two US POWs held in the North chose to defect (0.5 per cent of POWs), while in the South the figures suggest that 33 per cent of North Korean prisoners and 66 per cent of Chinese ones chose to do so. As we saw earlier in this chapter, this was far from a true picture. What it did demonstrate was that the USA still felt they could win a conflict based on the moral and fighting superiority of the American serviceman. Never was reality and the lessons from the past so ignored, and the history of American-led military interventions since the end of the Cold War has continued to demonstrate that little has changed.

American involvement in Vietnam followed the decolonisation from French rule of Indo-China, territory that included neighbours Laos and Cambodia. The US had supported French attempts to beat down insurgents in Vietnam but had not intervened militarily when they were defeated at the battle of Dien Bien Phu in 1954. The Viet-Minh insurgents were a communist-led coalition formed in 1941 with the double aim of fighting the Japanese occupiers, and freeing Indo-China from French colonial control, which had been in place since the mid-nineteenth century. The peace treaty that followed the French decision to leave the region split Vietnam in two along the 17th Parallel. As with the post-war division of Korea, this was meant to be temporary pending nationwide elections, with a Communist-controlled North and Pro-US government in the South. The elections never took place and by the end of 1955 the Viet Minh in the South, who already controlled the rural hinterlands, were fighting the corrupt Saigon-based dictatorship of Ngo Dihn Diem, in an attempt to attain reunification with the North. Here, efforts were being made to rebuild the country along socialist lines, with common ownership and an improvement in the lives of ordinary citizens. The Americans filled the vacuum left by the French in a deliberate effort to fight off communism, and maintain their puppet regime, rather than (as in the British examples discussed earlier) to defend their own colonial interests. Their presence and military involvement increased over the years as Americans, in the words of Welsh photo-journalist Philip Jones Griffiths, failed in their 'soft-sell' to convince the Vietnamese people that their ideology and way of life, epitomised by Coca Cola and hamburgers, was what they wanted (Griffiths 1971). By 1965 they had large numbers of troops on the ground to enforce that ideology, even if it meant killing the people they were there to save (ibid).

The American military had considerable jungle warfare experience gained from fighting the Japanese in the Second World War, and had fought communists in Korea. What they lacked, having only limited colonial involvement compared to the European powers, was knowledge of counterinsurgency warfare against a guerrilla army capable of melting away at a moment's notice. This they borrowed from the alleged successes of the British in Malaya and Kenya, and, strangely, from the Nazi experience of fighting partisans in Ukraine and elsewhere during the war; a 1956 US Army publication draws heavily on Nazi sources (see Chapter 2) and introduces them as of 'value to the Army staff and schools as a reference work in partisan warfare' (Howell 1956, p.iii). All this, as we shall see, was of little value as the Americans continued to rely on their own absolute belief that their way of life was the only path to freedom, alongside what, after the Cold War, became known as 'shock and awe' – the use of overwhelming power and

Vietcong Soldiers, Vietnam 1966. (*Unknown origin via Wikimedia Commons*)

Americans watch the murder of a Vietcong suspect on TV February 1968. (*W. Leffler via Wikimedia Commons*)

display of force to destroy the enemy's will to fight. What all these examples did show them was that on battlefields far from home, it was possible to get away with the use of tactics that might have destroyed faith in the cause being fought for. This they never seemed to learn, even though by the mid-1960s the war was televised daily, warts and all, to audiences across the world.

The Americans deployed increasing numbers of troops and firepower in Vietnam and, quite illegally, in their neighbours Laos and Cambodia. Tactics in South Vietnam against the Viet-Cong (as the Viet Minh became known in the South) borrowed from the British but on a much larger scale, included the use of torture and murder of civilians suspects and captured fighters, relocation of communities to 'safe' compounds, the destruction of jungle and cultivated areas with defoliants and other chemical agents, and general mayhem and destruction. They carried the war to the North by air to destroy the base of support and supply to the insurgents in the South; Operation Rolling Thunder, which lasted for over three years from 1965, was followed by further offensives in the 1970s, including an intensive operation over the Christmas holiday period in 1972. Carrier-borne aircraft and giant B-52 bombers dropped a total of 7.5 million tons of bombs on Vietnam, Laos and Cambodia between 1965 and 1975, double the amount dropped in the entirety of the Second World War. Many of these landed harmlessly on uninhabited jungle, but others indiscriminately killed civilians in large numbers. None of this resulted in any military success and the Americans began to realise that this was a hopeless war unsupported by the public at home. Peace talks began in 1972 and by the time the North Vietnam Army swept through the South in April 1975, there were few Americans left. Those that were still there, ignominiously departing by helicopter from the roof of the embassy in Saigon as the city fell to the communists.

Wilfred Burchett reported regularly from North Vietnam and Cambodia during the conflict. He wrote about the bravery, resilience and determination of the Vietnamese people North and South (Burchett 2007). In 1964–65 he spent six months in Viet Cong controlled liberation areas, where the popular fight against the Army of South Vietnam forces (ARVN) and their US 'advisers', involved the sophisticated linking of hamlets by tunnel systems. These had been built through the efforts of young men and women peasants to defend their communities. He met two young women, Blossom and Lissom, who described an action where they and five others had used these systems to drive off a force of 70–80 ARVN troops. In the North, Burchett described the defence against US air attacks with Soviet-supplied anti-aircraft weapons and the sparing use of fighter aircraft that were both very effective and accounted for significant US losses.

This contrasts with the account of Griffiths, who reported the war from the US Army side through the later stages of their ground involvement between

US forces leave Saigon, Vietnam, 29 April 1975. (*US Marine Corps via Wikimedia Commons*)

1968 and 1970. He accompanied US army patrols on murderous missions into the countryside where justification for their actions was almost unbelievable. One Captain from the US 9th Division surveyed a village his men had just destroyed and told him: 'The people know it was Charlie's [Viet Cong] fault. They know we had to do it to save them from the VC' (Griffiths 1971 p.137). He saw for himself how utterly counter-productive such tactics were, and that the Viet Cong could not have produced more support through their own efforts. He also noted the effect all this had on ordinary American soldiers, many of them drafted involuntarily. Any illusions they might have had in the US cause were quickly shattered, many turning to drug use and any form of diversion that might be available, including the supply of unenthusiastic, and venereal-disease-infected, local prostitutes. Some even turned to the murder of their own officers if ordered to make particularly unnecessary and dangerous attacks. In the cities where the South Vietnamese government were in some control, the streets were rife with pickpockets and muggers, theft being an essential form of income for the economically discarded.

The Vietnam War left a terrible legacy; not just the multitudes of war dead (including 56,000 US personnel) and those whose deaths came later from agent orange and other chemicals, but also those whose scars were psychological, including hundreds of thousands of young American vets. Their sacrifices had been entirely pointless and resulted in the defeat of the most powerful nation on earth by a poor nation of peasant guerrillas. The outcome gave a lift to the USSR

Soviet Postcard depicting Vietnamese women 1960s. (*Author's collection*)

and its allies; the war of liberation they had supported had ended in victory, and communist ideology seemed vindicated. However, as Afghanistan was soon to prove, other lessons had not been learned.

France and Algeria

France felt indignity at the loss of Indo-China and seemed determined not to suffer the loss of their principal North African colony in Algeria. However, its attempt to do so caused worldwide condemnation of its oppressive tactics and torture against the Muslim population that eventually turned home and international opinion into a force sufficient enough to make them grant independence in 1962. The liberation campaign was launched in 1954 by the left-leaning, but Islamic and anti-Marxist, National Liberation Front (FLN), who very effectively fought both through persistent military guerrilla action, and the winning of universal popular approval for their cause. They sought and received Soviet support (arms, technical and material assistance), but on an ambiguous enough level to cause the US eventually to back their call for independence to woo them back into the Western camp. The FLN included communists who recognised their hegemony in the freedom struggle, but quickly dissolved the Algerian Communist Party once they won independence. The FLN's campaign proved significant in its example to others seeking liberation from oppressive rule; the French Martinique born Franz Fanon's book *Wretched of the Earth* is still widely read, describing the process of psychological degradation imposed on

Algerian FLN guests in North Vietnam 1959. (*M. Nguyen Duc Minh via Wikimedia Commons*)

colonial peoples by the dominant white power. Fanon worked as a psychiatrist, secretly supporting the FLN, and treated both oppressors and oppressed, until forced to flee Algeria. Post-independence the Algerian government supported the Non-Aligned Movement, but still courted Soviet support, and in turn lent active support to other liberation movements on the African continent. Imminent Algerian independence led to political crisis in France, being regarded as betrayal by the large French-Algerian population (known in France by the derisively racist term 'Pieds-Noirs' (Black Feet) and by right wing elements in the French military establishment. Some launched a terrorist campaign through the secret OAS organisation that included assassination attempts on President De Gaulle – the backdrop to the popular novel and movie *The Day of the Jackal.*

Latin America – the USA's Back Yard

In Chapter 4 description was given of American covert backing of the Chilean coup of 1973. Prior to that, American special forces had been involved in defeating the guerrilla threat in Bolivia in 1966–67. US involvement in violent episodes when their interests were threatened was nothing new. In 1953, the CIA, working in tandem with the British secret service MI6, engineered the overthrow of the elected Iranian Prime Minister, Mohammed Mossadegh, to prevent nationalisation of the British owned oil company and any Soviet access to Iran and its resources. In Central America their involvement after defeat in Vietnam, was also motivated by a desire to prevent further socialist and communist advance in their 'backyard'. This happened irrespective of the democratic wishes of the people involved in the countries of Grenada, Honduras, El Salvador, Nicaragua and Guatamala (the other nation in the region, Costa Rica, has enjoyed stability and security for US investment since 1948). These republics had gained independence after the breakup of Spain's colonies in the nineteenth century. In 1954 Guatamala's democratic attempt at agrarian reform was stifled by a US backed coup that secured the interests of the United Fruit Company, a banana producing corporation that has long been a major player in the region. Honduras, El Salvador and Guatemala were prone to corrupt and self-seeking political leadership, and left-wing opposition stifled, often with US assistance.

In the 1980s, under President Reagan, the covert means of suppression of popular opposition were increased using proxy countries like Argentina, and funnelling arms to right-wing mercenary paramilitaries by quite devious means. In 1985 the story broke that the US had secretly been selling arms to Iran, who were not US allies, in order to use the proceeds to fund the Contras, a right-wing group opposing the Sandinista government in Nicaragua. Their Sandinista leaders, the Ortega brothers, had been trained in Cuba and had taken power with popular support in 1979, ousting the Somoza dictatorship that had been in place for decades. With Cuban support, they were keen to support similar insurgent movements in Honduras and El Salvador, all of which threatened American interests. The Sandanistas sought and received Soviet support but this was not unconditional; they were expected to pursue socialist measures at home and follow Moscow's line in foreign policy matters abroad, but even so were keen to pursue their own agendas independently (Fall 1993). As elsewhere the US response was to provide support to murder gangs and rebels whose lethal and undemocratic activities far exceeded those of any of the movements they were opposing (Williams, Peace and Kuzmarov 2018). The US tested Soviet resolve when it invaded the tiny island nation of Grenada in October 1983, ending a communist inspired government that had courted the USSR's support, on the pretext of instability caused by infighting within the leadership. The US action was allegedly requested by their allies in the Caribbean but condemned by the United Nations. For the Soviets this confirmed the lesson learned in the early 1960s that they could support emerging socialist nations so long as it was not seriously challenged by the Americans. Despite their growing Naval might and defensive capability, they had no wish to promote global conflict (Fall 1993). This was not lost on Reagan, and the hawks who surrounded him like National Security Adviser Zbigniew Brzezinski, who pushed this advantage as we shall see in Chapter 10. The end of the Cold War eventually put an end to these anti-communist activities, although US interference in the region has never ceased (as seen when they ousted their erstwhile ally Noriega in Panama in 1989, and in more recent years in Venezuela).

Popular insurrection that overthrew the Somoza dictatorship, Nicaragua 1979. (*D. Tellez via Wikimedia Commons*)

Soviet Involvement in Anti-Imperialist Struggles in Africa

The general Western narrative suggests that the Soviet Union and the Western powers fought one another in a series of proxy wars in faraway places, over ideology and influence. While there is an element of truth to this, it discounts (as seen in Central America) the very real attempts of the people directly concerned to improve their own lives and free themselves of those external influences that sought to exploit and control them. Viewed from this perspective, Soviet interventions and supports in Africa must be seen as more honourable and less self-serving than those of the USA, Britain and the declining colonial powers, France, Portugal and Belgium. This is the view of American doctoral student Douglas Rivero whose analysis looked at the evidence from both sides and alternative interpretations made since the Cold War ended (Rivero 2009). This becomes clear when examining events in Africa, a continent that had been divided between the principal European powers during the nineteenth century, the continued presence of which went against the 1941 Atlantic Charter and the founding principles of the United Nations after the Second World War.

Under Khrushchev's confident and bullish leadership, the USSR were active in support of the left-leaning government of Patrice Lumumba that assumed control of the Congo after the departure of the Belgian colonialists in 1960, sending food aid and other forms of civilian support. This only served to convince the Americans that Lumumba was a communist (which he wasn't). The Belgians had attempted to secure their financial interests through open military support for a pro-Western secessionist movement in the mineral-rich Katanga Province; the United Nations were asked to intervene to end the secession but refused, unreasonably in the eyes of many – including the USSR. The Soviets consequently offered to support Lumumba to defeat the secessionists, but other forces were at work to convince the UN and its leadership that Lumumba's removal was essential for a peaceful settlement (i.e. the securing of Western interests) in the Congo. With US support a military coup ousted Lumumba which then had him murdered. Khrushchev had no effective military means to support Lumumba and had to view events from afar without any means to intervene (Haslam 2011). A lesson was learned for the future about the need to build Soviet armed forces that were capable of global intervention. After his death Lumumba became an icon of anti-colonial liberation martyrdom in the Soviet world, but criticism from within the leadership was fired at Khrushchev for this foreign policy failure, which, together with the outcome of the Cuba crisis in 1962 and what was seen as a retreat over Berlin, led to a nervousness about foreign interventions that could not lead to success. Within, their own sphere of influence however, there was no relaxation of control. In 1968, after Khrushchev's removal in 1964, the USSR announced the 'Brezhnev Doctrine' that warned of intervention in countries where socialist rule was threatened; this followed, as retrospective justification, the military invasion of Czechoslovakia where a communist leader, Alexander Dubcek, had begun to introduce popular reforms.

1962 Soviet postcard depicting the orphaned children of murdered Congo politician Patrice Lumumba. (*Author's collection*)

Following the defeat of US interests by communist forces in Vietnam in 1975, the Soviet leadership were emboldened by success and felt that history was again on their side. Article 28 of the 1977 Constitution reaffirmed a commitment to 'supporting the struggle of peoples for national liberation and social progress' (CPSU 1982). Directly (and indirectly through Cuba) they set out to support liberation movements in southern Africa where the last vestiges of white colonial power were holding on with varying degrees of oppressive control over the indigenous populations. This was a significant chess move in the Cold War game of position, but was driven by the presence of liberation movements seeking support rather than their manufacture by the Soviets or their proxies. This is stressed from the outset to differentiate Moscow's strategy from the Guevarist notion of the 1970s that revolution could be exported from outside to a country if the conditions were favourable; this was a strategy which saw its epitome in 1967 in Bolivia, when Che Guevara and small band of revolutionary adventurers sponsored by Cuba were surrounded, starved and finally liquidated by local forces backed by the CIA. Information analysis in this brief section owes a debt to the insider author Vladimir Shubin, whose book detailing Soviet actions and motives is both honest and well researched as well as being based on personal involvement (Shubin 2008).

The Portuguese colonies of Angola and Mozambique in southern Africa had seen political and armed resistance to colonialization since the 1950s, as had Portuguese Guinea (Guinea Bissau) further north. All were important to the post-war economy of Portugal as the sources of cheap labour for farming, mineral and oil production which developed rapidly. All had Marxist-orientated anti-colonial movements and sought support from the USSR from the early 1960s onwards. The Soviet Union welcomed black Africans from these and other colonies for general education purposes, and for military instruction. They went back home committed to training others and leading their guerrilla armies both ideologically and tactically. The war for freedom in Guinea Bissau and (to a lesser extent) Cape Verde was especially vicious and became known as 'Portugal's Vietnam', and Guinea Bissau was consequently the first Portuguese colony to be granted independence, on 10 September 1974.

In Angola three competing movements emerged, based on tribal identity but morphing under external influence, into alliance with American interests on the one hand (FNLA through the CIA) and the Soviet Union on the other (MPLA through the open support described). The third, junior liberation movement was UNITA, restricted to the south-eastern fringe of the country, which really only came to prominence post-independence. Thus were sown the seeds of post-colonial civil war. In Mozambique, FRELIMO, a Marxist organisation, enjoyed unrivalled supremacy. In 1974 Portugal underwent the Carnation Revolution – led by socialist army officers tired of their war in the African colonies and keen to replace the dictatorship at home. Events in Portugal terrified NATO leaders, and with their encouragement, alongside hesitancy and caution on the part of Soviet leaders, a safe pro-Western democracy was in place within a year or so. Portugal almost immediately handed over power to the insurgent PAIGC in Guinea Bissau and to their counterparts in Angola and Mozambique in 1975, withdrawing its interests and most of its colonists. While this settled matters in Guinea Bissau and Mozambique, in Angola it led to civil war between the ruling MPLA and the FNLA. The MPLA were supported by Cuban troops and Soviet 'advisers', while the FNLA were actively supported by the South African Defence Force (SADF) and covertly, the US.

Formed in 1910, South Africa had proved pragmatically moderate until the 1948 whites-only election swept the Afrikaner ultra-right-wing National Party to power and so was born the system of apartheid ('separateness') which was diametrically opposite to the values fought for by the alliance that included the US, Soviet Union and Britain and its Commonwealth dominions, dependants, and colonies. This also ran against the Atlantic Charter of 1941 and the founding principles of the United Nations. Here races, just as with the defeated Nazi ideology, were raised one above another: those at the lower end, who were in the majority, were condemned to poverty and hard work so that the white minority at the top could enjoy wealth and privilege while their minds were poisoned by insecurity and hatred. As anti-colonial movements developed in Africa, South Africa assumed Cold War importance as a strong state who would fight Marxist influence in the region. Although it was officially derided by the West because of its state racism, it was tolerated and investment and trade flourished, so that it could fulfil this Cold War role. Without this tacit support from the West, apartheid South Africa could not have survived. The main opposition to apartheid in South Africa came from the African National Congress (ANC), within which the South African Communist Party (SACP) was prominent. These were banned organisations and if captured their leaders faced long jail sentences, including Nelson Mandela, who was sentenced to life imprisonment in 1963, serving twenty-seven years before being freed in 1990. The ANC's armed wing, Umkhonto we Sizwe ('Spear of the People', or phonetically abbreviated to MK), sent members for training in the Soviet Bloc (including Eastern Europe and Algeria), many receiving military and political instruction in a special centre in Odessa, Ukraine. These cadres formed the leadership of a movement that spanned generations and found expression in legal and semi-legal forms of protest and activism, including the black-led trade union movement and community organisation in the vast satellite townships that served the white-dominated the cities. The intransigence of South Africa was eventually broken when the Cold War ended, Soviet support for anti-imperialist movements in Africa ceased, and the West no longer had reason to tacitly back the apartheid state. Very rapidly, Mandela was released, the ANC unbanned, and then negotiations could take place openly to establish democracy in South Africa. The transition was not without initial violence, but Shubin comments that thanks to Soviet influence the leadership of the ANC were not imbued with anti-white feeling which facilitated a more orderly transition, (opening the way to the Truth and Reconciliation Commission's work in healing wounds), than otherwise might have been the case. Although the armed conflict had been a persistent irritant to the white rulers, military victory by the MK was never a possibility. Mandela, however, was clear in later years that without the support of the Soviet Union, an ANC takeover of power might never have happened (Shubin 2008).

Winnie Madikizela Mandela at the ANC funeral of Ida Mntwana, 1960. (*A. Dyile via Wikimedia Commons*)

South West Africa was administered as a separate state by South Africa after a 31-year period as a German colony came to an end in 1915 after a short, sharp South African campaign. The League of Nations mandate of 1920 authorising this control was abolished by the United Nations in 1966, when the state became officially known as Namibia, but direct South African rule continued until 1985 when 'independence' was granted by South Africa and a puppet government answerable to Pretoria was installed. Of the groups fighting for true majority independence, SWAPO emerged as the dominant and best organised force, and as a Marxist-based organisation, was backed by the USSR from the mid-1960s, in the same way as liberation movements among their neighbours. After Namibian people were displaced to neighbouring Zambia by South African Defence Force actions that destroyed whole communities, the Soviets also provided food and emergency aid. SWAPO fighters were trained and armed by the Soviets and waged a guerrilla campaign until 1990, when SWAPO won the first free election in the country.

The privileged white minority who enjoyed a comfortable existence in the fertile and pleasant climate of Southern Rhodesia dealt with the threat of decolonisation by declaring UDI (unilateral declaration of independence) in 1965 and consolidating permanent white rule in the former British colony. Southern Rhodesia had been a self-governing territory (i.e. settler-run) since

1923. In 1953 the short-lived Federation of Rhodesia and Nyasaland was formed (comprising Northern and Southern Rhodesia and Nyasaland) but was dissolved in 1963 due predominantly to black nationalist pressure. Northern Rhodesia became independent Zambia in 1964 and Nyasaland became independent Malawi in 1965. The UDI declaration was not unlike the situation faced by the French in Algeria a few years earlier that had led to a bloody war and crisis in France. The British had no wish for a similar war with their own kind (the new Prime Minister, Ian Smith, had been an RAF fighter pilot in the Second World War) and dealt with this act of rebellion with sanctions and condemnation of the regime, while the British queen continued to be recognised as monarch (until 1970 when the country became a republic). Rhodesia survived international approbation with support from South Africa and (until 1974) Portugal. The black majority already had their own anti-colonial movements, and in 1966 these became involved in internal armed conflict with the new white racist regime which was stepped up from 1972. The two movements, ZANU led by Robert Mugabe, and ZAPU led by Joshua Nkomo had only split from one another in 1963, reflecting loyalties to other black nationalist leaders in Africa but sharing Marxist leanings. ZAPU leant ideologically towards Moscow and was strongest among urban workers, while ZANU looked to the rural peasantry for support and growth, and as such drew inspiration from Communist China. While the Soviets trained and supported ZAPU fighters it built links with ZANU and encouraged joint activity and strategy, the two eventually forming a Patriotic Front in the mid-1970s. The Bush War, as it was known, was escalated after the end of Portuguese rule in Mozambique, which added further safe bases for the insurgents to those already in place in Zambia. The Rhodesians, backed by South Africa, launched special forces raids into Mozambican territory and the war intensified, resulting in massive casualties – civilian and military – that were reported by the Rhodesians as combatants and by ZANU as civilians. The Rhodesian forces also used chemical warfare to poison water supplies and food in camps in their home territory, but especially in Zambia and Mozambique (Cross 2017). Tactics of the government troops were otherwise based on those used by the British in counter-insurgency operations described earlier in this chapter: 'winning hearts and minds', engaging in hot-pursuit operations, and bombing from the air using ageing British-made Canberra and Hawker Hunter aircraft (see Chapter 4) with covert South African support. The insurgent forces also involved themselves in acts of atrocity including, on one occasion in 1978, the murder of twelve British missionaries including their children. Eventually, in 1979, under international pressure, the internal Muzorewa government (that had superseded the Smith regime in 1978) entered negotiations under British direction in Lancaster House, London. The war ended, and elections took place, resulting in black majority rule and international recognition of the new state of Zimbabwe. The Soviets continued support for the new regime led by Robert

Mugabe, whose North Korean-trained 5th Brigade systematically destroyed ZAPU, and were on the point of selling them the latest MiG-29 jets (they had trained Zimbabwe's pilots) but this was cancelled under American pressure in the late 1980s (Shubin 2008). By then the USSR was in no position to press its case.

Afghanistan – the USSR's Vietnam

According to Haslam (2013), the Soviets were tricked by the Americans into invading Afghanistan in 1979, which if true, demonstrates an ultimate responsibility for a conflict that the US has certainly pursued more directly in the post-Cold War period (making all the mistakes the Soviets made) and which continues to bedevil global security to this day. A pro-Soviet regime in which the Afghan Communist Party was a powerful influence had instituted reforms that had freed women from traditional oppression and brought in other socialist measures that were popular among more educated Afghans in the cities. They were, however, deeply unpopular in the rural hinterlands of the country where other measures sought to reduce the power and authority of local leaders that had been in place for centuries. The tensions were exploited by opposition political forces and the crisis was deepened by leadership feuds within the governing party. The Americans knew that if this was fomented enough, the Soviets would be forced to act in line with the Brezhnev Doctrine. National Security Adviser to US President Jimmy Carter, Brzezinski, knew exactly what the consequences would be when he persuaded the administration to send arms to Afghan anti-government rebels at the same time as courting moderate opinion in government circles. Moscow would have preferred to avoid military intervention but faced with the proposition that the country seemed to be heading in the direction of American influence, decided at the end of the year to send in up to 80,000 troops to bring stability to government in its own favour. When the news reached Washington on Christmas Day that the Soviets had sent an invasion force to Kabul, Brzezinski is said to have exclaimed: 'They have taken the bait', and later wrote a note to Carter stating that, 'We now have the opportunity to give the USSR its Vietnam War.' (Haslam 2013, p.326).

The Soviets were unable to bring about the quick result they had hoped for, and nine years of war followed which, like Vietnam, took a toll among the conscript troops involved, as well as a devastating one among the Afghan population. The resistance to the Soviet occupation soon took on a religious flavour, with populist religious leaders declaring *Jihad* – Holy war – against the infidel occupiers. Supplied from the outset by the Americans (and British) via Pakistan, the conflict became bloody and unwinnable by the invading side – just as it always has been since with Western coalition forces replacing the Soviets in the early years of the millennium, but fighting essentially the same war. The Afghan resistance was never a united force and involved competing fundamentalist groups and local warlords (going under the collective name of *Mujahideen*) all of whom, quite indiscriminately, were supplied with the latest hand-held weapons by the USSR's Cold War adversaries. The Americans put on a public face of outrage about the Soviet invasion that justified increased military spending and an aggressive stance when Carter was succeeded by Ronald Reagan in January 1981. The Soviets established some sort of stability in the cities with their Afghan puppet government but were never able to exercise control in the countryside, despite numerous small, heavily defended enclaves. TV shots of their aircraft coming into Kabul airport with visible anti-ground to air missile measures, showed graphically how vulnerable their forces were even in the areas of their strongest citadels. The Soviet occupation only hardened resistance and really took the country back to the Middle Ages. As with all wars in faraway places, often out of the eye of the media, there were awful atrocities; a process that becomes self-perpetuating, endemic to both sides and a poison that long outlasts the conflict itself. Civilian deaths, perhaps as many as several million, far outnumbered those of combatants. However, Soviet deaths at over 15,000 shocked a nation who had become inured to massive casualties in the Second World War, but who had thought those days were over, and for whom Afghanistan was no Great Patriotic War in the sense that the 1941–45 period was remembered. Finally, after nine years, and with the USSR facing internal problems the war was only increasing, the Soviets withdrew under international

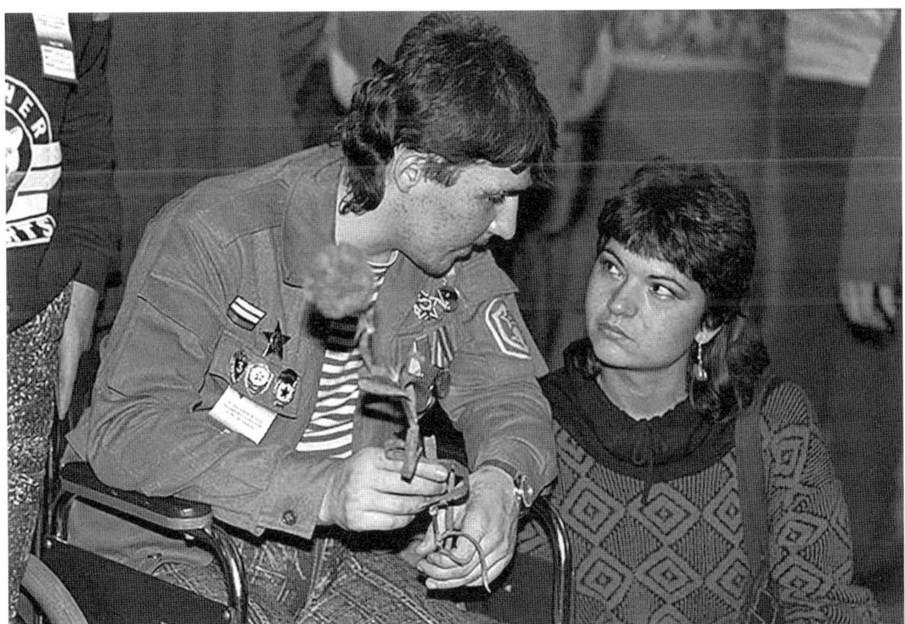

Wounded Afghan Vet in the USSR, 1990. (*Oleg Lastochin via Wikimedia Commons*)

pressure, having achieved little. Without their support, the regime was replaced by its warring Mujahideen opponents who started fighting among themselves almost immediately, leading to a very repressive state and enduring problems that seem impervious to external interventions.

Conclusion

Because the general perception reflected in much of the literature is that the Cold War became 'hot' in areas where armed conflict took place throughout the period, it has been necessary in this chapter to clarify that position. Korea and Vietnam were essentially unfinished business from the end of the Second World War, while others involved attempts at various stages by people to free themselves from colonial rule. The conflicts in Central America and Afghanistan, while different in many ways, were in the immediate vicinity of the two superpowers and involved respective efforts to stabilise regimes in these countries that would respect and further the USA and USSR's national interests. The evidence suggests that in general terms, the USSR were generally cautious about the extent of their support for anti-imperialist causes, while the Americans were more prepared to test the limits with confrontation and aggression if they perceived a communist threat. These conflicts have all been described quite briefly and further reference can be found in other chapters; Chapter 10 describes the end game of the USSR as an entity within which the Afghanistan conflict played no small part. The next chapter moves on the themes to look at those who voiced opposition to their own governments and how this shaped the Cold War period.

US Aircraft cemetery, North Vietnam 1965. (*G. Burchett*)

Chapter 6

Resistance, Dissent and Protest at Home

> The enemy is anybody who's going to get you killed, no matter which side he is on.
>
> Joseph Heller, *Catch 22*

Introduction

The focus of most accounts of the Cold War concerns the conflict between the protagonists, with mention typically, of the largescale anti-Soviet uprisings in Hungary (1956) and Czechoslovakia (1968), and the Solidarnosc movement in Poland towards the end of the period. The main superpowers enjoyed general political support at home in the sense that neither ever faced serious internal threat (although arguably the USSR did as its end neared – see Chapter 10), both faced opposition and dissent: at different times there were movements of various degrees of significance on both sides, ranging from the large-scale armed uprisings in Budapest and Prague, to a large anti-war movement in America, and into brave but almost unknown individual protest. This chapter will start with protest and anti-establishment movements in the West and move on to look at the Soviet Union and Eastern Bloc, and how these were used by both sides to further Cold War aims and objectives.

United Kingdom and Europe

The principal opposition to the immediate post-war consensus in the UK came from the Communist Party of Great Britain and their sympathisers (often referred to as 'fellow travellers'). CPGB members pursued opposition to anti-Soviet policies as Cold War tensions increased in the late 1940s but were too small to make much impact (averaging about 40,000 members according to their own figures from 1945 to 1950 – Branson 1997). Their *Daily Worker* newspaper offered a pro-Moscow account of events and only became slightly critical after the CPGB adopted its own *British Road to Socialism* (accepting a democratic parliamentary road to power) in 1951, and increasingly after 1956 when many members voiced criticism of Soviet actions in Hungary. British voters were quite conservative, and this did not change. The last Communist Party MPs, Willie Gallacher, who represented a Fife mining constituency in Scotland where his party's legacy had been strong since the days of industrial unrest in the 1920s, and Phil Piratin in London's East End, lost their seats to Labour in 1950. They had both raised issues in the House of Commons that would not have come from Labour. In 1949 Gallacher spoke up for striking black miners in colonial Nigeria, dozens of whom were killed by the police in one incident (Gallacher 1966). Where there were initiatives, such as the 'Peace Petition' launched by the British Peace Committee in 1950, CPGB members were prominent. This petition, part of a worldwide campaign in response to the explosion of the first hydrogen bomb by the Americans, gained over a million signatures despite opposition by the Labour Party and the start of the Korean War. The peace movement became a permanent feature of British civic society from then on, reaching new heights with the launch of the Campaign for Nuclear Disarmament (CND) in February 1958, an organisation that continued to campaign against nuclear weapons held by both sides throughout the Cold War. CPGB members were also prominent in anti-colonial campaigning and organised a conference in London in 1947 in which support for liberation movements across the British Empire was discussed and debated. In 1954 a coalition of left activists, including from the CPGB, set up the Movement for Colonial Freedom (MCF) and organised solidarity activity with freedom movements and struggles throughout the world. Although never as large or prominent as CND, MCF opposed racism, organised parliamentary activity and protest at Britain's involvement in the wars described in Chapter 5, and against the war in Vietnam in the 1960s. Its founder and prime advocate was the veteran pacifist Fenner Brockway. He was clear that colonial freedom was given an impetus by the Russian Revolution and the Comintern's commitment to ending imperialism and treating races equally. Brockway was also very forward-looking in his belief that the key to progressive change in British politics lay in an understanding of its own colonial history of division and exploitation based on race and white superiority – an issue still being raised and debated as a result of the Black Lives Matter movement of our own times (Gopal 2019). MCF changed its name to 'Liberation' in 1970.

Canon John Collins at a CND Demonstration, Trafalgar Square, London, 1960. (*T. French via Wikimedia Commons*)

One outcome of the 1962 Cuban Missile crisis (Chapter 3) was to build support for the consensus in UK politics that nuclear multilateralism had worked. Faced with the prospect of mutual annihilation there was a popular belief that the superpowers had backed down from war and reached agreement. CND support dwindled, only rising again with the ending of détente in the early 1980s, mass opposition to the siting of cruise missiles on UK soil, and the continued investment in Britain's own submarine-based 'deterrent'. In the meantime, in the UK and elsewhere protest focused on the Vietnam War. This was also an era of rising standards of living and expectations relating to consumerist aspiration that were new to working people. The reaction to the Hungarian Revolution and later, the Prague Spring, resulted in a diminishing belief that the USSR was progressive. Social trends resulting in growing student populations, combined with these other factors to produce new movements demanding change. In the universities the questioning of left orthodoxies across the Western world led to the growth of the 'New Left', many of whom put faith in neither Washington nor Moscow, but found inspiration in a variety of causes and movements, from support for Third World revolutionary movements (such as the cause of the Vietnamese people) to feminism, gay rights and trade union battles in the workplace. Some were inspired by Bolshevik icons long discarded in the USSR, notably Leon Trotsky (murdered on the orders of Stalin in 1940), others by anarchist ideas, some by reformed versions of Soviet ideology (especially involving the pre-War Italian writer Gramsci) and others by Mao's China.

The rise of leisure and the creation of a youth culture also resulted in alternative values and aspirations that often questioned the establishment. Pop culture and the growing use of recreational drugs (associated with social improvement because people had the disposable income to spend on non-essentials), also led to some questioning of establishment values. There was some irony in this given that many who promoted such alternative cultures became very wealthy establishment figures. In the USSR the political protest movement in the West was welcomed and publicised, while some aspects of youth culture were described as examples of western decadence and discouraged when they began to appeal to Soviet young people (see below). This was certainly a very different Cold War battleground to the military one! The new youth movements and cultures were not always understood for their potential on the traditional left; Beckett (1995) cites examples of YCL (Young Communist League) members being censured by their CPGB elders for a male organiser having long hair, and organising a debate about drug legalisation.

The zenith of New Left growth came in 1968 when the anti-Vietnam War movement reached a peak with mass demonstrations across the Western world, and popular condemnation of US imperialism. In France, the student movement, led by New Left figures, challenged the narrowly focused university system, and grew to involve at one stage, a general strike of French workers demanding change. This was cautiously backed by the French Communist Party and Trade Union confederation and the country ground to a halt, President Charles De

Gaulle temporarily fleeing to Germany fearing revolution. The growing unrest was spread through revulsion at Police repression, street battles leading to occupations and widespread discussions about alternative ways of organising society (Posner 1970). However, after seven weeks of turmoil, the movement evaporated as quickly as it had started, and the centre-right Gaullists emerged from the election in its wake with an increased majority. 1968 left a lasting impression on Western society, best expressed through the popularisation and iconic celebration of Che Guevara as a Christ-like martyr. He had been murdered by CIA-supported government troops the previous year when leading an ill-fated attempt to foment revolution from deep within the Bolivian rainforest.

New Left ideas and anti-establishment protest from a generation who could not remember the Second World War took place all over Europe, challenging the traditional left as well as the right in politics. In Western Germany, young people were more forthright than their parents in disassociating themselves from their country's recent past, completing the de-Nazification process dropped pragmatically by the Allies in the immediate post-war period (see Chapter 2). Some of these involved extremes of violence perpetrated by the anarchist 'Red Army Faction' (also known as the 'Baader-Meinhof Gang' after two of its leaders), and the 'Revolutionary Cells', a less well-known group who

Paris student occupation, May 1968. (*China News Agency via Wikimedia Commons*)

actually carried out most of the bomb attacks of the period. Their targets were industrialists and leading members of society whom they held responsible for an authoritarian capitalist regime that suppressed left ideology. The Red Army Faction did enjoy a measure of support among young Germans that was never achieved by similar groups elsewhere (the 'Red Brigades' in Italy had similar origins and organisation). They were opportunistically funded and supported in secret by the DDR's secret police, the Stasi, and this would have been known and approved of by the KGB in the USSR. Despite the imprisonment of many of their leaders (some of whom apparently committed suicide together in 1977), the Red Army Faction continued intermittent operations until the 1990s (Aust 2008).

The events of 1968 and the development of alternative cultures in the UK, led some to fundamentally question the establishment, but the political consensus was never seriously endangered. When it came to electing their political representatives, most workers still chose the Labour Party. This had always been fiercely anti-Communist since the early 1920s, refusing any unity even at the height of wartime when the USSR was united in an anti-fascist struggle with the UK (this history is discussed in my *Anglo-Soviet Alliance* 2021a). There were though, anti-establishment Labour MPs prepared to become involved in an extra-parliamentary struggle, and who were against the UK's Cold War policies and military interventions. In 1947 Dick Crossman founded the 'Keep Left' group to attempt to win Labour to a position of non-alignment to either superpower, but mainstream Labour in government needed US dollars to keep the economy afloat, so committed themselves totally to the American side in the emerging Cold War (Northedge & Wells 1982).

The most notable dissenters of the Cold War period were Tony Benn (1925–2014) a prominent MP from 1950 until 2001, and Jeremy Corbyn (1949–), a 1968 generation activist and MP from 1983. Corbyn attended a CPSU Congress in Moscow in 1989 as the USSR was in the final stages of its decline and has been kept firmly on the backbenches for most of his political career. Both were prominent in their support of the 1984–85 Miners Strike in the UK, an important battle between a government determined to deflate trade union power, and a powerful union led by Communist and other leaders who could be described as fellow travellers. The government were determined to prove that the National Union of Miners was receiving money from the USSR but failed to do this, despite the financial support that their cause received from throughout the world, including from Soviet miners. This was the last occasion when the British establishment sought and failed to find 'Moscow Gold' funding worker's opposition to their policies – a search that started in the 1920s (Turbett 2021a). The Soviets did purchase large quantities of the *Daily Worker* and the *Morning Star* (as it became) during the Cold War period, enough to keep it afloat in difficult times. The police in the UK, in conjunction with their secret service colleagues in MI5, kept a watchful eye on left-wing political groups and trade unions, including through infiltration and agent-provocateur style mischief making. The irony here perhaps is that the Labour Party was infiltrated at this time – not by the USSR's agents, but by the American CIA in order to turn it towards Washington rather than Moscow (Wilford 2003).

Dissent in the USA

The US establishment promoted their nation as having a way of life that was superior to that of all other nations. Post-war there seemed merit to this point of view; America emerged physically intact, unlike the nations of Europe and the Soviet Union, and thanks to the permanent arms economy (see Chapter 4) the awful poverty of the 1930s became a memory for most (the large black minority remained disenfranchised and outside of this social progress). There was, therefore, little resistance to the virulent anti-communism of the McCarthy era and the white majority felt generally that work was plentiful, affordable consumer choice was increasing, and life was getting better and better. Politics in the USA has always been dominated by two parties, the Democrats and Republicans, who shared the same values including wholehearted opposition to socialism and communism; their policies differed only in detail, much of which stemmed from geography and history. The Socialist Party of America was never a large electorally successful organisation, and its influence was small. The Communist Party of America, for most of its history loyal to Moscow, suffered serious decline through the 1950s, and was nominally banned in 1954. In 1957 it was reported by the FBI to have fewer than 10,000 members, 1,500 of whom were informants (Gentry 1991) . As elsewhere, many left in the wake of the Soviet suppression of the rising in Budapest in 1956.

The absence of dissent and protest was to change in the late 1950s and 1960s. A significant reason for this was the rise of the Civil Rights Movement from the mid-1950s in response to the continued oppression of black Americans, especially in the Southern States of America one hundred years after the Civil War ended slavery. Despite some legislative improvement, black Americans suffered segregation, discriminatory laws and violence from white supremacists supported by police and local authority institutions including the Courts. The Civil Rights campaign drew in many young people both black and white – through the Student National Co-ordinating Committee (SNCC), and as repression increased, the formation of the militant Black Panther Party in 1966 (originally called the Black Panther Party for Self Defense – reflecting its initial emphasis). The new generation of militants began to reframe Civil Rights in terms of Black Power – they demanded not just an equal place in society, but took pride in their heritage and identity. This expressed itself in a rise in Muslim religious identity through the activities of Malcolm X and the Nation of Islam Church. Their aggressively defensive stance was only increased when the moderate black Christian Minister Martin Luther King was assassinated by a white supremacist in 1968. Black celebrities were not all silent despite their reliance on white support – the boxing champion Cassius Clay renounced his 'slave name', renamed himself Mohammed Ali, and was stripped of his honours when he refused to be drafted in the US Army in 1967, famously stating 'I ain't got no quarrel with those Vietcong.' The acknowledgement of slave heritage led many activists to create an alternative history to that usually offered; one that recognised the place of imperialism and capitalism in enslaving their ancestors and continuing to oppress them as black people.

Black US Athletes John Carlos & Tommy Smith, Black Power protest, Mexico Olympics 1968. (*A.Cozzi via Wikimedia Commons*)

One of the most remarkable individuals to rise to international prominence during this period was Afro-American Angela Davis. Born in 1944, Davis grew up in Birmingham Alabama where she experienced racism and violence against black people as a child. Moving to New York for education she became involved in Civil Rights activism when still at school. She went on to study in Paris, Frankfurt and East Berlin, and eventually San Diego University, California, by which time she had achieved some prominence in the Black Power movement, associating with the leading figures in the SNCC and the Black Panthers. She had also been drawn to far-left ideas under the influence of New Left theorists, particularly Herbert Marcuse in Germany. In 1969 she joined the Communist Party in California, finding there both anti-racism in practice and acceptance of the need for black self-organisation. In 1970 a gun she had purchased legally for self-protection was used in an armed action by black activists in which four people were killed. Although claiming innocence of any involvement, Davis went on the run and when captured, spent a year in prison before being acquitted on all charges in 1972. During her period evading the law, Davis was placed on the FBI's 'ten most wanted' list and was described as a dangerous terrorist. This whole episode led to international fame as one of the best-known communists outside the Soviet Union and its allied countries. She visited Cuba, the Soviet

Union and other Eastern Bloc countries and continued her activism throughout the Cold War period (Davis 1974).

The USSR's press supported the Civil Rights campaigns and made much of the disparity between America's intent to defend freedom across the world, and inability to protect and look after the interests of its own citizens. Parallels were drawn between racism at home and racism in the places overseas where their military were active. Court cases were highlighted where there was obvious injustice but those that resulted in acquittal went unreported (Roman 2018). A book about space travel for a home readership in the mid-1960s compared the fact that US astronauts were all white with their own (limited in reality) ethnic mix; it also joked that if the US could not even bus black children to school safely, it seemed unlikely to make much progress with its plan to land a human on the moon (Turbett 2021b). The Black Panther movement maintained a distance from the USSR but found international support among liberated nations, notably Algeria, where several who were being targeted by the US establishment, including leader Eldridge Cleaver, relocated (Roman 2018). Angela Davis and other less well known CPUSA members like Kendra Alexander, were unique in their loyalty to the USSR among black activists and so enjoyed favour in the USSR. Davis was awarded the Lenin Prize for Peace in 1979, a move criticised by Soviet dissidents who saw a difference between her espousal of freedom for critics of the US establishment at home, but refusal to recognise their legitimacy in the USSR and Eastern Bloc.

The post-war Peace Movement in the USA that developed in the shadow of McCarthyism was largely based around religious beliefs rather than socialist politics and grew out of awareness that nuclear war was unwinnable. A RAND Corporation (a non-profit-making think tank set up to serve the needs of the US Military Industrial Complex) analysis from 1962 discusses the Peace Movement (using capitals) as a homogeneous organisation, when it actually consisted of various organisations, individuals and Church bodies. These included the US Women's Strike for Peace, the US Committee for a SANE Nuclear Policy, and 'peace candidates' in congressional elections who were members of the two main parties but supported anti-nuclear policies. The RAND paper starts with an assumption that its readers will believe that the peace movement is inhibited by the 'lunatic fringe' but explains that they have indeed to be taken seriously (Wesson 1962). SANE was started in 1957 as a pacifist pressure group and included the Civil Rights leader Martin Luther King among its supporters. By 1958 it claimed 25,000 members in 130 local chapters (groups) and was able to sponsor full page anti-nuclear advertisements in national newspapers. Such was the publicity that SANE and other organisations gave to the issue of nuclear fallout from bomb tests affecting public health, that public pressure contributed to the American decision to enter into the Partial Test Ban Treaty in 1963 with the Soviet Union and the UK which banned above-ground testing. A SANE activist, Norman Cousins, was proactive behind the scenes in liaising between Khrushchev and Kennedy to bring about the talks.

The system, however, remained intact and anti-communism was still driving foreign policy as we saw in Chapter 5. As the decade wore on, US involvement in Vietnam increased with no visible victory in sight. Young American men had been liable to be drafted into the armed services since 1940 whenever vacancies could not be filled voluntarily and as more troops were needed, this came increasingly into play. During the years of the Vietnam War, over 2 million were drafted involuntarily, some of whom went to Vietnam, although the majority of those who went did so voluntarily. Many avoided the Draft and risk of being sent to war by various means, including prior enlistment in another service such as the National Guard or Coastguard. The fact that these included future Presidents Bush Jr and Trump, illustrates how it was the well-off who took advantage of any method they and their influential families could manage. Large numbers of young men saw no just cause to fight for and campaigned against the Draft and the Vietnam War, burning their draft cards in public gatherings. By the late 1960s they were being joined by embittered and psychologically scarred returning soldiers (Vets) who spoke of the horrors they had witnessed and tossed away their medals. The mass anti-war movement involved SANE and Civil Rights Movement activists, SANE organising some of the earlier mass demonstrations such as the 35,000-strong march in Washington in November 1965. This was a bitter campaign that divided America and only began to heal when American involvement ceased in 1973, and the war ended in victory for America's enemy in 1975. Writes one such anti-war campaigner, Caleb Rossiter:

> Millions of citizens, unpaid and ostracized, took the patriotically traitorous and apparently futile step of opposing their own country's unjust foreign war … and succeeded. Everyone who attacked their officers, sabotaged their patrols, burned a draft card, fled to Canada, dodged the draft, marched in protest, put up a poster, signed a petition, voted for a peace candidate or just griped to their neighbors can take pride in being part of that success.
>
> Rossiter 1996, p.191.

The climax of the anti-war movement was not a protest or formal mobilisation but a cultural event – the Woodstock Festival of 1969; attended by hundreds of thousands and seen by millions more in the movie of the event. Many of the top rock and folk stars of the day made anti-war gestures that captured the imagination of a generation of American young people and spoke of an emerging anti-establishment counterculture being fuelled by the war. The following year, movie star Jane Fonda visited North Vietnam and was photographed symbolically with an anti-aircraft gun, before broadcasting an anti-war message to American troops. Not that they needed this, by 1970 the usual GI wartime

US Flower Power peace protester 1967. (*US Dept. of Defense via Wikimedia Commons*)

grunt 'Get some!' had been replaced by 'Not even' – a phrase signifying non-cooperation in a war not worth risking one's life for (ibid). 'Hanoi Jane', as she was dubbed by critics who likened her to the traitors who had made broadcasts for the Nazis in the Second World War, was by then funding the vet soldiers' anti-war movement back home.

Woodstock Festival 1969. (*J. Shelley via Wikimedia Commons*)

The young American anti-war generation found more political sympathy with the Students for a Democratic Society (SDS) than the traditional left. This was a new left organisation that emerged in the early 1960s from supporters of the Civil Rights Movement and SANE, but in 1969 it split and disappeared. The SDS were behind many of the campus protests that characterised the period. The most notorious took place at Kent State University Ohio in 1970, when National Guardsmen opened fire on a student demonstration, killing four and wounding nine. The 300-strong demonstration had been called to protest escalation in Cambodia and several of those killed were simply watching between classes. More than 4 million students and school children

'Hanoi Jane' Fonda Hanoi, North Vietnam 1970. (*Alamy Stock*)

1970 US protest poster depicting the Kent State University shootings. (*Library of Congress via Wikimedia Commons*)

reacted by walking out of classes across the country, and anti-war sentiment deepened. Once the war ended the movement evaporated quickly, and most of the radicalised generation of young Americans were absorbed back into the American mainstream. There was a lesser revival in Peace Movement activity with the ending of détente under Reagan, but the 1960s had passed and such upheaval was not to be repeated during the Cold War period.

The period from the 1960s onwards also saw the popularisation of various novels that carried a strong anti-war and Cold War sceptic message. *Catch 22*, originally published in 1961, was based on author Joseph Heller's own experiences as a USAF bomber crew member in the Mediterranean during the Second World War. In satirical style it highlights those who gain from war and how for the profiteers, which side you happen to be on matters little. It also humorously illustrates the cynical manner in which generals sacrifice the lives of others. Heller was clear in his public statements that his book was about McCarthyism and the Cold War atmosphere in the USA; it became popular among young people after the escalation of the Vietnam War (Heller 1977). The title refers to the paradox of system-created situations from which escape is entirely rational, but prevented by the rules of the system responsible, and the book eschews heroism in favour of survival. The science fiction novels of Kurt Vonnegut were also very popular in the West, reflecting their author's experiences as a POW in Dresden as it was fire-bombed with devastating consequences. Volunteer firefighters crop up regularly in these books, and one, *Slaughterhouse-Five*, has as its central character a young American soldier held as a POW in Dresden. Vonnegut always said that they were about the Cold War and the destruction of the American dream of service and prosperity for all, by rampant capitalism and aggression, and he wanted to fix these things, not replace them with another system (Sumner 2011). These books were also popular in the USSR, translations into Russian appearing there from 1970. Sarah Phillips, an academic from Indiana University, USA, has researched this and considers that his appeal to young people in the USSR stemmed from their identification with his characters: 'decent people trying to survive in an indecent world', and helped them independently question capitalism's excesses and the nature of hatred and evil (thedailyvonnegut.com 2021). Vonnegut's experience as a victim and witness to an Allied wartime atrocity found favour with Soviet authorities, even though they had silenced native writers such as Vasily Grossman who wrote critically about wartime from a similar perspective.

The generation who opposed the Vietnam War, while absorbed into mainstream life, gained the resources to air their views on contemporary America. Probably the most climactic example of this is the movie *Apocalypse Now* which was planned while the Vietnam War, its subject matter, was still underway. It eventually emerged in 1979, the result of multi-million-dollar expenditure including an all-star cast. Unlike the patriotic movies of previous times (some discussed in Chapter 7), the US Army refused to assist with production. The film, based on Joseph Conrad's classic novel *Heart of Darkness*, laid bare the brutality and dehumanisation endemic to the war; while it focused entirely on US perspectives and reflections, its depictions of American firepower and its needless destructive use, demonstrated a message that was universal. The Vietnam Vet Oliver Stone made a trilogy of movies at the end of the Cold War period; one, *Born on the Fourth of July* was unambiguously anti-war in its depiction (based on a true story) of how a disillusioned war-wounded vet becomes a leader in the anti-war movement.

The Soviets took delight in the American anti-war movement and reported it faithfully in their papers and magazines for home and foreign consumption. They had no need to influence it even if they could. The US government was doing the job of undermining cohesion in American society much better than they could ever have done.

Dissidence and Protest in Eastern Europe

Western accounts of life in the Eastern Bloc and USSR during the Cold War (and since in many cases) characterise their populations as either brainwashed or discontent, but oppressed into silent compliance. Both these traits are probably true about some people, but the fact is that most citizens were accepting of the regime under which they lived under for most of the Cold War period, and loyal to their respective governments. It was only when they began to crumble under the weight of their own contradictions in the late 1980s that dissidence became popular and openly pro-Western. Dissent, however, always existed and was expressed in multiple ways.

In the countries that fell into the Eastern Bloc by the end of the 1940s, there was always a resentment by many about Soviet domination and it is important here to differentiate between resistance (involving armed actions) and dissent (involving peaceful forms of organisation – both collectively and individually). Armed guerrilla activity took place in Poland, Ukraine, Romania, Bulgaria and the Baltic countries of Estonia, Latvia and Lithuania, based on bands that had emerged during the war. In Poland these were loyal to the wartime London based government, had fought the Nazis, and wanted a return to the pre-war Poland. Elsewhere they were a mix of right-wing nationalists and anti-communists, many of whom had fought with the Nazis and were guilty of holocaust involvement and genocide and what we now call ethnic cleansing. By the mid-1950s they had all been wiped out from their forest and rural bases, some survivors escaping to the West, only to re-emerge as heroic figures with the crumbling of communism several decades later (discussed in Chapter 10).

In the cities of Eastern Europe discontent about economic issues could suddenly explode into mass confrontation with the authorities. The first Eastern

Bloc mass anti-Soviet action occurred in the DDR in June 1953. A strike of building workers in East Berlin against 10 per cent work quota increases resulted in rapid backdown by the authorities who were taken by surprise. This emboldened workers who broadened their demands to include free elections, returning to the streets with clear displays of anti-Soviet feeling. After police and local authorities failed to persuade the demonstrators, numbering thousands, to return home and avoid provocation, Soviet troops were deployed to break up the protests, resulting in violence and mass arrests. Word quickly spread and over the next week there were protests throughout East Germany's cities, towns, and villages. In the face of determined repression and intransigence these petered out after a week or so, the state blaming Nazi elements for provocation. There was widespread loss of faith in the regime and many left the ruling Socialist Unity Party (SED), but stability was restored with reforms, investment from the USSR in the economy, the release of remaining prisoners of war being held in the USSR, and the ending of reparation payments. Afraid of what they had experienced the government also invested heavily in the Stasi (secret police) to monitor and deal with dissent, a feature of life in the DDR for the next thirty-five years. The DDR's workers learned that direct confrontation was risky and would not be supported from outside. Although the FDR and Western nations did not intervene, the suppression of the East German revolt was remembered with a National Public Holiday on 17 June, celebrated as a permanent reminder of communist oppression until reunification in 1990.

DDR 1954 – leaders of the previous year's strike movement on trial accused of espionage for the West. (*Bundesarchiv via Wikimedia Commons*)

In Poland, workers in the city of Poznan went on strike in June 1956 in protest at their deteriorating standard of living (and demanding free elections), resulting in violent clashes with the police and the deaths of fifty-eight demonstrators (almost as many as died in East Germany three years earlier). The Polish ruling party (the PZPR – Polish United Workers Party) responded with reforms and self-reflection designed to reassure the population that they realised their mistakes and agreed with the economic demands of the demonstrators. This helped further similar demands elsewhere, particularly in Hungary, where similar agitation arose in Budapest the capital. There, the demands were quite political and were reflected within some leadership elements of the ruling Party – Hungarian Workers Party (MDP). Matters escalated quickly and large numbers of demonstrators took to the streets in openly anti-Soviet protest, symbolically burning out the communist hammer and sickle form the middle of the national flag. Students drew up a list of 'Demands of the Revolutionists', which ranged from the right to free opinion and general elections, to the removal of the giant statue of Stalin from the city centre. No response was awaited to the latter and crowds destroyed it themselves. An armed response by riot police led to the arming of demonstrators and confrontation with hastily deployed Soviet troops, who withdrew. Budapest was by now in the effective hands of the insurgents who were supported by most of the population. The government under Imre Nagy announced free elections, the dissolution of the MDP and its replacement by a new democratic socialist party. Khrushchev by this time had seen enough and saw this as a threat to communism and the security of the USSR. In this he was backed by all his allies, including China and Yugoslavia. Over 30,000 troops and 1,000 tanks were mobilised by the wartime hero Marshall Zhukov and, led by another wartime leader, Marshall Konev, invaded Hungary to brutally put down the revolution. The insurgents fought back, and Red Army casualties rose to over 700 killed, with over 3,000 deaths on the Hungarian side. The outcome, however, was never in doubt.

The Hungarian Revolution tested the anti-communist rhetoric of the West. Although the 'free' radio stations (see Chapter 7) assured the Hungarian people that NATO would intervene to help them, this was never a plan of the Western powers. Talk of 'liberation' was replaced with that of 'loosening up the ideology' (Rethly 2006). There was a profound impact on supporters of the USSR in the West. Eyewitness reports from convinced communists like the UK *Daily Worker*'s Peter Fryer, cast doubt on Soviet integrity, and resulted in thousands leaving communist parties in Europe and elsewhere. The respect and admiration enjoyed by the Red Army for having played the major role in the defeat of fascism eleven years earlier was shattered forever.

History was to repeat itself in Prague in 1968, when the Czechoslovak party leadership under Alexander Dubcek began experimenting with reform, events known as the 'Prague Spring'. These involved freedom of speech and

Soviet tank confronts protesters Budapest, Hungary 1956. (*CIA via Wikimedia Commons*)

media, and the lifting of travel restrictions, alongside some decentralisation of government – all attempts to give socialism, in Dubcek's words, 'a human face'. After attempting to negotiate the end and subvert these changes, the Soviets sent in half a million Warsaw pact troops to enforce their wishes, who were met with passive resistance and no organised armed opposition. Soviet Union objectives were eventually achieved after several months of tense negotiations and compromises by Dubcek and the leadership, who were eventually replaced with Moscow loyalists. President Johnson in Washington was advised of the invasion by Soviet diplomats and assured that there was no intent to cross into NATO territory. Several NATO countries bordering Czechoslovakia went onto a war footing, but the USA would not sanction any move to protect democracy despite all the rhetoric, having no wish for confrontation over Czechoslovakia when they were so bogged down in Vietnam. For the new left in Europe, fresh from the barricades in Paris, this was further proof for many that their aspirations for socialist change would not come through the USSR (Mastny 2005).

Until events in Poland in the 1980s turned regime opponents westwards in outlook, many Eastern Bloc dissidents were convinced socialists and looked for reform of the system rather than its dismantlement. This was true in Poland itself; in 1964, Jacob Kuron and Karol Modzelewski published an open letter to the PZPR leadership, criticising their creation of a new ruling class of bureaucrats and calling for workers' democracy. This led to their imprisonment

Leaflet distribution Prague 1968. (*Czech National Archives via Wikimedia Commons*)

for three years and when sentenced in court, Kuron sang the 'Internationale'. Their semi-clandestine activity continued and in 1976 Kuron and others formed KOR (Workers Defence Committee), aimed at supporting political prisoners and their families, and social movements defying the state. Socialists like Kuron were instrumental in forming the independent trade union Solidarnosc (Solidarity) in the Lenin Shipyard, Gdansk, in 1980. This aimed, because of the violent suppression of strikes in 1970 and 1976, to better organise workers. By 1981 membership across Poland had reached 10 million, but a leadership had emerged who were more interested in replacing Polish socialism with Western style labour relations and freedoms, than in reform. The most prominent leader was Lech Walesa, a staunch Catholic who was happy to be courted by Western leaders, many of whom, like Ronald Reagan and Margaret Thatcher, were no friends of the free trade union movements in their own countries. Solidarnosc provided a powerful lead to Poland's workers and very successfully represented their aspirations for change. When it became apparent, due to changes in the Soviet Union in the 1980s, that the Polish state would have to deal with its own internal problems and that military intervention by the Warsaw Pact was not going to happen (in effect the ending of the Brezhnev Doctrine), the leaders of the PZPR capitulated and organised free elections in June 1989. After this the countries of the Eastern Bloc fell one by one to similar change as will be discussed in Chapter 10, and one-party rule ended.

It needs to be emphasised that the intellectuals, often socialists, who contributed directly to the unfurling of events in Poland and elsewhere, were not involved in launching the major uprisings in East Germany, Budapest and Prague – these were spontaneous outbursts based on fractures and turns within the ruling party leaderships (Pollack & Wielgohs 2005). The socialists were dissidents trying to achieve reform through change to the system, rather than replacing it. Such dissidence featured across the Eastern Bloc countries. These individuals were as opposed to the creeping influence of Western culture (for example Coca Cola and blue jeans) as they were the grey uniformity of Soviet style socialism. A young Hungarian writer, Miklos Haraszsti, who spent a period working in the Red Star Tractor Factory in Budapest, published a book *Workers in a Workers' Sate* in 1973. This looked closely at the system of piecework in the early 1970s, where Western systems (and Western manufactured machinery) had been introduced to increase production and reduce labour costs. He describes levels of labour exploitation in a so-called workers state that would have been familiar to any trade unionist in the USA, UK or France in the same era. The book was immediately suppressed, and its author put on trial in 1974 for 'incitement to

Lenin Shipyard, Gdansk, Poland, occupied August 1980. (*European Solidarity Centre via Wikimedia Commons*)

subversion' – that he had authored a book with a view to distribution likely to stimulate hatred of the state. Haraszti was found guilty and given a suspended prison sentence (Haraszti 1975). He went on to become an academic and then politician in post-communist Hungary.

In the view of Pollack and Wielgohs (2005) the attempts of socialist intellectuals to reform their respective regimes had largely foundered as the USSR and Eastern Bloc countries entered the period of stagnation during which living standards began to fall and aspirations for a better life under socialism withered. During the late 1970s and 1980s emphasis was placed on human rights and this became a potent force in Czechoslovakia with the launching of Charter 77 in 1977. Its founders, including Vaclav Havel, soon linked up with KOR activists in Poland, and their influence was also evident in the rise of opposition activity in the Baltic States. The Human Rights narrative also encouraged dissident voices from within Church institutions, not just within Poland and its strong Catholic Church, but also within East Germany's Protestant Church.

The history of opposition to communist rule in Romania is different to that of other Eastern Bloc countries due to the distance created by the regime there from the USSR, from the 1960s onwards – and certainly not because it was in any way more liberal. Romania, under Nicolai Ceausescu, was the only Warsaw Pact country to condemn the Soviet invasion of Czechoslovakia. This strangely

Nikolai and Elena Ceausescu State Visit to Britain, 1978. (*Romanian Communism Online Photo Collection via Wikimedia Commons*)

led to Western support for a totalitarian regime that controlled all aspects of life at home, because of its liberal attitude to events abroad. In 1978 Ceausescu became the only communist head of state to be invited for a state visit to the UK, which followed not just his regular slights to Moscow, which the West saw hope in, but because a £200 million aircraft sales deal was in the offing. The queen bestowed him with an honorary knighthood, and he conferred her with the 'Order of the Star of the Socialist Republic of Romania'. A year earlier, emulating events in Czechoslovakia, intellectuals in Romania launched their own human rights charter to address their woeful absence within the country, despite guarantees within the constitution. This was violently supressed by the Securitate (secret police) and its authors imprisoned, events conveniently ignored in the West (Petrescu in Pollack & Wielgohs 2005).

Dissent in the USSR

Resistance within the USSR, mostly arising from supporters of the Czarist regime overthrown in February 1917, was ended with Bolshevik victory in the Civil War in 1921 (I exclude here the armed resistance in several of the Western republics mentioned above). Through the period of Stalin's rule (1924–1953) dissent from his opponents, real and imaginary, was dealt with harshly through the most overt means of state repression – millions of citizens were subject to long prison sentences or simply executed for alleged political crimes. This served the twofold purpose of stifling any real opposition before it could emerge and providing the vast slave labour force the country needed to implement its plans for rapid industrialisation. Change to this general picture only began after Stalin's death and the Khrushchev 'thaw' from the mid-1950s, when relaxations were made on censorship and cultural life. The thaw did not mean relaxation on general labour discipline and freedoms – in 1962 a strike over economic issues in the city of Novocherkassk in Southern Russia, spread from one key factory to the whole community, leading to street demonstrations and confrontation. Troops were sent from elsewhere and the outbreak rapidly suppressed at the cost of twenty-eight dead and many others wounded (Lewin 2005). The thaw was anyway always disputed within the CPSU leadership and came to an end with Khrushchev's removal.

It is from the mid-1960s on that the Western notion of the Soviet dissident began to take shape, a theme that quickly became a Cold War weapon used against the USSR, filling more press columns than the glaring human rights abuses perpetrated by the US at home and abroad. The starting point for this process was the publication of works by Alexander Solzhenitsyn (1918–2008), a wartime decorated artillery officer from Rostov-on-Don who had spent eight years in penal camps for criticising Stalin in 1945. His first book *A Day in the Life of Ivan Denisovich* was published, with official permission, in 1962, and its description of life in the camps won Solzhenitsyn worldwide fame. This unnerved the Soviet authorities to the extent that his work was banned from publication and when *The Gulag Archipelago* was published in the West in 1973, it caused a sensation; although it graphically described the effects of Stalin's brutal regime on his domestic victims, the contemporary treatment of the author associated its content with Soviet authority in the minds of Western readers. Solzhenitsyn was expelled from the USSR in 1974 and after a spell in Germany, went to live in the USA, where his Orthodox Christian religious ideas and reactionary views alienated him from liberal opinion.

There were other celebrated Soviet dissidents in the Soviet era, and the usual emphasis of their activity was around human rights, echoing that in the Eastern Bloc satellites described above. These include the nuclear physicist Andrei Sakharov, the writers Vladimir Bukovsky and Anatoly Kuznetsov, and the Medvedev brothers Zhores (a biologist) and Roy (a historian and socialist). The USSR did not sign the United Nations' 1948 Universal Declaration of Human Rights, and even when it signed a similar declaration in 1973 (and as part of the Helsinki agreement in 1975 – see Chapter 3), monitoring groups (themselves persecuted) were concerned about its recognition. The importance of socialist thought that stemmed from the ideas abundant in the early years of the revolution then crushed by Stalin, is important. One such was Alexander Zinoviev, who survived both serving as a pilot in the war, and Stalin, despite expressing oppositional views and sharing thoughts about assassinating Stalin as a youth. He was expelled from the USSR in 1978 after samizdat copies (see below) of an allegorical and satirical novel critical of the regime, *The Yawning Heights*, appeared in 1975. Zinoviev was as much a critical outsider in the West as he had been at home, believing that communism represented the future even though the Soviet model was flawed. He attacked other dissidents as paid stooges of the West and mourned the passing of the USSR after 1991.

Lewin (2005, p.192) discusses the 'prophylactic' interventions of the KGB to limit the influence of targeted citizens who were leaning towards dissidence; these could be triggered by 'suspicious contact with foreigners, treasonable intentions or harmful political interventions'. Prophylaxis involved an interview and warning by a KGB officer, and between 1967 and 1972, 13,000 individuals were subject to this method of dealing with dissent. Dissidents included Jews who were persecuted in civil life, some of whom were 'refusniks' who refused military conscription, and many sought refuge in Israel. Other religious faiths suffered the closure of churches, especially under Khrushchev when the policy of promoting atheism was most vigorously pursued.

Serious repression of dissidents could include internal exile, imprisonment, expulsion and forced psychiatric treatment. Zhores Medvedev, Vladimir Bukovsky and the poet Joseph Brodsky were among those regarded as mentally ill and detained in special psychiatric hospitals (Психушка) because their belief systems were seen as signs of madness. Soviet psychiatrists came up with a special diagnosis for this condition – 'creeping schizophrenia' (вялотекущая шизофрения) which explained the sufferer's paranoid obsession with 'truth and justice'. While not denying this human rights abuse, all this was grist to the mill for Western propagandists, few of whom took much interest in their own vast psychiatric institutions where human rights abuses were also an issue and that were in major need of reform. One of the examples of such Soviet incarceration concerned two of eight demonstrators who conducted a brief and violently supressed protest against the invasion of Czechoslovakia on 25 August 1968 (five others were exiled and imprisoned). This did receive attention worldwide, was condemned by the World Psychiatry Association, and became a source of embarrassment to Soviet medicine in general. Under the Glasnost reforms and international pressure, it was effectively ended in 1989 after a permitted visit to institutions and subsequent report by American psychiatrists (Human Rights Watch 1990).

The people of the USSR were avid readers – the official publishing houses turned out more books than were printed anywhere else in the world. A varied movement of self-publishers got round censorship by hand-producing books and newspapers that were passed from hand to hand. These 'samizdat' publications involved celebrated writers and poets when these were available for copying. Some were typed and duplicated, others were stencilled and copied, and circulation

Samizdat literature from the USSR. (*Nkrita via Wikimedia Commons*)

was obviously limited unless copies reached the West and were published there. Penalties for possession of such material could be harsh. Some samizdat material was hardly liberal or progressive, reflecting the views of Stalin apologists or the right-wing nationalists who emerged from the shadows in the 1990s.

Political jokes had a long history in the USSR, event through the time of Stalin when their telling could have consequences:

> An Englishman, a German and a Russian were arguing together about which of their three nations was the bravest. 'We're the bravest,' insisted the Englishman, 'because one in every ten of us drowns at sea.' 'Nonsense,' protested the German. 'We are the bravest, because one in every six of us dies on the battlefield.' 'You are both wrong,' said the Russian. 'We are the bravest, because although every second one of us is an informer, we still tell political jokes.'
>
> Benton and Loomes 1976, p.85

As the period of pride in achievement and general improvement in living standards under Khrushchev lapsed into economic stagnation under Brezhnev, ordinary people found ways of sharing their growing cynicism with their rulers through jokes and these would be passed on to those who were trusted. These could be self-deprecating but poked fun at the establishment:

> Brezhnev was walking across Red Square when he heard a ghostly voice: 'Comrade Leonid, bring me a horse …' The same thing happened the next day, and the next. He decided to report the affair to Kosygin, and the two men went down into Red Square to investigate. Suddenly the ghostly voice started up again: 'You fool. I said bring a horse – you've brought me an ass!'
>
> Benton and Loomes 1976, p.96.

The USSR long had a concern with 'hooliganism' – a broad description of any behaviour deemed anti-social. This was often associated with drunkenness, an endemic problem in a cold nation where life was hard and alcohol cheap, and present before and since the Soviet period. In the 1960s concerns mounted about Western-inspired hooliganism among young people attempting to emulate the youth culture of the West. This was usually associated with music and clothing – Western items were sought after and those that came into the country, typically through the Northern Baltic ports close to Sweden, could reach high prices on the black market. Youth culture even expressed itself through motorcycle gangs and Western style customising of the crude Soviet machines. As in the West, the state were not quite sure how to deal with this – attempts were made to accommodate rock music into popular Soviet culture, but the lure of the forbidden

West (travel was strictly controlled and beyond the reach of most citizens) was enduring. Yurchak, whose book (2005) describes the life and aspirations of what he calls the 'last Soviet generation' (those born in the 1950s to 1970 period who came of age before the collapse in 1991), talks of the 'imaginary West', much better, as it turned out, than the real thing.

Conclusion

This chapter has discussed internal resistance and dissent both East and West. In the case of the USA and USSR neither was liberal towards their internal critics when they felt especially threatened during most of the Cold War period. The shooting of workers in Novocherkassk was no less brutal than the shooting of students at Kent State University; armed force was used in both against angry but unarmed protesters. Similarly, the McCarthy purge of communists from public life had parallels with the later treatment of dissidents in the Brezhnev era – both were based on a belief that their own systems were beyond reproach and serious opposition had to be criminal (or in the case of some in the USSR, insane). Those whose sympathies lay with the other side, like the CPGB in the UK or some dissidents in the USSR, were a minority and played no great role in oppositional movements East or West – these emerged through other factors and often involved people whose loyalties and values lay with their own country. Many of the oppositionists in Eastern Europe in the 1960s and

President Reagan meets with expelled Soviet dissident Anatoly Shchransky October 1986. (*White House via Wikimedia Commons*)

1970s were socialists and Marxists; many of those in the USA and the UK who opposed their governments on various issues were implacably opposed to the totalitarianism of the USSR.

Naturally, each side in the Cold War made every effort they could to exploit stories of dissidence and protest in their adversary's country. This probably made little impact on events or opinions abroad – except perhaps in the case of Soviet dissidents deemed mentally ill. Propaganda and the efforts each protagonist made to keep on side their own people, and get their values across to the other, did play a role in shaping opinion, and this will be examined in the next chapter.

Women peace protesters at Greenham Common Cruise Missile site, UK, November 1982. (*Ceridwen via Wikimedia Commons*)

Chapter 7

The War of Words – Ideology and Propaganda

> Ideology – that is what gives evildoing its long-sought justification and gives the evildoer the necessary steadfastness and determination….
>
> Alexander Solzhenitsyn, *The Gulag Archipelago*

Introduction

Capitalism and communism, the basis of the Cold War, are different economic systems determined by very different ideologies. It follows naturally that these differences should flavour the way in which each side sold the Cold War to their own populations and across the divide. This chapter will explore some of the methods and means used and will examine fundamental differences in the meaning of citizenship East and West. Failure to grasp this concept pervades much of the Cold War literature, especially that written since the early 1990s. It is assumed perhaps that the rush from the East in 1990 to adopt the West's systems and values tells its own story about what people really wanted all along. In fact, as we shall see, socialist or communist values were embedded within most of the population, certainly in the USSR, but also elsewhere in the Eastern Bloc. US hegemony of outlook might be a reality for much of the world in the present era but cannot be said to be universally true of all periods in recent world history. Chapter 11 will explore this further from a viewpoint thirty years on. This is set out based on general agreement within the Cold War literature that the period was characterised by ideological rather than military confrontation. This is important as it differentiates the Cold War from conflicts based on national economic interest and difference.

The British Way and Purpose

'Britishness' and what it means to be a British citizen is hard to describe; for some it sums up an idea built around the empire and racial superiority, others would contest this and see it in terms of a long tradition of democracy and peaceful transition. Nowadays those who seek British citizenship must pass an exam that most UK born people would fail miserably. There is no written constitution, but an accumulation of laws and customs going back to the Magna Carta of the eleventh century. During the Second World War, when concerted effort was made to motivate troops through compulsory education, a programme was drawn up titled *The British Way and Purpose.* This sought, among many other things, to define citizenship in terms of responsibilities and rights, and appreciation of key factors of 'Britishness': free choice, understanding the reality of totalitarian alternatives, and active participation in democracy (Directorate of Army Education 1944). These can serve as the template the UK carried into the era of the Cold War, except that now, Nazi totalitarianism had been replaced by the USSR's perceived desire for world communism. The fact that the Soviet Union had so recently been a close ally was quickly clouded in a mire of altered memories and narratives, mostly told by former officers who had never taken much comfort from the wartime pragmatism of the alliance (Turbett 2021a). This was the ethos that British troops were supposed to take with them into the hot wars in Korea, Malaya and elsewhere, and which drove popular support for them at home.

In the Introduction to the book mention was made of the patriotic war movies produced in Britain in the 1950s. While still exciting to watch as they describe experiences of a generation who are almost gone but who were the parents of my own, they present a carefully crafted image in keeping with Cold War values. Central characters are usually white middle-class English officers, with a sprinkling of support roles for plucky working-class 'other ranks' with caricatured accents, and faithful women looking after the country cottage while the men are fighting. The Red Army, who did most of the fighting against Nazi Germany, rarely get a mention, so that audiences could easily substitute them in the here and now for the wartime enemy (Turbett 2021a). Boys' comics were full of similar heroic stories, as was popular literature for adults. Working-class people, as strong rather than dependent characters, only began to appear in the late 1950s, with gritty Northern novels, movies and TV shows. Even these portrayed drabness and poverty (not just in the material sense) rather than the pride and solidarity that characterised many working-class communities in that period. The underlying messages of the British Way and Purpose were hardly being challenged. This began to change in the 1960s with the social changes discussed briefly in the last chapter; more alternative accounts in literature could be found without recourse to books and newspapers circulating among the small cohorts of leftists and peace campaigners. However, the establishment still ensured that their interpretation of past and current events was passed on. The main organ of media manipulation of opinion was of course the mainstream press, owned by a wealthy and privileged group whose interest lay in maintaining the status quo. Even though they differed in party loyalty, all were anti-communist and clear on their Cold War affiliations (Barnett 2018). This was the pattern that was to continue for the duration of the Cold War. A 1985 study by a group of peace activists of school textbooks in Britain found that children were being offered a history of the end of the Second World War and the start of the Cold War that was 'distorted or extreme' (Sykes et al 1985, p.39).

The UK government was not above censorship if it felt this was necessary. The best-known example concerns a movie made in documentary style about the aftermath of a nuclear attack on Britain – *The War Game* made for the BBC in 1965. The BBC themselves decided that the film could not be shown on television, and the government agreed (Chapman 2006). The film was shown to private audiences, often hosted by peace-movement groups, but not broadcast publicly until 1985. As mentioned elsewhere in this book, the presence and role of the British Labour Party in suppressing communist ideology and influence from within the labour and trade union movement was largely effective, and the government had little need to move directly to restrict civil liberties as had happened in the USA (Mahoney 1989). Neither had they much need to intervene to propagandise within the education system or the press – although such moves were considered in the early 1950s (ibid). This was not the attitude always taken overseas where influence was considered necessary.

Selling the British Way and Purpose abroad involved the sponsorship and promotion of books that promoted the right values. In the early 1950s the *Don Camillo* novels of Giovanni Guareschi humorously described the post-war battle for hearts and minds of a rural Catholic priest and a Communist mayor. The priest, Don Camillo, was generally portrayed as being the smartest, and the values and practices of the mayor, Peppone, as wily but easily outwitted. These first appeared in 1948, a time when communists were popular in parts of Italy and electoral victory was a possibility. The first stories appeared as magazine pieces, and it was British MI6 funding that secured their publication as popular and widely circulated books. This was a form of subtle psychological warfare that accompanied American CIA funding of the rival Christian Democratic Party (Haslam 2011). The use of George Orwell's works at home and abroad was equally subtle. *Animal Farm* described the descent into totalitarianism of animals who had freed themselves from the coercive rule of the human farmer – the parallels with Stalin were obvious, which is why the book's publication was deferred until just after the war ended in August 1945. In 1943, when the book had first been written, victory had very much depended on Red Army success and neither the USA nor the UK wanted to upset Stalin. Orwell's other best seller was *Nineteen Eighty-Four*, published in 1949 when anti-communism had become embedded in Western thought and action. One of its precepts is the 'doublethink' practiced by the ruling party in Orwell's depiction of a future totalitarian state: 'war is peace', 'freedom is slavery' and 'ignorance is strength'. This was quoted in the press to illustrate the insincere doublethink of communists at home and abroad (Barnett 2018). A World Peace Conference was to be held in Sheffield in 1950, called by the USSR-backed 'World Committee of Partisans for Peace' following a similar but controversial conference in Paris in 1949. Such was the outcry in the press that the Labour government took steps to make participation difficult, withdrawing consent for eighteen charter flights from the Eastern Bloc and

Italian writer Giovanni Guareschi, secretly sponsored by the UK, reading communist *L'Unita* 1953. (*Unknown origin – Wikimedia Commons*)

refusing visas to would be delegates. 'Peace' as a concept was successfully turned on its head to suggest different motives from the communist backers. In the face of such obstacle-laden opposition, the conference was hastily moved to Warsaw. After this, any mention by the Soviets of their peaceful intentions was generally interpreted differently by British people imbued deliberately with Orwell's ideas about doublethink and totalitarianism.

Stretching longer into the Cold War was the UK government agency, 'Information Research Department' (IRD) originally founded under Labour in 1948 and dispensed with in 1977. Starting with a mission to promote the British idea of social democracy, it quickly extended into forthright anti-communism (Smith 2010). Their activities reached a wide and unsuspecting audience through the publications of the 'Background Books' publishing house, established in 1953. Their small pamphlets were enhanced with further republication by Bodley Head and others of bound versions that lent both quality and respectability. These were all designed to look objective and neutral: according to their own backcover explanations, 'They will not interpret current history for you but they will help you interpret it for yourself.' (Quoted in Smith

2010, p.117). Explicit 'Red scare' material included Labour politician Francis Noel-Baker's *The Spy-Web: A Study of Communist Espionage* which argued that Western Communist Party membership could inevitably led to spying for the USSR. Other publications were more subtle: the 1966 *Glossary of Political Terms* edited by Maurice Cranston purported to offer a neutral explanation of everyday terms such as communism and anarchism. The IRD ensured that the books received a worldwide audience.

The IRD also operated through authors and British publishers who are said to have had no idea (according to Smith, ibid) of the manipulation involved, including the prestigious Oxford University Press. In the early 1960s they republished an IRD promoted work entitled *Books on Communism* (Kolarz, 1963, 2nd edition); this was praised by academics for its scholarly appraisal of other titles, and there can be little doubt that it influenced many academic books whose prestigious authors used it as an information base (Smith 2010). Reading this book today it seems extraordinary that it might be regarded as objective; its description of Senator McCarthy's book explaining his anti-communist crusade takes up a single uncritical sentence. Lenin's entire output is reduced to reference to his *Collected Works* with no comment attached. The section titled 'The Appeal of Communism' has nine pages of anti-communist titles without a single objective view of – let alone in favour of – its ideology. There are a few Marxist classics dotted about but the book is transparently anti-communist despite its claim to be 'of lasting value to librarians, research workers, teachers, students and all who are concerned with the theory and practice of communism'. (Kolarz page v). With its notable lack of titles published in the country of its principle subject matter, the USSR, this book contrasts strikingly with a similar volume published in 1942 at the height of the wartime alliance (Grierson 1942). Orwell's prophesies were closer to home than many chose to imagine!

The British Way and Purpose, and the UK government's view of world events was also broadcast to most corners of the world in the neutral sounding tones of the BBC World Service. Their place as the world leader in terms of hours broadcast was only overtaken, by the USSR, in the mid-1950s. The BBC could be relied upon to project the government view, but at times went their own way by rejecting attempts at interference; this happened most notably during the Suez Crisis in 1956 when they broadcast opinion from the Egyptian side and angered the Conservative government. Projecting objectivity, the facts from both sides if there was conflict, became the watchword of the BBC, and led them to be more trusted than the more combative Western stations funded by the CIA (see below). The BBC was also apparently commended for its calming influence at times of turmoil; it suggested restraint, and this is remembered by activists in Hungary in 1956, and by others during the later Polish events (Nelson 1997). Soviet citizens listened in to hear news that could not be accessed through their own radio stations; in 1961 the funeral of the writer Boris Pasternak, whose popular novel *Doctor Zhivago* had been published in the West but banned in his home country, was attended by thousands who had heard about it through the BBC (ibid).

The American Way

Promotion of the freedom-loving American way of life as a positive opposite to the despotism of communism was vigorously pursued throughout the Cold War period. This difference, and the fear of the poison of communism, reached paranoid-ridden heights in the late 1940s and early 1950s, with Senator Joe McCarthy's Congressional House of Un-American Activities Committee (HUAC). The HUAC's brief was to root out communist influence, particularly in the spheres of American life where ordinary innocent citizens might be open to persuasion. The HUAC worked hand in hand with the FBI, whose director, J. Edgar Hoover, was an enthusiastic anti-communist whose experience in the field went back to the 1920s. The movie industry was a particular target, and among those films investigated by the FBI was the blockbuster *It's a Wonderful Life*, because of the characterisation of the town banker; however, the finding that two of the screenwriters had alleged communist connections did nothing to harm the movie's success. Others, though, fell victim, and lives and reputations were destroyed. The FBI under Hoover was later found to have exceeded its brief in its anti-communist activities, amassing huge blacklists of suspects and infringing civil liberties in its pursuit of its goals over a long period, until his death

Senator Joe McCarthy briefing a Senate Hearing, 1954. (*US Senate via Wikimedia Commons*)

in 1972. The HUAC's activities were deliberately open but there was nothing rational about their deliberations and bullying; these were more reminiscent of the witch hunts of the seventeenth century than of civilised free debate. By the mid-1950s liberal opinion was winning over and the HUAC's interrogations were brought to an end.

One of McCarthy's supporters was the ambitious politician, Richard Nixon. In 1960 Nixon spoke at length in his (unsuccessful) presidential campaign on the persuasiveness of communism, contending that while it was no longer attractive in the USA, it certainly was in the emerging states of the Third World. He offered an intellectual case for rejecting communism (and socialism) as a failure past and present. By the time Nixon was fighting his 1968 campaign he had considerably refocused his anti-communism, and was now suggesting dialogue and negotiation with Moscow in keeping with the era of détente (Rzepecka 2012). What Nixon's example demonstrates is that anti-communist rhetoric changed in the USA during the Cold War, rising and falling according to the need to convince the electorate of the requirement for policy turns and expenditures, but never going away. Some of this, as discussed in Chapter 4, was driven by the needs of the Military Industrial Complex. Chapter 10 will look at anti-communism's zenith under Reagan in the 1980s.

Anti-communism in the USA stemmed from a particular view of citizenship arising from the American Constitution and its accompanying Bill of Rights. This all contributed to the popular image of the frontiersman who carved out his own future in the Wild West – typified in the real-life story of Davy Crockett. Crockett was born of humble origins, received little formal education, but gained experience from childhood in learning how to hunt, track and live off the land. After a period as a politician in Washington he died a hero's death defending the Alamo against the Mexican Army at the age of 50 in 1836. His immediate contribution to the Cold War was to have a short-range nuclear weapon named after him; if Crockett, as legend held, could kill a bear at the age of 3, then this piece would enable the ordinary soldier (or a crew of three) to readily knock out Soviet tanks on the battlefield. The Bill of Rights placed curbs on a government's ability to restrict individual freedoms, the most famous example being the right to bear arms. While it would be wrong to stereotype the citizens of any country, what is being suggested here is that there was (and perhaps still is) a shared image of the All-American that was fostered and promoted during the Cold War as an opposite to communist values.

All-American values were expressed in quite unsubtle and simple terms through movies and literature. No one represented the rugged individualism of the frontiersman, cowboy and war hero better than the Hollywood actor John Wayne (1906–1977). All of his movies (179 Screen and TV shows) celebrate American values. Two that will be touched upon here directly concern the Cold War. The first, *Jet Pilot* was made in 1957 and features a beautiful female defecting fighter pilot, played by Janet Leigh, who embarks on a love affair with USAF flyer John Wayne. The plot criss-crosses between the USA and the USSR, the couple acting as double agents. The characterisation of the Soviet Union is reminiscent (and perhaps based upon) the very drab and basic Northern Arctic ports American seafarers would have visited in the Second World War. This memory also shaped the female lead – by the 1950s there were no Soviet female air force pilots, but there had certainly been some celebrated ones during the war. The plot is simple and light-hearted, involving matching flying skills, superior American hardware, and a predictable victory at the end for Wayne and the USAF, who assisted in the movie's production.

John Wayne, Janet Leigh and the USAF star in *Jet Pilot* 1957. (*Universal Pictures via Wikimedia Commons*)

Perhaps you remember the scene from the film "The Alamo", when one of Davy Crockett's Tennesseans said: "What are we doing here in Texas fighting - it ain't our ox that's getting gored." Crockett replied: "Talkin' about whose ox gets gored, figure this: a fella gets in the habit of gorin' oxes, it whets his appetite. May gore yours next. Unquote. And we don't want people like Kosygin, Mao Tse-Tung, or the like, "gorin' our oxes".

Perhaps it is presumptuous on my part to write direct to your Office for guidance, but I feel this picture can be extremely helpful to the Administration. Your assistance in getting us Defense Department cooperation will certainly expedite our project, as we are anxious to move ahead on it immediately. Therefore, we would appreciate hearing from your Office concerning your reactions.

Best wishes for the coming year.

Respectfully yours,

John Wayne

JW:ms

Excerpt of letter from John Wayne to President Johnstone seeking support for his planned movie *Green Berets* 1965. (*Library of Congress via Wikimedia Commons*)

More serious in its content and message is *The Green Berets* launched in 1968 and featuring American special forces opposing rather two-dimensional enemy Vietnamese forces at the 1966 stage of the conflict. Co-directed by Wayne the film follows a deliberate and very long mission to combat not the Vietcong, but anti-war elements in the USA. While panned by film critics it escalated polarisation of American opinion on the war, pleasing those who supported US involvement, but ridiculed by opponents – especially those with experience of the war. Oliver Stone went on to make his trilogy of Vietnam movies partly as a critical response to *The Green Berets*. A staunch right-wing Republican, Wayne was very anti-communist and expressed this directly in the documentary *The Challenge of Ideas* that was shown to lower-ranking US servicemen and women on their way to Europe, NATO's front line against communism. Following on from a crude description of communism by the broadcaster Ed Murrow, Wayne quaintly reminds the viewer of the 'American Way of Life'.

US Comic Book depiction of Nuclear War, 1953. (*Wikimedia Commons*)

An advert from the inside pages of *Atomic War*, 1953. (*Wikimedia Commons*)

American comics of the 1950s and 1960s also embody a patriotic and simplistic anti-communist message. Superheroes conquer enemies single-handedly; some, like Captain America during the McCarthy era, confronting 'commies' set on destruction and anarchy. All took on insane criminal masterminds who were also intent on domination of contemporary America. It wasn't hard to substitute communists for criminals in the reader's imagination. The American hero, like John Wayne, was usually a wealthy white male individualist concerned with freedom and the defence of the weak. Women, black people, Puerto-Ricans and others were fairly invisible unless saved by the Superhero.

An effort to disseminate literature across the world, especially the undeveloped nations in Africa, South America and elsewhere was taken by both government agencies, publishing houses and not-for-profit agencies (including church missionary bodies). The global south was a particular target as impoverished people were most likely to be attracted to communist ideology. These efforts varied from explicitly anti-communist tracts, material explaining the workings of American institutions and corporations, technical instruction books, and classics like Louisa May Alcotts *Little Women* and Jack London's *Call of the Wild* (Laugesen 2010). Other books tried to deconstruct the attractions of Soviet communism and suggest that Russians themselves were at heart opposed to the regime. *Books on Communism* (op cit, also published in the USA) lists dozens of such titles; one title of 1961 made its purpose obvious, Werner Keller's *Are the Russians Ten Feet Tall?*, which argued that every Soviet advance originated in the capitalist West.

While an underlying aim of much promoted literature was to demonstrate American values and way of life, it also reinforced the significant phenomenon of the Americanisation of Western culture. The impact of this drive, as we shall see in Chapter 10, eventually reached the USSR itself. It involved the export of Hollywood movies and other American icons, as well as the products of culturally influential US corporations – clothes, soft drinks, fast-food, and other consumer products that were sold as must-have items. Clever advertising ensured that some products became associated with attributes that were sought after by the fashion-conscious younger generation. Only the music reflected the other side of American culture – that of its minorities and its women. From the 1970s of course there were also the anti-war and counter-culture movies, promoted by the music and film industries, but not by the US government.

The main weapon of propaganda deliberately aimed at the people of the Eastern Bloc and USSR was the voice of radio. The American equivalent of the BBC was the *Voice of America* – funded directly by the US government and, in effect, their voice overseas. Its activities during the Cold War were supplemented by the CIA-funded *Radio Free Europe* which broadcast to the Eastern Bloc countries outside the USSR, and *Radio Liberty* which aimed specifically at Soviet Citizens. The CIA-funded services involved emigres who were native speakers of the countries they broadcast to, and so had a pretence at least of offering the views of an internal resistance. These offered more overt propaganda and anti-communism to their listeners, whereas the *Voice of America* was more about projecting news and stories from the USA itself as examples of freedom and democracy. The *Voice of America* played a major role in promoting Americanism and winning the culture war, which was an important factor among young people in ending the USSR's communist experiment. *Radio Free Europe* and *Radio Liberty* were also influential but, after the debacle of the former's role in the Hungarian uprising in 1956 (see Chapter 6), perhaps less trusted as a news source (Nelson 1997). Despite the various efforts of the Eastern Bloc governments to reduce and negate their spread (discussed below), the Western radio stations were listened to by millions. In the late 1950s American researchers calculated that between 2.5 and 5 per cent of the Soviet population listened to Western broadcasts (5 to 10 million listeners). They believed that while they would not have influenced loyal communist-supporting citizens, they would have impacted on the worlds within which they moved (Nelson 1997). By the 1980s, as we shall see in Chapter 10, this had become irresistible.

The Builder of Communism in the USSR

Citizenship had a different meaning in the USSR, one never entirely understood in the West even though it emerged out of centuries of Russian history rather than suddenly appearing in 1917. It is important to examine this so that it can be contrasted with US and British citizenship where the individual's rights and freedoms take precedence in most cases over that of the community. The discussion then needs to move on to look at how well citizenship ideas fared in the Eastern Bloc satellites where they were more or less imposed in the late 1940s.

The ideal of the Soviet 'Builder of Communism' was laid out in expectations of CPSU members agreed by the Party Congress in 1961. This 'Moral Code' stated:

- devotion to the communist cause; love of the socialist motherland and the other socialist countries;
- conscientious labour for the good of society – he who does not work, neither shall he eat;
- concern on the part of everyone for the preservation and growth of public wealth;
- a high sense of public duty, intolerance of actions harmful to the public interest;
- collectivism and comradely mutual assistance: one for all and all for one;
- humane relations and mutual respect between individuals – man is to man a friend, comrade and brother;
- honesty and truthfulness, moral purity, modesty, and unpretentiousness in social and private life;
- mutual respect in the family, and concern for the upbringing of children;
- an uncompromising attitude to injustice, parasitism, dishonesty, careerism, and money-grabbing;

- friendship and brotherhood among all the peoples of the USSR; intolerance of national and racial hatred;
- uncompromising attitude to the enemies of communism, peace and the freedom of nations;
- fraternal solidarity with the working people of all countries, and with all peoples.

(*Programme of the CPSU*, October 1961, pp.108–9)

While this was to provide an example through the behaviour and actions of the country's leadership at all levels, the 'Law of Honour at Work' was displayed in workplaces and explained what was expected of ordinary workers. This was rather in the fashion of the mission statements found in the reception areas of enterprises today and brought the moral code into the main area of public life – the workplace. It explained duties to strive for quality and to help one another to achieve this. The underlying theme in USSR society was the desire to place the collective needs of society above those of the individual, in the belief that all would ultimately gain from common endeavour. Workers who performed well were highlighted on workplace 'honour boards', and this did not arouse jealousy as it might in Western society, but genuine admiration and wish to emulate such success. The curbing of freedom to accumulate personal wealth and opportunity was at the centre of difference with capitalist societies, and along with the hypocrisy and double standards of some of the leadership and their privileged layer of state bureaucrats who administered the system (the 'nomenklatura'), a source of criticism abroad and private cynicism at home.

In the West there was an acceptance in the wake of the prestigious victory by the Red Army over Nazism – the Great Patriotic War – that the Soviet people in general were loyal to the regime despite the privations and tyranny of Stalinism. Attempts were made to understand this, especially in the early 1960s when the USSR seemed to be advancing in terms of science and technology (for example in the Space Race) and living standards for citizens were improving dramatically. The Khrushchev thaw after 1956 seemed to herald new individual freedoms as well. The 1961 publication *Soviet Society – a Book of Readings* (Inkeles & Geigher eds. 1961) brought together a number of papers that tried to explain the USSR and how it worked. These included a 1955 paper by the sociologist C. Kluckholm that described the Russian national character: Soviet people, it argued, were essentially subservient and needed a strong leader; they were less concerned about personal achievement and the views of others, and more with the collective good and values such as loyalty and honour. This the author contrasted with the typical American citizen who places self and family above all else. In another paper the British sociologist MacCrae describes Marxism as attractive only to the gullible, and that the doctrine itself was little more than cruelty dressed as kindness. In rather more sophisticated contrast, a 1960 attempt by an English writer who had spent some years in the USSR did offer a useful description of the factors that created what could be called a 'Russian character' (Wright 1960). He described how collective identity was placed above that of the individual, a feature very evident in the willingness to make sacrifices in order to win the war against fascism. This author discusses how the idea of community permeates life and although proudly described as a 'communist' trait, is also found among emigres opposed to the regime, and among its imprisoned victims. He calls this the 'community-individual relationship', emphasising the significance of the former in Russian historically, and on life in the USSR. Wright also talks about the optimism and enthusiasm commonly found, and how solutions are found to big problems while small ones are overlooked; a friend tells him 'We are an extraordinary people, we can defeat the German armies but we cannot organise the exits from a railway station…' (ibid p.83).

There is an old Soviet era joke that depicts Alexander the Great, Julius Caesar and Napoleon watching a Red Square Moscow parade of the Red Army and its weaponry. While Alexander the Great and Julius Caesar are in awe at the missiles (spears) and tanks (chariots) that could have won them eternal glory and power, Napoleon is busy reading the newspaper *Pravda* (Truth), the punchline being that if he had a weapon like this, no one would ever have heard of his defeat at Waterloo! The underlying joke here is of course that although in the USSR the state controlled all media and imposed censorship at all levels, everyone knew that what they read and heard from state organs was a version of events, and probably not the whole story.

'Pravda' and other daily newspapers provided coverage of events at home and worldwide, and the satirical magazine *Krokodil* poked fun at the West. Other popular magazines extolled the virtues of Soviet citizenship. Women enjoyed an ambiguous place in Soviet society; while equal under the law and given work opportunity (including good childcare facilities) denied to women in the West for most of the Cold War period, an underlying patriarchy meant that they were subservient to men in the home, and responsible for most homemaking tasks. Even the husband of the celebrated first woman cosmonaut Valentina Tereshkova, was promoted quickly so that he outranked her (Turbett 2021b). While Western women's magazines celebrated consumerism and fashion, Soviet ones like *Woman Worker*, *Peasant Woman* and *Soviet Woman*, promoted their place as workers *and* homemakers, and discussed the skills they might need to undertake both roles at the same time. Soviet radio and later television spread the state's message to the population through a restricted set of mediums. Such was the censorship requirement to check everything before it was broadcast that people already knew of events from Western radio stations long before Moscow told them (Nelson 1997).

Movies were popular and many were made to high artistic standards and recognised as such universally, but all contained messages that upheld the values

1950s Soviet postcard cartoon depicting the Nazi undertones to NATO sponsored German rearmament. (*Author's collection*)

1950s Soviet postcard cartoon depicting the cynical use of Europe as a base for US nuclear bombers. (*Author's collection*)

1960s Soviet postcard cartoon of the celebrated Bolshevik poet Mayakovski looking down disparagingly on Wall St finance. (*Author's collection*)

'US Out of Vietnam', Soviet cartoon from 1967. (*Author's collection*)

Soviet poster of British troops in Belfast, 1969. (*Author's collection*)

of the Soviet State. Any critical films would simply not have been made. Books were a different matter, and as described in Chapter 6, samizdat copies of banned literature were passed from hand to hand in urban intellectual circles. While the inward flow of media considered subversive to the state could be controlled, and that produced internally at least made difficult to circulate, there was little that could realistically be done to prevent the population listening to Western radio broadcasts. Not that this stopped them from trying; from 1948 until the late 1980s, vast amounts of state expenditure (over £600 million annually according to the BBC) was made on jamming the *Voice of America*, *Radio Liberty* and the BBC, and likewise in the satellite countries (Nelson 1997). Jamming was never more than partially effective. The problem here was that communication of state messages to the population was primarily though state short-wave radio stations, long after this ceased to be used as a medium in the West itself. The USSR was the largest manufacturer post-war of short-wave radios – millions and millions were made and distributed across the country, effectively supplying the people with the means to listen to the enemy's message. Articles in the Soviet press decried the Western stations as propaganda tools that disseminated anti-communist lies, but this clearly made little impact on what people could do in the privacy of their own homes. A 1973 pamphlet that contained a compilation of fourteen such articles translated into English for US and British readers argued, not unreasonably, that in the period of détente when attempts were being made

US actor Gregory Peck on Radio Free Europe, 1953. (*Radio Free Europe via Wikimedia Commons*)

Polish anti-Free Radio Europe poster, 1981. (*Muzeum Historyczne w Sanoku via Wikimedia Commons*)

to promote peace and mutual understanding, such Western propaganda efforts had no place (Novosti 1973). Interestingly none of the articles refer to the BBC, focus being on the American-funded stations. In 1985 a Soviet movie thriller, *Can-Can in the English Park*, depicted infiltration of *Radio Liberty* by a KGB agent, who exposed their lies and the traitors who informed them (Nelson 1997).

The USSR state publishers produced massive quantities of approved literature, and some of this was translated for distribution in the West as well as the countries of would-be and actual influence. Many of these have been quoted throughout this book. It cannot be said that any of this output reached a wide audience in the West; such publications were distributed at trade fairs and through embassies and specialist bookshops like Collets in London (opened in 1934 and closed in 1997). Some of the publications were very obviously propagandist, *Soviet Life* being an example: a large colourful photographic magazine showing life in the USSR to be on a wonderful level that many citizens might not have recognised (an attribute it must be said, of many Western lifestyle magazines). The Soviets and their satellite countries also had multiple foreign language broadcasts, but in truth, few listened to them outside the Party faithful, and probably not many of them either (see, however, Iain Morrison's story in Chapter 8).

The Satellite and Other Socialist States

The regimes in the Eastern Bloc that joined the socialist/communist experiment in the late 1940s had an arguably harder job in selling their virtues to their people. Romania, Bulgaria, Hungary and of course the DDR, had all had actual or fascist-leaning regimes and had been on the other side for at least part of the Second World War. Other satellites had strong nationalist movements opposed to the imposition of communism. Nonetheless, the governing communist parties in each set about trying to popularise the ideas of collectivity and opposition to the values and actions of the capitalist West. This was achieved through education and the promotion of civic responsibility and involvement. Each of the regimes also set about socialist measures that would genuinely improve people's lives: care of the workforce, equality for women, universal education, child-care, the social wage and health services. These were developed alongside economic changes – central planning for large scale production, cooperative farming, small cooperatives, and support for small businesses (Green & de la Motte 2009). All of this was reflected in state publications and other media that demonstrated socialist progress. Another idea imported from the USSR was the erection of monuments to socialism and its heroes in prominent settings throughout Eastern Europe. We saw in Chapter 6 how one such icon was treated in Budapest in 1956; many others did not survive for long after the anti-communist regime changes in the 1989–91 period.

The uprisings described in Chapter 6 all resulted in increased internal security to address paranoia over dissent. While show trials and executions characterised the Stalinist period up until the mid-1950s, repression continued almost unabated throughout the Cold War on levels not experienced in the USSR where most citizens had grown up with the system already in place. Many citizens who remembered the uncertainties of previous times, welcomed the social security and full employment benefits of the socialist one-party states – not all were forced onto the streets to attend the May Day and other celebrations. However, the activities of the Stasi secret police in the DDR were notorious for their extent – over a quarter of a million individuals passed through their hands during the Cold War years. They employed over 90,000 people and about 2 per cent of the population acted as their regular informers, resulting in the growth of files to cover 5.6 million citizens. This despite (or perhaps a cause of) the fact that the DDR never had any opposition movement. The East German regime were so afraid that their people might be infected with new ideas that they even restricted the circulation of Soviet publications (Funder 2003). The USSR tried to bolster its satellite regimes by offering a beacon eastward that would outshine the attractions of life in the West; soon after the Berlin Wall went up in 1961 this was exactly the message broadcast by the cosmonaut Titov from East Berlin, as an ambassador of Soviet achievement (Turbett 2021b).

West Germany (the FDR) had the most virulently anti-communist official outlook which worked its way into law and employment practice, and was arguably, the cornerstone of the state's raison d'etre (Graf 1984). The KPD (German Communist Party) was banned from organising, and from 1972, anyone considered to have 'extreme' views was banned from public employment with 'Berufsverbot' legislation. As one in ten workers were in the public sector, this barred anyone with leftist views from work in key sectors where trade unions were strong. At the same time successive West German governments were pursuing 'Ostpolitik', a rapprochement with the DDR that they thought would swing opinion in their direction in the longer-term due to their higher standards of living. Although there was a wave of migration from West to East in the early 1950s (about 350,000 people) most of the traffic was the other way, lives being risked to cross the Wall. Later, labour shortages resulted in further economic migration to the DDR, some from Africa and the Middle East. There were also refugees who were welcomed in the USSR and Eastern Europe from countries where communists were subject to persecution – particularly Greece at the end of the 1940s and again in the 1970s, and Chile after the Coup in 1973.

In Romania the regime was especially despised by its people, the self-enrichment of the leader Nicolae Ceausescu being obvious; in power from 1965 until the sudden popular uprising that forced his removal at the end of 1989, he was the only communist leader to be executed (after a rapid summary trial) as payment for his crimes. His regime in Romania was brutally repressive; as at the Berlin Wall in the DDR, would-be escapers trying to swim the Danube to freedom were shot by border guards. Just as in the USSR in the 1930s, people arrested for political reasons were used as slave labourers to construct the Danube-Black Sea Canal, perhaps as many as half-a-million people over a thirty-year period, brutal conditions and murder leading to over 200,000 deaths in the 1949–53 period alone (Applebaum 2003). The casual thuggery of the regime can be witnessed in the Romanian TV show from the 1980s *Comrade Detective*. Dubbed into English (with, I gather, quite literal translation) after its discovery by a Hollywood producer in recent years, its two heroes take on criminals in Bucharest, who are typically US agents, torturing suspects and ignoring legal niceties in their efforts to 'defend socialism'.

Poland developed a Cold War movie industry of which it was justifiably proud. Although its output was controlled for many years, by the early 1980s its most famous director, Andrzej Wajda, was able to depict the birth of the Solidarnosc movement in his *Man of Iron*. Of most influence throughout Eastern Europe were the Western Radio stations, the CIA-funded *Radio Free Europe* broadcasting the native-language voices and views of emigres opposed to the respective regimes. Jamming efforts and Stasi-like surveillance of the population were not always considered enough; in 1978 a Bulgarian agent murdered the émigré writer and broadcaster Georgi Markov with the poisoned tip of an umbrella as he walked over Waterloo Bridge in London. Markov was a regular broadcaster on the BBC and his recently published memoirs had been put out through *Radio Free Europe*. A few years later, in 1981, the broadcasting centre of *Radio Liberty* and *Radio Free Europe* in Munich, FDR, were bombed. This was ineffectual and within an hour, broadcasts had recommenced. American intelligence initially believed the Czechs were responsible, but in 1991 the convicted international terrorist Illich Ramirez ('Carlos the Jackal') admitted that he had carried out the bombing on behalf of Ceausescu, the Romanian leader. However, sources that later emerged suggest the involvement of the KGB and other East European agencies (Nelson 1997). The KGB were also believed to be implicated in Markov's assassination.

Conclusion

The best measure of the success of the ideological warfare of the Cold War is through the efforts each side made to minimise the impact of the propaganda of the other. In this sense the Soviets' most effective weapon did not involve any effort on their part; it lay in the attractiveness of its anti-capitalist, anti-imperialist ideology. This was fought by the West by diverse means such as anti-communist McCarthy witch hunts in the USA, the CIA's influence on the British Labour Party, and later Berufsverbot in the FDR, all of which could be said to demonstrate the fear of communism. From the USSR and its satellites' point of view, the greatest threat to their security lay in the ability of the Western radio stations to unsettle their population by providing alternative information and challenges to their own messages, and their reaction was an expensive and counterproductive jamming exercise. Ultimately, the attempt to suppress the audience only served to increase it as people were curious to see what all the fuss was about. The outcome from 1989–91 suggests who was most successful.

Iconic portrait of Che Guevara – a symbol of rebellion in the West since the 1960s. (*A. Korda via Wikimedia Commons*)

Having looked at the forces that affected ordinary lives East and West in this and previous chapters, the next two will look at how some of this was experienced.

St Peters Day Parade, Gloucester, Massachusetts, 1950s. (*Glenn via Wikimedia Commons*)

Mayday Parade USSR 1964. (*Author's collection*)

Chapter 8

Tuning In to The Cold War – Stories 1

> We want to achieve a new and better order of society: in this new and better society there must be neither rich nor poor; all will have to work. Not a handful of rich people, but all the working people must enjoy the fruits of their common labour. Machines and other improvements must serve to ease the work of all and not to enable a few to grow rich at the expense of millions and tens of millions of people. This new and better society is called socialist society.
>
> Vladmir Lenin, *To the Rural Poor* (1903),
> Collected Works (Volume 6, p.366)

Introduction

This chapter and the next will look at some of the events described in the book through the prism of some ordinary people from East and West whose lives were shaped by the Cold War, if only in a small way. It can only cover a small breadth of experiences in events, after all, that encompassed the entire globe. Some of these are first-hand accounts given to the author, others are drawn from previously published but perhaps not widely known sources. Emphasis in this and the next chapter are on narratives that differ in background and perspective from most that appear in the voluminous Cold War literature, much of which focuses on those who regard themselves as victims of Soviet inspired terror and aggression. Readers interested in ethnographic narratives from the former USSR and Eastern Europe are directed to Svetlana Alexievich's various books, and to the lesser-known works of Kristen Ghodsee – some of which are referenced in the bibliography. These are writers from very different backgrounds but whose work contains some interesting reflective similarities.

Chapter 7 highlighted the significance of the Cold War Radio Stations, suggesting that the flow of information and propaganda from West to East made more impact than that in the other direction. Given their significance, it is no surprise that they should be reflected in several of the accounts that follow.

Friends Across the Divide – Olga Kevelos and Lida Rutkova

This is a story of an unusual (for its time) friendship made through sport at the height of the Stalin era, but which lasted throughout the Cold War period. What these two young women had in common was skill and prowess in the man's world of motorcycle sport. Olga Kevelos, born in 1923, was the fiercely independent and adventure-seeking Birmingham woman, who took up motorcycle sport in the late 1940s (Turbett 2017). She worked for many years in the family café business in Birmingham's city centre. In the early 1950s she met Lida Rutkova from Czechoslovakia at an international motorcycle trials event and the two became good friends, mostly by letter as opportunities to meet were rare. Lida was born in Pilsen in 1927 and grew up with knowledge of several languages including English. By the time the two women met, Lida was working in the CZ/Jawa motorcycle factory in Prague. Although primarily engaged in administrative work in the export department (using her language skills), her flair for motorcycling discovered through membership of the factory sporting club, enabled her to ride factory machines in events. Lida's husband (she married in 1954) was also a top Czech motorcycle sportsman and the couple had their first child in 1955.

Olga Kevelos 1948. (*Author's collection*)

What has survived among Olga's personal effects from her family's Birmingham home in which she spent much of her life, are letters and postcards from Lida. Most of these contain family news and updates about motorcycle sport, but one, dated 5 March 1953, offers a fascinating insight into life and the difficulties in maintaining such a relationship at that time. The letter is typed and must have been posted from outside Czechoslovakia, but Lida is nonetheless worried about the possibility it might be intercepted. The letter starts with discussion about an idea previously posed by Olga that she could ride a CZ/Jawa motorcycle in events in the UK and abroad, including the ISDT (International Six days Trial, a key international event due to be held in Czechoslovakia in September 1953).

Lida Rutkova 1953. (*Author's collection*)

Friday 6 March 1953
Olga, my dear,
You have written in your last letter you would like to ride Jawa or perhaps a CZ motorcycle for some trials in England or in the ISDT. Olga your great occasion is here! I shall tell you shortly what to do to get a favourable reply from our authorities. I have made some private steps to find out. It looks Olga, like a great YES. Real interest is expected in in the participation of an English rider in the ISDT to be held in our country, riding a motorcycle of Czechoslovak production.

Write to the export department in Prague telling them what you told me in your last letter about your interest in riding a Jawa 250cc or CZ 150cc (I do not know which you prefer) in the ISDT in September 1953 in Czechoslovakia. Tell them too that you have tried these machines belonging to Dutch people in Italy at the 1951 ISDT and that you were very fond of them. Please do not use my name in this letter, but if you like you can say that you are looking forward to competing with the well-known Czechoslovak woman rider you have heard about during the ISDT – or something like that. I shall explain the reason for this personal request of mine too.

I am using a special occasion to mail you a brief and open letter again and beg of you Olga, to confirm receipt of same by sending me a card with the best greetings from a Sunday-trip. Please do not forget to do so immediately so I can be informed you received this. Should I not be compelled to take certain circumstances into consideration when writing letters to England and other Western countries I am convinced I would be able to reply within two or three weeks. I have already told you in my last letter ('black letter'), I suppose you have received that one dated September 1952 and mailed from Switzerland – that it is very dangerous for any citizen of our country to have congenialities to Western countries, or people of those countries, and more dangerous to send and get correspondence from them. The moment this is known about you as a person, you are a 'politically and untrustworthy element', some letters and in many cases all your correspondence is censored. When you then, for instance, have some friends and relatives in various countries belonging to the Western states, if you speak two or three foreign languages and are single, it is quite impossible to get a passport, and sure it is a ground and a beginning of an endless run of unpleasantness, disadvantage and troubles in your private life, in your work, and in the sport.

The letter then discusses Olga's request for some information about the Czech women riders for the UK motorcycle press, and the reasons this might be difficult to provide without official sanction, and continues:

I believe Olga, you will understand me a little at least and when the visit to my country comes true, it will be the most splendid time for me. I mean your coming here in September to participate in the ISDT. I will explain everything personally to you. I do believe Olga, that you will not hesitate to spend most of your free time with me. I know today perfectly, I will not mind what 'they' say and how 'they' look – I am everywhere with you. It is a happy thing I shall be for sure the only woman rider for Czechoslovakia and many people here know I speak English and so they cannot wonder we two shall be together. I'll be your 'official interpreter' – do you agree?

Olga, please say promise you will try to come here to see me and be my sister for these few days will you?

I have to close now with much love and asking you not to tell anybody any word about the content of this letter. Thank you.

I am yours for ever.

Loving sister.

The plan succeeded and Olga was taken on by the Czech factory to ride one of their machines in the 1953 ISDT in Gottwald, Czechoslovakia. This involved travel to the country several weeks in advance of the event and participation in intensive training alongside the Czech team, including Lida, one of the only three lady entrants. Olga was known at this time for what we might now call 'partying' and had something of a reputation for this, and for her conquests of men, but the gruelling schedule left little opportunity for either. The two women won prizes for their performances: Lida a Gold Medal, and Olga a Silver, and factory advertisements consequently appeared in the British motorcycle press celebrating their success and the machines they were riding. This did not all pass without remark; Major Watling, the President of the British Motorcycle Manufacturers Association, was enraged at this breach of patriotism at this stage of the Cold War. Olga continued an intermittent association with the Czech factory for many years, and was soon followed by other top British male riders keen to take advantage of the simple but competitive nature of the Czech machines. Lida had expected and hope to attend the next ISDT in Wales in 1954 as she was now one of the top women trials event riders in Europe, but this was denied, as was other international opportunity for some years. Perhaps her friendship with Olga had come to the attention of the authorities? Her brother, Ludek, later expressed the view that she was deliberately denied travel abroad and that her international career ended after the birth of her first child in 1955 (Rutka 2015). Her correspondence with Olga continued, and featured motorcycling and her needs as a young mum; Olga could obtain items in the UK that were scarce at home and pass them to Czech riders at international events she was attending. They did meet again, certainly as late as 1968 at an event organised by the Women's International Motorcycle Association, with which Lida was involved. Olga's links with Czechoslovakia were recognised in 1993 when she attended a reception in the Czech Embassy in London to mark the country's accession to the European Union. Olga Kevelos died in 2009.

Ian Morrison – Kilwinning Ayrshire

Ian Morrison's account, which follows, is both unusual and unique. It describes how a Scottish schoolboy from a working-class background in Ayrshire, Scotland, went against the norm for his time and sought out information from the other side, not to reinforce already held beliefs, but to help shape them. His actions might be compared to those of young people of own time, perhaps through a feeling of alienation, who seek out alternatives though the internet. The comparison, though, is limited; there was nothing about Ian's activity that was illegal, dangerous or destructive, his interest was spurred by a wish for a better world and not revenge on his own society.

> I was born in 1973, and from as early as I can remember – and for me that is very early, as I have memories from when I was as young as 2 years old – I have always had a keen interest in the world around me. I was also intrigued, like many children, by 'how things work' and my fascination

Iain Morrison 1988, aged 15. (*Iain Morrison*)

Iain Morrison 1988, listening to his shortwave radio. (*Iain Morrison*)

with the science of communication was there from an early age, and when I got my first radio-cassette player in 1984 for Christmas, that's when I got really hooked. You see, the radio had the usual FM, Medium Wave and Long Wave bands, but it also had this thing called 'Short Wave'. I had heard this mentioned before by my uncle, as he listened to Radio Moscow's English-language service from time to time, and I had heard at bit of Radio Moscow when visiting his home, but I hadn't really tried tuning the radio on shortwave myself by that time. That was soon all to change, and it was going to change a lot more in my life besides.

Up to that time, my experience of 'international' radio had been limited to hearing a station that most people of my age and older in Britain will have some recollection of, and they will probably also remember how they listened to it: the station was Radio Luxembourg (on 208 metres Medium Wave) – generally under the blankets in bed using an earpiece to avoid detection by mum and dad. When I started fiddling about with my own shortwave radio, the first station I stumbled upon was Radio Moscow in English. In those days it was broadcasting 24 hours a day as the 'Radio Moscow World Service' on virtually every shortwave band. It also broadcast on Medium Wave in the evenings, when the signals can travel much further distances due to the darkness, or rather due to the lack of solar activity. Radio Moscow really was the 'big daddy' of international broadcasting in those days. In addition to English, it was broadcasting in over seventy other languages and could be heard in virtually every part of the world. What you could hear wasn't just limited to what people would regard as 'propaganda' such as news and commentaries on current events. Radio Moscow offered an extremely diverse range of programming which included the arts, radio plays, all sorts of music and fascinating feature programmes about many aspects of life in the Soviet Union, to name but a few.

Now, for most people this may have been just a bit of curiosity and it would have ended at that. But for me, even at that age, there was another crucial dimension: politics. My political views were already shaped by the environment I was in, as my home area, like other working-class parts of Scotland, was more or less a one-party state. Labour MPs were consistently elected with large majorities and Labour also controlled the local authorities at district and regional level. In addition, this was the era of the momentous 1984–85 miners' strike, so for a youngster with a very inquiring mind, my outlook moved in a profoundly leftward direction.

Added to this was my family. My parents were not political, but like most people in the area at the time, they were consistent Labour voters. However, my grandpa was distinctly political, and he helped to shape my political views into something more coherent, consistent, and radical. He had been politically motivated from an early age, growing up in the Vale of Leven in Dumbartonshire in the 1920s and 1930s – an area which was dominated politically by the Communist Party to such an extent that it earned the nickname of a 'Little Moscow', along with mining areas in south Wales, Fife and northeast England. Such was the strength of the Communist Party in the Vale of Leven that in the 1920s, it was one of the few places in Britain which even had a communist children's organisation -- the Young Pioneers, of which my grandpa was a member until he graduated into the Young Communist League as a teenager. Ultimately, he joined the Communist Party as a young man in Clydebank in 1942. This was the year when the Party reached its peak membership of almost 60,000 as thousands rallied to the cause, inspired by the heroic example of the Red Army as it tore the guts out of Hitler's army in the Battle of Stalingrad.

He remained a Communist Party member until 1956 and then joined the Labour Party, which he remained a member of until the mid-1980s. A skilled plumber and an active trade unionist through all those years, he later told me that the year of his departure from the Communist Party actually had nothing to do with the Soviet military intervention in Hungary and Nikita Khrushchev's 'secret speech' to the 20th CPSU Congress that denounced Stalin and the 'cult of the individual' – the factors which led many thousands to leave the Party's ranks that same year. He said it was due to a dispute with 'leading Party comrades' over a lack of democratic discussion of issues about Party work in his union, the Plumbers' Trade Union.

For him, there wasn't the same degree of disillusionment with socialism or the Soviet Union that had affected many others who left the Communist Party, and his admiration for the USSR and his belief in socialism remained undimmed. His was a very practical socialism. He was not a theoretical person and I doubt that he ever read the works of Marx and Lenin. He told me that his political education was largely derived in his youth from street orators, the comrades in his area, and reading pamphlets, the *Daily Worker* and the *Soviet Weekly*. This meant that as a 12-year-old, it was very easy for me to grasp his concept of socialism, and to understand and appreciate its logic.

The time when this all fell into place remains crystal clear in my memory to this day. A family dinner in the summer of 1985, where he explained that socialism was a society where everyone had work, everyone had a home, and everyone could have a decent and fulfilled life. In that polarised world of the mid-1980s, he saw the socialist countries as where that agenda was being implemented. It was a clear choice, and it was a sort of 'lightbulb moment' for me, the moment when I arrived at the conclusion that I had become a communist. I was hungry and eager to learn as much as possible, and my little shortwave radio gave me the ideal opportunity to do this. In those pre-Internet days, it was one of the very few ways to get information directly from foreign countries in a way which conveyed their outlook and opinion.

This information was provided not only in terms of the radio broadcasts, but also a wide range of publications sent by some of those stations in Eastern Europe. These included free subscriptions to the very professionally produced and colourful magazines *Czechoslovak Life* from Radio Prague and the Kontakt youth magazine from Radio Berlin International in the German Democratic Republic. There were many pamphlets, books (some of which were large coffee-table illustrated books), magazines and a wide range of souvenirs such as badges, pennants, t-shirts and calendars from the radio stations in all of the Eastern European socialist countries, as well as from China, Cuba, Vietnam and even North Korea. There were also some other quite fascinating things, prizes for various contests run by these stations: cassettes of music from Albania to LP records from the Soviet Union, folk crafts from Czechoslovakia to a lovely table cover from China, won in a 1989 Radio Beijing contest for the 40th anniversary of the founding of the People's Republic of China.

My parents were not exactly overjoyed with this to begin with, and I don't blame them; I just think that they were victims of the quite extreme anti-communist propaganda that pervaded large parts of the media during their formative years in the 1950s. Another factor was that they were rather quiet people, so they had very few friends and, as a result, it was harder for them to understand things and put them in perspective. They had this exaggerated fear that my name would go 'on a list' if I wrote letters to those radio stations in the socialist countries, or that I would get blacklisted by someone (who on Earth they thought it would be, I don't know) and that I wouldn't get a job, or that my dad would lose his job, or that we would get a 'brick through our window'. I'm not naive enough to think that the security services didn't pay attention to some 'subversives' or that people weren't blacklisted from employment, but to think that this would happen to a teenager for writing some letters to radio stations and getting some mail from them really was taking paranoia to the extreme. Being rather 'quiet' people, my parents did not realise that there were actually communists and left-wing people around them in the workplace and community, and these people were not destitute beggars because of their opinions. Anyway, even I knew at that age that my parents' outlook was unrealistic, so I just carried on regardless and they were fine when they soon realised that the world wouldn't end! In fact, it wasn't long before my dad was posting the letters for me. He travelled to work by way of a major sorting office, so the mail would get to its destinations a bit quicker than sending it from my home town of Kilwinning.

Listening to the socialist countries' radio stations not only provided a diversity of programme content, but also showed that there was diversity among the socialist countries themselves. This diversity was a reflection of their own national conditions, historical experiences, level of development, and how advanced politically they had been before their 'revolutions'. For example, Yugoslavia was non-aligned and relatively liberal (including no restrictions on its citizens travelling abroad), so Radio Yugoslavia had a relatively relaxed and friendly tone and didn't really try to sell their ideology in any serious way. Meanwhile, the GDR and Czechoslovakia were more politically hardline. Before the socialist era, these countries already had highly developed economies, and had long and strong traditions of labour and trade union movements on a par with Western countries. Their way of selling themselves was highly sophisticated: very professional programmes, news coverage which didn't bash you over the head with slogans but adequately got their message across, and very slick publications that were as good as anything produced in the West. The overall standard of living and level of development politically and economically in the GDR and Czechoslovakia led me, and many other communists in those days, to point to them as the closest possible examples of what socialism might be like when it came to Britain. In those pre-1989 days, that didn't seem outlandish! The Hungarians, Poles and Bulgarians (with Radio Budapest, Radio Polonia and Radio Sofia) also had quite decent programmes and a common form of presentation, and I quite enjoyed hearing their broadcasts. But there were two countries that stood out: Albania and Romania.

Albania had managed to fall out with just about every other socialist country that had been its friend (apart from Vietnam and North Korea), so listening to Radio Tirana was quite an experience. Tuning in to other Eastern European stations was certainly like another world as they offered a much more multifaceted view of life in their countries than was presented in mainstream British media at the time. In comparison, listening to Radio Tirana was like listening to another planet, as virtually nothing was known or said in Britain about that remote Balkan nation in those days. That was enough reason for me to get hooked, as I was intrigued by its mystery. Their programmes were an odd combination of shrill rhetoric (every other socialist country in the world was a 'revisionist' sell-out). Their over-the-top criticism, especially of the Soviet Union (who they called 'social imperialists') could be quite off-putting at times, but it was made up in large measure by broadcasts that gave an insight into this totally unknown country. They described its rich folk culture, and presented its wonderful folk music and lovely 'light music' (there was no decadent 'pop' in socialist Albania). I learned of the amazing history of its people's resistance against all sorts of foreign invaders and occupiers, all the way from Skanderbeg (a national hero in the Middle

Ages) to the virtually single-handed battle against the Italians and Nazi Germany in the Second World War. Albania was the only country that completely liberated itself from the Nazis with no foreign army coming in to help them. That perhaps explained its very single-minded approach and the staunch defence of its independence, but it also contributed to them making enemies of virtually everyone in world for which they eventually they paid a high economic price. Anyway, rhetoric aside, I was willing to make the radio journey to this other 'planet' almost every day and became a very loyal listener of Radio Tirana from 1987 to 1992. I wrote to them regularly with reception reports and asked them questions that were answered in the programme 'Answering Our Listeners' Questions'. I remember that I asked them (rather naively) what their attitude was to 'bourgeois culture' (as though that could be summed up in a few minutes!), and they got some professor in to the studio to give a talk on it! They also had a contest in 1988 called 'What Do You Know About Albania?'. The top prize was a holiday in Albania. Sadly, I didn't win, but I got a runner-up prize of a cassette of Albanian 'light music' which I still love to this day. In fact, my knowledge of Albania was so extensive that by 1989, in the written essay part of my French 'o' Grade exam, I wrote about an imaginary trip to Albania. I described many of the places I had heard about on Radio Tirana and got a good grade, so it must have impressed the marker of the exam!

Then there was Romania, unusual in so many ways. A non-Slavic country in Eastern Europe with its language being closer to French and Italian, very independent (it denounced the Soviet-led invasion of Czechoslovakia in 1968) and a style of leadership under Nicolae Ceausescu that still had a very strong personality cult. My enduring memory of Radio Bucharest was the first time I heard a programme of Romanian traditional folk music in 1987. Those lively and exciting melodies literally felt like a burst of colour was coming out of the speaker of my radio and I will never forget that experience. The other enduring memory of listening to Radio Bucharest, and also one of the great things about listening to shortwave radio broadcasts from foreign countries, was that you could hear history in the making. One special day was 22 December 1989; I had tuned in at 2 pm expecting to hear the regularly scheduled English broadcast and was listening with particular interest as there had already been protests against Ceausescu in some parts of Romania; the day before a big pro-government rally was held in Bucharest addressed by Ceausescu and this turned out to be his last appearance as the country's leader. The previous day's broadcast reported that rally without mentioning the chaos that erupted which had forced Ceausescu to stop speaking while order was restored and the event was falsely presented as a great reaffirmation of support for his leadership. Anyway, on 22 December, here am I waiting for that day's broadcast to start. The first thing that seemed unusual was that it started without the regular signature music or opening announcement. Instead, the familiar voice of one of the male announcers came on and started to read what sounded like a news bulletin, with the first few words sounding like there had just been more pro-Ceausescu rallies. He said: 'Following the great popular manifestations in Bucharest and all over the country, today, 22 December 1989…' and then came the words which, when you hear something historic, give you the feeling that an earthquake had just taken place … 'the dictatorial regime of Nicolae Ceausescu was overthrown.' He went on to say that a new government was established, and the old regime was finished. It was a strange and exciting feeling to experience this so directly, as that broadcast was likely also to be when the major media in Britain and other countries had become aware of what was going on. It really made me appreciate the great value of my little radio.

The other historic bolt from the blue I remember was on 19 August 1991. I had tuned into Radio Moscow World Service just before midday (as I often did) to catch the news bulletin on the hour. The first sign that something was not quite right was that there wasn't the regular programme on the air, there was some classical music being played which was often a sign on Soviet radio and television that there was some major announcement coming up, such as the death of the leader of the country. It was followed by the regular station identification announcement 'This is the World Service of Radio Moscow', details of what wavelengths the station was broadcasting on, and the playing of the theme tune of the station, a jazz version of the famous song 'Moscow Nights' (also known in the West as 'Midnight in Moscow'). At least that was all normal and my worries were allayed momentarily. The Kremlin clock chimes on the hour heralded the start of the news.

Here we go again, listening on my little radio to big history in the making: the coup attempt against Mikhail Gorbachev. I couldn't believe what I was hearing as the announcer started going on about the State Emergency Committee being established to run the country and that Gorbachev 'could no longer perform his duties for reasons of health'. I immediately phoned my grandpa to get his opinion on this. He was quite philosophical and said it probably meant the end of the Soviet Union. Over the next few days, for me, and for many communists around the world, it felt like the world had ended. The unthinkable was happening: Soviet power was collapsing, the CPSU was banned and just faded away, and numerous Soviet republics were declaring their independence in rapid succession. What many of us had thought could only happen if there had been a nuclear holocaust was happening without a war, without invasion and with very little fighting: the world's first socialist state was collapsing before our very eyes.

> I was a young and very optimistic communist and thought Gorbachev's reforms of Perestroika and Glasnost were a renewal of socialism and a return to the ideas of Lenin. The accepted wisdom had been that, even if the republics in the Baltics or others such as Ukraine broke away (which was becoming increasingly likely by 1990), that socialism would continue in Russia. To have that removed so suddenly was like a prop shoring up my beliefs had just been pulled away, and the certainty that socialism would remain a force in the world had just been smashed to smithereens. I had just finished secondary school that year, I was on the brink of adulthood and preparing to go to college. I had thought that it could be very likely that one day I would maybe continue my studies in the Soviet Union and work in some way to make a small contribution to help promote British-Soviet friendship. I had already had some contact with the British-Soviet Friendship Society in London and was hoping to follow in my grandparents' footsteps and travel to the Soviet Union for a holiday. That day felt like something had died. It meant for me a realisation that socialism would not come courtesy of any foreign power, and that I had to focus my efforts on the struggle taking place in Britain, which inevitably led me to joining the Communist Party of Britain in 1993.

Veniamin Nikitsky – Ukraine USSR

In contrast to Ian's account from the West are the earlier memories of Veniamin Nikitsky, born in 1937, who grew up in a rural area of Eastern Ukraine, not far from the city of Kharkiv. His memories describe rural poverty and the impact of the failed state agricultural policies of the 1950s; these turned wheat growing areas of Southern Russia and Ukraine over to pasture and animal food production, and areas of virgin land elsewhere, over to wheat production. Although initially successful, a series of poor harvests resulted in a grain shortage in the USSR, with the consequences he remembers. Veniamin also describes the impact of Western radio broadcasts; these include Anatol Goldberg who was an émigré Russian BBC broadcaster who rose to be head of the Russian Service. In the 1950s Goldberg was criticized by the British government and certain sections of the media – the Spectator accused him of 'esoteric right-wing Marxism' (Nelson 1997 p.105) for refusing to use his regular factual broadcasts to castigate the Soviet system. The testament here suggests that Goldberg was trusted to an extent he might not have been had he adopted a stridently anti-communist style. As Goldberg correctly understood, his listeners were intelligent enough to make their own minds up about the system they lived under. Veniamin became a technical translator and patent specialist in a state switchgear plant in Kharkiv, where he utilised his language skills, and spent his working life.

Veniamin Nikitsky New Year, 1962. (*Nikitsky family*)

The Nikitsky family's TV and shortwave radio, 1960. (*Nikitsky family*)

I began listening to the Voice of America and BBC in the late 1940s or early 1950s, using a crystal radio receiver. These radio stations were prohibited in the USSR and their radio broadcasts were jammed. My favorite radio host was Anatol Goldberg. His voice was like voice of Yuri Levitan, the principal Soviet radio announcer during and after World War II. Most of the people in my circle of friends listened to these prohibited radio stations. At the time I was close to my cousin Lydia and we met often but never talked about the radio – her husband was a KGB Major! By the 1960s I was not very patriotic to the USSR.

Electricity came in our village in 1958. After that we got an electric suburban railway which we used to get to Kharkiv. Now we could listen not only to rural valve radio sets (with heavy batteries weighing several kilograms) and we could watch TV. The first TV set I saw, being a student, in the 'red corner club' of my college was probably in 1955. We bought our first 'Zarya' TV set in the early 1960s. It had a little screen and there was only one channel – our Kharkiv local television broadcasting station. Television reception was not perfect and a good aerial was necessary.

In the 1950s we were quite poor, because only my father earned money from his work as chief of a mail coach. Our usual meal was soup and porridge made from different cereals. We kept hens and rabbits so we did not have to buy meat. We bought cheese and sausage only for parties. My parents liked to invite our relations to our place. We often put tables in the garden, if the weather permitted. Our relations from Kharkiv left us with bouquets of lilac or other flowers, with apples and other fruits.

The Khrushchev Corn Company began to grow wheat only in small areas, and this led to a situation where white bread products disappeared. We could not buy biscuits. Wheat was sold only to people who needed diet food prescribed medically. They tried to grow corn in the Northern regions which were not suitable for it. This was for not a very long period (maybe a couple of years) and when the authorities changed their policy, areas of wheat growing increased.

As my father Vasily always went with his mail coach to the Far East (Khabarovsk), he brought from there fish delicacies, like salmon and red caviar. He bought these from poachers, because it was cheaper than in stores. I remember that father brought red caviar in a 3 litre jar and as we had such a lot, we ate it with teaspoons. One time my mother suggested we serve caviar in this way to guests, and someone told her the proper way to eat it, putting several roe-corns on a piece of bread and butter. When Brezhnev came to power after Khrushchev the life became a little better. At least the shortage of food decreased for a while.

In my workplace I considered the Board of Honour as just a formality, though my portrait was often on it. People were indifferent to the Board and didn't try to get onto it. Good salary and bonus were important, not things like the Board of Honour, certificates of honour for dedicated labour, challenge banners of the best working collective and so on … they were only flashiness.

Over the years I didn't feel there was any growing dissatisfaction with our system of government. In our circle though we mocked the regime and told political jokes and stories to one another. I knew the regime was false, but all along I was sure Soviet power was absolutely stable. When Gorbachev came along I thought he was a chatterbox. I didn't see his real actions improving the economy of the country. Throughout the period I never worried about war with the West

Rita Bannatyne – Romania

Rita came to the UK over twenty years ago with her British husband who had been working in Romania to help establish an adoption agency. She regards herself as a socialist and traces this back to her experiences as a child in Romania and her witness to what has happened in her country and across Europe since those times.

I was born Rita Zbojan in 1974 in the city of Oradea, Translyvania, just a few miles from the border with Hungary in north-western Romania. My mother was a secretary in the theatre and then the sports high school until disability forced her retiral at the age of 42. My father was a crane operator who worked in various factories including one that made asbestos panels – he died of lung cancer at the age of 70 which may be to do with that, or possibly because he was a heavy smoker. I don't remember much of my early life but I'm told it was a happier time before the country started suffering from shortages.

I was 15 years old when the Berlin Wall fell, but sure, I have many pleasant and some unpleasant memories, the latter more to do with the dictatorship and having to learn praising songs about our (puppet) leader and trying to hide any negativity from the world. My experiences as a child were mixed – there was a collision of ethnicities and Hungary, whose radio signals we could pick up, seemed freer than Romania. We knew quite a lot about the outside world though not necessarily from official sources – we listened to the BBC World Service and Radio Free Europe. Some people we knew had travelled outside the country and my own brother backpacked to East Berlin. As we were close to the border, people had special passes to go across and visit family and friends on the other side. This compensated for the rather careless drawing of the border after the War – our region had been part of Hungary. We didn't know much about Western European history or about contemporary life in the USA, Australia or Canada – these were taboo subjects only talked about behind closed doors. The American TV shows and movies that showed these were rarely seen anywhere: we only saw costume dramas, fantasy and sci-fi: *Star Wars*, *Gone With the Wind* and *Indiana Jones* made it into the country as they were far enough from reality to be deemed acceptable. I loved *Star Trek*!

Of course at school we had to have pictures of our 'valued leader' in every classroom, and you were sent home to put on your Socialist Romania badges and ties if you somehow forgot them. But otherwise, I think school was pretty much the same as anywhere else at that time, with some corporal punishment seen as acceptable. We had history and geography of the world which included everything. I remember Great Britain being vilified from a historical perspective, but who could disagree with that? My favourite teacher, he had us play games where we were put in several groups and then had to see everyone's actions from their perspective – it was fun and informative.

I can't say that the dictatorship affected us although we had to stand in queues every day to get our milk allocation, and to get candles to light during the scheduled power cuts in the evenings. It was just part of life – just the way it was. My grandfather had lost quite a lot of land although he still managed to live off what was left to him, running his own business selling produce. After 1989 he lost even more because of inflation which he never understood. In Romania our prices had been stable for decades, and suddenly his savings reduced to zero because he hadn't used them to buy something concrete.

Rita Zbojan, Young Pioneer, c.1984

My parents were asked to do 'voluntary work' on Sundays – building parks and other recreation areas in town. I don't remember them objecting though; in the Summer it was used as a social gathering with a lot of beer drinking, partying, and making friends. If my parents had feelings against the regime they didn't say anything in front of me. My father dreamt of travel outside the Eastern Bloc and to experience more of life. He had a side business selling decorating materials and travelled a lot within Romania to sell them. One of his friends was persecuted because he was gay and spent some time in jail. That was the East European mentality at the time and still hasn't been shaken off.

My father was an ethnic Hungarian, an ethnic group who were the majority in our region, but who suffered because of Ceausescu's policy of Romanianisation. His mother could not even speak Romanian and it would be important to them that government services were available in their language, but apart from in one other autonomous region (Mures-Magyar) this was not offered. The government organised mass resettlement of Romanians into our region so what was a predominantly Hungarian town became a Romanian one: Hungarians reduced to about 30 per cent while I was there and are even less now. Romanianisation started in Kindergarten; there was a single Hungarian one for 170,000 people and no Hungarian higher education until after 1989. In my time growing up, most children spoke both languages from early on because of children playing together out in the street, in schools and mixed households (like mine as my mother was from Bucharest). There were also ethnic Germans from the time of the Austro-Hungarian Empire and we learned some German from playing with them as well. I also had Roma friends as my grandparents lived near the Roma quarter – a multitude of overcrowded blocks of flats in an area by the river that regularly flooded – almost a reservation for them to lead a separate life. We children didn't make distinctions – a playmate was a playmate and we didn't care that our parents were prejudiced and had warned us about them. It was generally believed that Romas were dirty, passed on disease and stole, so they had a difficult time holding down jobs. Probably because of this I didn't have much contact with Romas after a certain age.

There were a lot of positives in Romania, such as zero unemployment as everyone was guaranteed a place of work and an income. If, for example, four people were needed in a particular office, possibly six or seven people were employed to do the job. This way, everyone had an easy life. For instance, my brother was guaranteed a workplace in his hometown the moment he graduated university (which was obviously completely free by the way). Old people were guaranteed their pension and everyone had pretty much an equal chance in life. With the plentiful nurses and doctors included, there were no waiting times in health care and it was sure you would be seen the day you turned up. So people didn't really understand when I complained about the NHS when I arrived in Scotland over twenty years ago.

Western Brands rarely made it into the country apart from Pepsi and so nobody knew Nike or Adidas existed to fight over and mostly everyone wore whatever clothes were made in the area or other communist countries, not overpriced branded clothing to make huge differences between individuals.

I also knew people who were self-employed or operated small businesses. It was only restricted for anyone to own large scale farms or businesses and become exploiters themselves.

What was bad in Romania in particular is that the leaders decided to pay back the full loan given to the country (how evil and unfair of them, right?) and thus the shortages happened. But it was nowhere near to North Korea's levels, there was no day where we had no food, but we rarely had chocolate, oranges, beef and bananas. However, we were given special portions of these at Christmas time, yes, the Christmas time that wasn't supposed to officially exist, but it did. The entrance to the church I was baptised in was right across the road from the local Securitate office.

You won't believe how many movies I watched in just a few months after December 1989 when they suddenly became available: from *Aliens* to *Terminator* and *ET*, it was a time of wonder and excitement, that ended in disappointment when I realised what the USA was really like – nobody told us about private health care and how workers were treated!

Nowadays lots of people look back fondly on the socialist times in Romania – especially older people who lived most of their lives under communism. So many things are missing now that people took for granted at the time and that is why. There was a slower pace of life with less hustle, competitiveness and people also feel a sense of betrayal because of the way it all turned out.

Fejzo Sela – Albania

Fejzo Sela is now a pensioner living with his wife in a flat in Tepelene, Albania, a great-grandfather whose descendants include the author's granddaughters. Born in April 1944, much of his life was spent under the socialist dictatorship of Enver Hoxa. Because two of Fejzo's uncles were partisans who had been martyred in the war against the Italian and German occupiers, his family enjoyed some esteem in post-war Albanian society. Sacrifices were made so that Fejzo could be educated up to eighth grade, and on leaving school in 1960 he was sent to Durres, the principal port in Albania, for further education. This was a naval school named after Mujo Ulqinaku, a hero who died resisting the Italian invasion in 1939. After two years Fejzo left and joined the Albanian Merchant Navy, serving on a cargo vessel that travelled abroad – a privileged occupation within the socialist state. He worked on the vessel for five years continuously.

It was at this point that Fejzo's life changed in a way that was not unusual for that period. His father was accused of theft of wood, one of the consequences being that Fejzo lost his job and was forced to return home to his family. At that time any stain on an individual that caused approbation from the state had implications for other family members unconnected with the alleged misdemeanour (Lea

Fjzelo Sela as a young man in the late 1960s.

Ypi's 2021 autobiography contains many such stories). However, having mulled it over for a few days, Fejzo decided that he would seek a meeting with the leader of the Albanian state to sort the matter out. The meeting took place and Fejzo was able to make a successful plea to return to gainful employment. He was given a job as a teacher in the town of Memaliaj north of Tepelene. This town, on the edge of the mountains of Southern Albania, was created just after the Second World War to serve the coal mines in the area. Fejzo worked as a teacher for six years, but now married and with family responsibility, took a better paid job as a machine operator underground in the coal mine in the town. He retired at the age of 50 in 1991 after twenty-five years of hard and tedious work. Fejzo's retirement came just before the closure of all the mines in the region due to the 'shock therapy' imposed as the country's economy changed from planned socialism to a free market, bringing in its wake stagnation and unemployment.

Fejzo recalls the communist years as being ones of poverty and hardship, in a collective work setting where the individual counted for little. There was also great fear of the state – people could disappear into prison for twenty-five years for simply criticising Enver Hoxa. However, these were also years of peace, and good health and education services. The end of communism brought Albania closer to Europe, a process that continues, but at first there was great instability with theft of savings and property that caused people to rise up and fight for their rights.

Chapter 9

Cold War Frontlines – Stories 2

Introduction

> 'Where were you born?'
> 'On a battlefield,' [Yossarian] answered.
> 'No, no. In what state were you born?'
> 'In a state of innocence.'
>
> Joseph Heller, Catch-22

This chapter continues the theme of ordinary lived experience and perspective, but this time from a military aspect. Soldiers were under orders to obey without question whichever side they were on, so the scene was determined for them by their officers and hierarchy. Although understanding of what they were being asked to do is not obligatory, successful armies ensure that their troops are motivated to support their country's cause. When this breaks down because the purpose is obscure, there is a consequential effect on morale and discipline, as seen among American troops in Vietnam and Soviet troops in Afghanistan. These themes are reflected in the chapter.

Europe's Frontline:

The FDR was NATO's forward military base facing the Soviet enemy. Hundreds of thousands of American and British troops were deployed there from 1945 onwards, their role changing from that of occupying army to one of defender.

In 1971, Dean Lewis, a young newly married American draftee, opted for a three-year assignment in Germany, a posting that would avoid the possibility of a Vietnam posting (Lewis 2018). Lewis was a well-educated 'New Christian' patriot, but had no wish to suffer wounding or death in Vietnam. Germany offered a home also for his wife. His job would be to crew a US Army Pershing Missile truck capable of sending a nuclear missile 450 miles eastwards from various locations in Southern Germany. There he would join another 265,000 US troops. What he found was a mixture of banality, bureaucracy, boredom and absurdity. The latter included the logistics of moving a huge missile along country roads to establish a launch site – a noisy and highly visible process that took five hours to set up. Morale was low, not helped by the presence of traumatised

US Army poster promoting presence in Germany, 1960s. (*US Army via Wikimemedia Commons*)

colleagues who had undertaken tours in Vietnam. Drugs and alcohol abuse were commonplace, the latter subsidised by the military establishment. After moving to a finance role life got easier ,but his cynicism about government never left him. Meanwhile, wife Nan, a New Zealander, got a job on base as a teacher at what she describes as a 'pathetic army school' (ibid p.39). Dean was later given a role 'screening malingerers' (ibid p.43), filtering out referrals for psychiatric treatment who had concocted symptoms to get out of the army. This was all based on increasing concern at the levels of drug overdose and suicide among US army personnel. Despite his many and varied experiences, which involved never actually meeting the enemy just over the border, Dean remained a convinced anti-communist who was sure that defence against the threat from the USSR was absolutely necessary, welcoming the overthrow of the Allende government in Chile. At this time in 1973, Dean and Nan moved to the UK where he started an army sponsored degree. Although a confirmed anti-communist, his account sees no irony in the couple's relief that their new baby would be born at no cost to them in a National Care Service hospital. Lewis's account ends with an admonition against communism's concern with the common good over that of the individual, and its consequences across the world; he makes no mention of American sponsored aggression, or the contradictions apparent in his own story.

In contrast to this published American account are the memories of Sergey Eremenko from Kharkiv, Ukraine, who was a conscript Soviet soldier serving in Hungary later in the Cold War period, 1984–86. Sergey was born in 1966.

Only the best Soviet young men served abroad, as they were the face of the USSR. In my school years I was a school Komsomol leader. Among my fellows-soldiers were students conscripted to the army before graduating from their colleges or universities. Such interruption of studying was normal practice.

I served in Hungary for about two years – from November 1984 until October 1986. Before leaving for Hungary I spent two weeks in Dnepropetrovsk Region, on a young soldiers' course. I then flew by plane to Hungary. For the first six months I was training on a medium tank as a commander in the training centre in Debrecen. A tank crew consisted of three persons: a commander, a

Sergey Eremenko Soviet Army Conscript. (*Sergey Eremenko*)

Sergey Eremenko and comrades, Hungary, 1985. (*Sergey Eremenko*)

gunner and a driver-mechanic. To determine these roles the young men had to do push-ups to chin level on a high bar. Whoever was able to do it ten times and more was selected as either commander or gunner. Those who could do pull ups to hip level became tank commanders. So only physical fitness was taken into account, not knowledge. The soldiers learned about tank equipment, had tactics classes and firing practice.

The rest of my service in Hungary was spent in Veszprem. We didn't mix much with local people. Soldiers could leave the military base only if accompanied by officers. We could ask for a glass of water or to ask for directions. Also, occasionally Soviet soldiers exchanged Soviet rubles (which parents sent them inside envelopes with letters) for Hungarian forints.

We were looked after well in the army. Our diet was better than that of soldiers inside the USSR. We were fed what was normal for cadets in military colleges and the menu changed every day. The food was quite tasty!

I was proud to be a defender of the USSR on the far boundaries, and supported our system and government. I never regarded myself as an occupier. We were worried about the possibility of war – we had political information lessons and were told about what could happen. Officers (with whom we soldiers communicated constantly) were all quite young, five or six years older than us soldiers. They lived there with their wives and small children. There were good relations between officers and soldiers. Several times I repaired TV-sets for officers. Once some officers asked me to look after their young children while they and their wives left the military unit to walk about the city. The wife of one of the officers hesitated as she wasn't sure if she should entrust the children to me. One of the officers assured her that I was the oldest son of a family with many children and I was used to looking after them. I felt anxious, as in reality I was the only son in the family and had no experience with babies! There were three small children and I stayed with them about three hours while their parents enjoyed their city visit in a large group.

The 30th anniversary of the Hungarian revolution of 1956 (for the USSR it was an uprising) took place in October 1986. In that period local people began to behave aggressively towards Soviet soldiers. Demands to get the Soviet troops out of Hungary began to be heard. Two Soviet officers were murdered by knife when they were in Veszprem. Magyars (as Hungarians called themselves) threw stones through windows at our base. Officers and soldiers were prohibited to leave the base grounds. Soldiers armed with live ammunition were on guard on the entrances. To normalise the situation and distract attention the Hungarian army held impromptu exercises in the training area not far from the Soviet base. Nobody in our unit knew about it: everybody woke up very early in the morning because of sounds of fighting, flying helicopters and so on. As we were only 150 km from the border with Austria, we were worried and tried to phone to our main command. There were problems with phone connections and these attempts took a while to succeed until we were finally told what was going on.

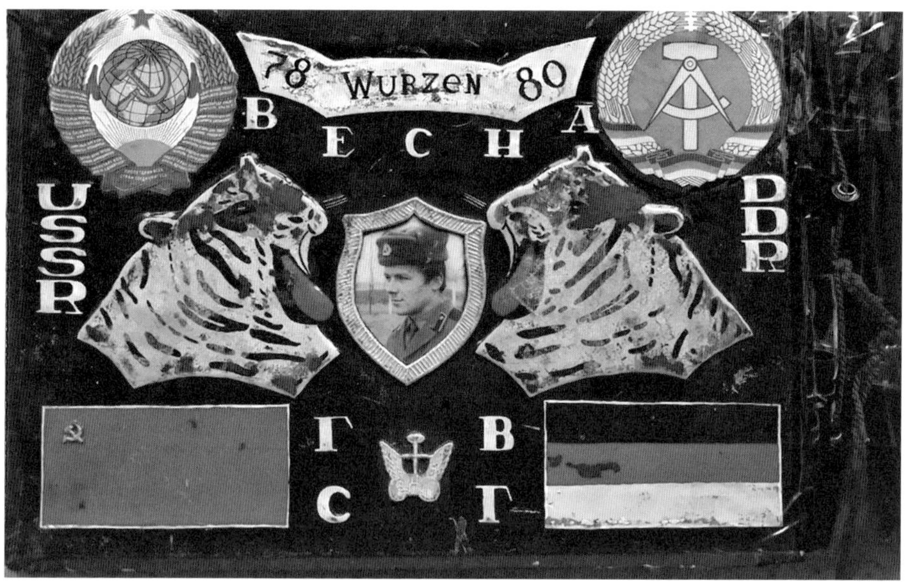

Photos from the 1980 demob. album of Soviet Army conscript Grigory Slutsky from Sumy Ukraine, whose unit was based in Wurzen, DDR. (*V.Kudinova*)

Diplomacy and Duplicity

During the Cold War there were many instances of acts of superficial friendship between the protagonists. The admiration shown in the West for the pioneer Soviet cosmonauts on their ambassadorial visits in the 1960s and 1970s is illustrative (Turbett 2021b). In 1961 Yuri Gagarin, the first human in space visited the UK and had dinner with the Queen as part of a trip that saw him applauded by large crowds in London and Manchester; the niceties stopped short of a photograph of the meeting although this was readily granted to the American lunar-landing crew of Apollo 11 several years later. Cold War friendship visits between armed forces personnel were rarer but one such took place in April 1956, when the Soviet Navy's *Ordzhonikidze*, escorted by two destroyers, brought leaders Nikita Khrushchev and Nikolai Bulganin to Britain for a diplomatic visit. This was a Sverdlov Class cruiser that had entered service in 1952, as one of a class of fourteen built on Stalin's orders for a larger capacity Soviet naval fleet; a further sixteen were cancelled after his death, his successor Khrushchev considering such vessels obsolete in the missile age. Although built to specifications adopted by the Italians and Americans from the Second World War period, there were aspects of their design that interested the West, one being the propellers. This was not the first such visit of one of this class to British waters: sister ship *Sverdlov* had taken part in the Coronation Naval Review off Portsmouth in 1953.

Elvis Presley (who was a US conscript in Germany) in the movie GI Blues 1960. (*Alamy Stock*)

The ships docked in Portsmouth Harbour's Royal Navy base amid the usual pomp and ceremony for such events and remained there for nine days. The two leaders travelled to London for extensive talks with Prime Minister Anthony Eden, and other British politicians. Their entourage included cultural and other representatives. This was the first such visit ever made abroad by the highest-ranking Soviet leaders, their aim being to win acceptance and have their views on the world aired and taken seriously. Meanwhile the crew hosted visits aboard the *Ordzhonikidze* and did some sightseeing, and this was captured on camera by an unknown Soviet sailor in the accompanying photographs. Probably unknown to the photographer were events taking place below the vessel's waterline.

Soviet Army guitarist. (*Author's collection*)

It seems extraordinary that British Intelligence should take advantage of such an occasion but that apparently is exactly what happened. In an effort to find

Soviet Navy cruiser *Ordzhonikidze*, Portsmouth, UK, April 1956. (*Alamy Stock*)

Royal Navy WRNS are welcomed aboard *Ordzhonikidze*, April 1966. (*Author's collection*)

out more about the propeller systems (or perhaps for other purposes) a retired diver who had made a name for himself during the Second World War, Commander Lionel 'Buster' Crabb, was secretly engaged by MI6 to dive under the ship and investigate. He did so on the night of the ship's arrival but was never seen alive again. His absence was reported by the Admiralty over a week later under a story that he had been trialling secret underwater apparatus in the Solent some miles distant from Portsmouth Harbour. However, the Soviets reported that a diver had been seen near their ship on the night of Crabb's disappearance, and a complaint was made about what was reported in the newspaper *Pravda* as 'shameful espionage'. Rumours and speculation abounded until a body turned up

A crew member from Ordzhonikidze posing on a visit to London. (*Author's collection*)

further along the coast the following year; although dressed in a diving suit of the type Crabb would have been wearing, the head and hands were missing, making identification uncertain. Some facts have emerged confirming the nature of Crabb's mission, including revelations in Peter Wright's book *Spycatcher* (1987) but much remains a mystery and still subject to British official papers that will not be released until 2057. The stories range from his death at the hands of Soviet personnel from the cruiser because the Soviets had been tipped off about the mission, to his death during interrogation after capture, and even that he might have defected to the USSR (Hoole 2007).

The British Army Of the Rhine (BAOR)

At its post-war peak in 1957, the BAOR comprised 80,000 troops spread across 129 locations in the British zone of occupation in North-West Germany (see Chapter 3) and West Berlin (Chrystal 2018). Over its forty-eight-year history, BAOR troops were never involved in armed conflict but where present as a deterrent, much of their time being taken up with training. As the British Army presence in Germany was its largest permanent deployment, it was regarded as a long-term posting, and families were housed and schools and other provisions laid on. After 1952 and the establishment of the GDR as a NATO member with its own armed services, the British Army were invited guests rather than occupiers. It took some time, though, for attitudes to change. During major exercises numbers could increase dramatically: Operation Lionheart in 1984 involved 131,000 personnel, many transported from the UK in chartered ferries and aircraft just as might happen in a real war (ibid).

Rather than later memory, this short contribution is based on a 1949 diary written by R.A. Johnston, a National Serviceman from Stanmore in Middlesex, that found its way into the author's possession. How typically it represents the views of BAOR soldiers in the immediate post-war period cannot be determined. Although after the Berlin airlift, and in the year the USSR acquired nuclear capability, there is nothing in the diary to suggest tensions or indeed reasons for being in the BAOR at all. The diarist served in the REME (Royal Electrical and Mechanical Engineers) and spent the last part of his service in Germany. Lance Corporal Johnston arrived in Hamburg in February 1949, and after a period of guard duties and searches of Germans in the quayside barracks, was transferred to the Ayrshire Barracks REME workshops in Monchengladbach (this British base is still in existence as the last in Germany). His diary is quite preoccupied with the life he has left behind at home including his plans to get engaged and marry his 18-year-old girlfriend Pat. He makes only a very few passing comments on world events (dock strikes at home and Eire becoming a republic), and Germany only seems of interest for its recreational opportunities: sailing, horse riding and photography. His comments on the cities of Hamburg and Dusseldorf express surprise at the amount of goods in the shops, presumably compared with austerity Britain. The Cold War and the Soviet threat are not mentioned once, and the feel one gets from the brief entries is that Lance Corporal Johnston saw himself very much as an occupier of Germany rather than a defender of Europe. Much of his leisure time was spent at the cinema seeing all the favourite movies of the day, such as *Paleface* with Bob Hope. Sightseeing and cinema clearly have more appeal to Lance Corporal Johnston than the drinking indulged in by his compatriots. He undertakes an intensive and well described 'Christian Leadership' course, but makes little mention of his work repairing Type X coding machines (the British forces standard cyphering and deciphering machine for sending coded messages), just a few references to his workshop duty. This sits alongside reference to parades, route marches, guard duty and occasional firing practice. Food and its quality were also worthy of note. Lance Corporal Johnston was 'demobbed' and returned to England in October 1949; after some leave cruising on the Thames he went to work for James Combe & Co. in North West London as a heating engineer, attending night school.

Later in the Cold War, maintaining morale and motivation was an important task within the BAOR, and NATO forces in general; 85 per cent of BAOR forces were on constant readiness to combat an enemy about whom little was known, apart from their impressive scale and equipment. Gaps in knowledge were filled by Intelligence staff tasked with presenting the enemy as formidable but flawed. Rather simplistic material aimed at the literary levels of ordinary infantry soldiers was put together that tried to explain things and maintain

A British serviceman on BAOR deployment, 1957. (*Author's collection*)

optimism. Presumably 'Threat – A Periodical Review of Developments in the Military Power of the Warsaw Pact' No.3 March 1977, is an illustrative example. Its roughly duplicated twenty-two pages contain basic information on Soviet equipment and the deployment of their forces – enough in fact to make the BAOR's job seem serious, although a lot of space is taken up with simple and rather pointless diagrams and maps. A comic-style picture story, that would not have looked out of place in one of the boys' weeklies of that time, provides a briefer than brief potted history of Soviet expansion and Western reaction. Another page compares basic conditions of service, telling the reader important truths such as the fact that the average weekly take home pay of a British squaddie is '£47 (enough to buy 134 litres of beer)' while the Soviet infantryman earns '50p (enough to buy 1 litre of beer – but he's not allowed to drink!)'. Typical menus are shown that tell the reader that the British are fed much better than the other side, and that while the Russkies get no leave, we (the Brits) get forty-two days. If there were any lingering doubts about the best side to be on, the next page offers a fictional account of the life and times of a Soviet officer. It is hard to take this seriously, especially when his bride-to-be is shown as a topless model who 'has some views on discipline'. This publication was concocted by '7 Intelligence Company' and rather surprisingly, considering the very basic literacy level required of the reader, states on the back cover that it is 'intended for Unit Intelligence Officers and Junior Commanders with information on the Warsaw Pact that can be given the widest possible dissemination'. Well done Major M.D. Durman CO and his Intelligence staff who probably knew exactly what they were doing! The reality though was probably spelled out by National Serviceman Geoff Barnett of the Lancashire Fusiliers who remembers that the generally shared view in the mid-1950s was that the only way to stop the Soviets would have been to 'nuke' them as an attack would have seen NATO forces rolled over and the enemy at the English Channel within a week (Schindler 2012).

The need to characterise the Soviet way of life as different and inferior pervaded other NATO literature; in the late 1960s *NATO Letter* magazine carried a series of articles that described aspects of life in the USSR, all in terms that, while posed seriously, would have relied on a negative reaction from the reader (NATO 1969). While no doubt accurate in its account, what is noticeable is what it doesn't say in relation to social benefits, free access to recreational and other facilities (especially in the cities), full employment and other facets of life denied to many citizens in the West. It pointed out that participation in university life for a student depended on Komsomol (Young Communist) membership, but then extended this to suggest that this involved interference in the lives of other students. While Komsomol and Party membership carried advantages in influence, it could be argued that the same principal applies in the West; participation for instance in a trade union branch is voluntary but can mean influence over conditions and pay at work that affect everyone. In this sense the series also failed to look at the difference in citizenship and responsibilities touched upon in Chapter 7; in fact it made no real comparisons, but, as so often with Western-inspired propaganda against the USSR, veiled attacks on the absence of perceived freedoms. This is of course hardly surprising, as the reader could not be left to make their own mind up.

By the time they left Germany after the end of the Cold War, the BAOR was well integrated into life there, providing jobs and incomes to many in the locality of their bases. It wasn't always like that; Hugh Hudson, a National Serviceman officer in the Royal Armoured Corps, recalls a very negative attitude towards German farmers and country people that saw tanks ruin their crops and blanks discharged around their buildings that blew out the windows. He also remembers the sexual encounters with prostitutes in Hamburg and with the bored wives of more senior officers. For him it was a good life; as a junior officer he had his own room, a batman (servant), officers' mess with lots of cheap alcohol – and or course, no war (Ibid). The infrastructure to support British civilians and troops increased as time went on; Paderborn Barracks was served by British pubs, a tax-free car dealership and other British shops. Communities such as the enormous base at Osnabruck had schools, health facilities, and social and recreational amenities to the extent that troops and their families had no need to go beyond them and mix with Germans.

Had there been war, the reality was that BAOR troops and their families were all very vulnerable; they would have been early targets for tactical nuclear weapons which would have accompanied a ground attack. The *British Army Of the Rhine NBC Guide* published in 1981 made for grim reading; the dangers came from not just the enemy's use of such weaponry, NATOs defence relied on their use. A change of wind direction could rain friendly nuclear fall-out onto BAOR families (Chrystal 2018). The British Army's *Infantry Training Manual* also offered little comfort for those on the battlefield; its 1960 edition suggested that troops exposed to nuclear attack who were in the open should 'shut their eyes, fall flat on the ground, hands under the chest and faces pressed to the earth. Men should lie like this for at least fifteen seconds before getting up.' With that kind of advice, it was probably best not to dwell too much on such matters.

Africa From Both Sides

Chris Cocks, born in 1957, was a white Zimbabwean who was swept up the war in Rhodesia/Zimbabwe, not through choice as with some of his contemporaries, but simply because he was of call-up age. Unlike most of his fellow white conscripts he was educated in a multiracial setting and took an early distaste to the apartheid he saw around him. He later wrote about his military experiences (Cocks 2018), explaining that he had intended at one point escaping to Mozambique to avoid conscription, but was persuaded not to bring shame upon his family. Once trained and in a situation where survival depended on trust and a close relationship with comrades, he put the morality of the war behind him and became a skilled combat soldier engaged in regular operations. This was to later take a personal psychological toll on both Chris and many of his fellows: their dangerous combat activities for a country generally regarded as a pariah state for a cause some like Chris, had no belief in, did not change any outcome; their efforts received little recognition or acclaim from any source.

> I was born and grew up in Rhodesia (now Zimbabwe). Being white and 18, I was liable for conscription in 1976 as the Rhodesian bush war – or the Zimbabwean war of liberation – gathered pace. I served in the Rhodesian Light Infantry, a crack airborne unit, for three years and saw action on an almost daily basis. I was opposed to the white regime of Ian Smith and his segregationist policies but I had no choice but to serve in the military. My enemies were the armies of Joshua Nkomo's ZIPRA and Robert Mugabe's ZANLA, based in Zambia and Mozambique respectively. ZIPRA was sponsored by the Soviets and ZANLA mainly by the Red Chinese, the latter indoctrinated in the teachings of Mao's Little Red Book. The country was on the front line of the Cold War, but not in the traditional way. The West did not support Rhodesia which it saw as a pariah. Today China is probably the biggest 'investor' in Zimbabwe, so justifying Chinese involvement. I never fully believed the liberation movements were truly communist, but more nationalists, fighting for majority rule.

Chris's completion of training and first deployment coincided with the beginning of ZANLA's 1976 offensive. He describes his first action and sight of the enemy – a short firefight that ended with an airstrike:

> Corporal Seward spotted what looked like a bundle of rags beneath a bush. In an instant his rifle was at his shoulder and her fired three or four quick shots. The bundle grunted and as it rolled over, a communist AK-47 rifle clattered to the side. I was astonished. So that was a guerrilla.
>
> Cocks p.54

Moulded together by a shared penchant for dope smoking and a devil-may-care attitude to life and death, Chris and his comrades became more confident and skilled at tracking down and killing their opponents. He witnessed some terrible things as they battled an enemy that could easily and frustratingly disappear into the local population. Abuse of suspects was not uncommon:

> A corporal … was particularly fond of forcing uncooperative suspects to lie naked on the ground. He would then with aid of a fine *sjambok* … lightly lash the soles of the victim's feet for a prolonged period. He would only move up to the genital area once he could no longer see what he was whipping because of the blood. The corporal couldn't speak Shona and his victims couldn't speak English so I wondered what was the purpose of the exercise. Such was the war in Rhodesia.
>
> ibid p.83

After receiving parachute training, Chris and his troop (platoon) in which he became an NCO in charge of a 'stick' (a group of four soldiers who could be carried together in a helicopter) were sent into Mozambique and Zambia in search of guerrilla bases and training camps, burning and looting their way through villages that showed any sign of support for ZANLA and ZIPRA. This was war at its most brutal, with scenes familiar from Vietnam war movies; one of Chris's friends later recounted to him how he had shot up an ablution block in which guerrillas were thought to be hiding only to learn as they tumbled out that it was packed full of women and children. Having already killed many of them, he proceeded to shoot the survivors, a matter he still found hard to live with some seventeen years later when he shared the memory with Chris.

Gradually the tide turned against the Rhodesian forces, politically and militarily; ZANLA and ZIPRA benefiting from intelligence gained from infiltrators at all levels, including high up in the Rhodesian military leadership, and showed their capability with their own commando actions in Salisbury, the very centre of white power. Chris completed his three years' service, thankful to have survived, in January 1979. He found readjustment hard and soon re-joined the war in an anti-terrorist police role, but peace was to come later that year.

Agrippa Mutambara, born in 1951, grew up in a black Christian family in Rhodesia where he and his family suffered all the indignities of white supremacy. His father, a teacher, had been dismissed from his teaching post for standing up to the white establishment, and thereafter worked as a medical orderly. Agrippa ended his education earlier than he should have, as higher education, for which he was quite suitable, was only available for a handful of black high achievers. He was later trained as an African Council finance officer

Chris Cocks serving in the RLI. (*Chris Cocks*)

– a local government post. A chance encounter with a wounded and captured ZANLA fighter being treated in his father's hospital convinced Agrippa to join the freedom struggle and in 1975 he crossed into Mozambique and after a spell as a tea picker, succeeded in joining a 'refugee' camp where he was politically educated about his country's history and later selected for training as a ZANLA fighter. This was a complex and staged process – infiltration was a common feature, so all potential recruits were under initial suspicion of not being true rebels. Gradually Agrippa proved his commitment and was soon promoted to senior positions within the movement, all the time educating himself further. By 1978 he had been appointed Acting Director of Politics for ZANLA. Agrippa later wrote about his experiences.

> I was one of the few who seriously studied the literature on capitalism and imperialism on the one hand, and socialism and communism on the other. Socialism made a very strong appeal then, as it still does today. I was convinced then, as I am convinced today, that the bourgeoisie, with their insatiable appetite for wealth, are the cause of social tensions within societies and hence the cause of the inequitable distribution of wealth among nations.
>
> As for the ZANLA forces in the camps and battlefield, the socialist gospel was easy to embrace. They had no wealth to distribute and therefore nothing to lose. But, for some of our political leaders and ZANU supporters, especially those living in capitalist countries, they emulated the glamorous lifestyles of the wealthy.
>
> Mutambara 2013 p.63

His account mirrors that of Chris Cocks – guerrilla fighting against a well-trained and supported enemy who could call upon air support when under pressure:

> The enemy forces were still moving towards our positions, oblivious that they had now entered our killing zone, when I opened fire. That was the signal for all my comrades to follow suit. As my fighters began firing, my own gun fell silent while I studied the effect of our fire and the reaction to it from the enemy. The enemy appeared to be in disarray, with a few returning our fire and the majority scrambling to seek cover. Evidently, command and control had been lost.
>
> For almost forty minutes we dominated the fire fight and I was sure the battle would end soon unless enemy reinforcements arrived quickly. Celebration turned to panic, however, when three helicopters appeared above and started attacking our positions. There were also two spotter planes circling above us, directing the attacking planes to their targets.

> We directed our fire power towards the enemy planes until jet fighters also joined the fray and began bombing our positions. Now our own command and control was lost. Each one of us sought refuge in some cave, under boulders or in whatever cover or protection the terrain could offer.
>
> ibid p.77

Agrippa vividly describes the impact of Rhodesian attacks on rebel bases deep in Mozambique and the loss of comrades, including women, and the senseless slaughter of unarmed people. He also describes successful operations. As the struggle reached its final phase, Agrippa was present in London when Patriotic Front leaders, including his ZANLA comrades, negotiated a settlement with the representatives of the Smith regime. He expresses disappointment and frustration at the compromise this involved; as a socialist he wanted to see land reform as central to a liberated Zimbabwe. However, under pressure from the 'frontline' states of Tanzania, Mozambique, Zambia and Ethiopia, whose support for the struggle was crucial, this promise was being negotiated away, creating frustrations that would explode in the years to come.

Agrippa Mutambara (centre) with Robert Mugabe. (*Chris Cocks*)

Chapter 10

The 1980s and the End of Really Existing Socialism

But the biggest thing that has happened in the world in my life, in our lives, is this: By the grace of God, America won the Cold War.

US President George H.W. Bush,
State of the Union Address, 28 January 1992

Introduction

To summarise what has been covered in previous chapters: peaceful co-existence was based on the maintenance of a balance of terror that reached preposterous scales and was unaffordable – at least to the USSR. The Soviet economy was faltering by the late 1970s; shortages of essentials and queuing for things as they briefly appeared in the shops, became a way of life for ordinary citizens. This was the cost of the massive defence spending discussed in Chapters 3 and 4, and other matters that will be discussed in this chapter. Neither could the country afford the attempts to spread its influence worldwide after the American defeat in Vietnam – the trade returns were negligible compared with the expense of supporting regimes in Cuba and elsewhere. For the West, the tipping point came with the invasion of Afghanistan in 1979 – this was extending the Brezhnev Doctrine beyond the satellite states into an unstable region where a Soviet orientated government had barely held power. As mentioned in Chapter 5, the fact that the invasion had to an extent been contrived by the Americans to weaken the USSR, was an important part of the equation. Détente had to end sometime and if there was ever to be an opportunity for the West to tighten the screw, it was now. Historical occurrence works in mysterious ways – come the moment, come the leader – and in this case the 1980s provided a combination of key personalities who were willing to take risks to change the game: in the West, Ronald Reagan of the USA and Margaret Thatcher of the UK were both fiercely anti-communist and anti-socialist, and were ready to up the stakes; on the Soviet side, Gorbachev represented a new generation of CPSU apparatchiks who sought popular change, while the old Stalinist style leaderships in the satellites, especially Poland, were under increasing pressure to democratise and reform.

Economic Stagnation in the USSR

Mikhail Gorbachev, who became Soviet leader in 1985, coined the term *stagnation* to describe the state the country had grown into during the years of his predecessors following Khrushchev's removal in 1964. This was a deliberately pejorative phrase; in Gorbachev's view the promise of socialism, which might develop into communism, had been lost through bureaucratic incompetence and the squandering of public support for the project he hoped to save through his own reforms. The popular support and willingness to make sacrifices had been lost through failures to improve freedoms and quality of life for ordinary workers. Industry was beset with corruption and inefficiency, with a thriving black market in pilfered goods and services.

Despite efforts to compensate for the USSR's poor geographical location in terms of agriculture, the country still could not feed itself and relied on imports of staples like grain from the USA. Comparisons are indicative of the scale of the problem; in the USA, according to American estimates, an agricultural worker in 1983 statistically could feed sixty-five fellow citizens, while in the USSR the figure was nine – even this was an improvement on previous years, although a very small one (CIA 1985). Food shortages impacted on the nation's health; despite increases in income and improved social benefits, infant mortality and life expectancy declined after 1970. Khrushchev had boasted at

Citizens Patrol in the USSR, 1980s. (*Author's collection*)

Different generations in the USSR, 1980s – where grandparents often provided childcare. (*Author's collection*)

the CPSU's 1961 Congress that the USSR would have a higher standard of living than any capitalist country by 1981, but economic growth (the measure then and now) had slowed down when compared with the US, falling to 51 per cent by 1984 (Brainerd 2006). Production targets of the consumer items Soviet citizens wanted, cars, televisions and washing machines, were consistently missed and with nothing in the shops to purchase, there was little incentive to work harder. This downward spiral lowered industrial output generally, and what was produced was of low quality, poorly designed and if mechanical, unreliable. Clothing seemed drab compared with Western fashion and the urban young especially, were becoming privately dissatisfied with what the system was offering them (Yurchak 2005).

Stalin's dream of socialism in one country, and Khrushchev's promise of communism by the 1980s, looked as if they would never happen – unless your vision was one of a perpetually totalitarian state whose alliances with close neighbours were based on the bullying might witnessed in Budapest in 1956 and Prague in 1968. The final years of Brezhnev's leadership until his death in 1982, had lacked direction; Brezhnev himself was too ill to impose leadership, his most able accomplice, Kosygin, had died in 1980, and his successors, Andropov and Chernenko, were also old men out of touch with the people. Both mistakenly and hopelessly thought that tightening labour discipline would bring about improvement. They were also set on a defensive outlook determined to maintain a balance of nuclear capability, whatever the cost. This depended on a popular belief in the integrity of the armed forces. Such support was in jeopardy and not just because of the failure to secure an outcome though military action in Afghanistan. In September 1973, Soviet air force fighters shot down Korean Airlines Flight 103 with the loss of 269 passengers en route from New York to Seoul. The airliner had strayed into Soviet airspace over the Kamchatka in the far east, and in poor weather had been mistaken for a military aircraft and had not responded to signals and warning shots. The West pounced on the incident and made much of initial Soviet denials of responsibility and clumsy attempts to cover up their error. It took a long time for the truth to emerge, and this included the fact that the US Air Force were in fact operating in the area and were far from blameless in their use of civilian aircraft to provide cover for their activities (a few years later the US Navy shot down an Iranian airliner in similar circumstances). Tensions were already high and there was genuine fear in the USSR that war might result, especially when the incident lent popular Western support to the siting of American cruise missiles in Europe.

By 1985, Andropov and Chernenko were both dead, leaving a comparatively young Gorbachev to try and change a Soviet Union under increasing pressure. Gorbachev's approach from the outset differed from his predecessors – more of the Khrushchev thaw reform attempts to win support from the population, but without the old Stalinist threat of armed force if others wanted to move faster than he did. His twin approach involved two main strands that won him fame internationally as a new type of Soviet leader: 'perestroika', meaning restructuring of the centralised economy involving workers in planning, a reduction in bureaucracy, and better production through improved technology. The other strand of his reform programme involved what he called 'glasnost' (openness), meaning freedom to criticise and discuss issues and problems so that socialist solutions could be found. There were many within the system who opposed his efforts – under Brezhnev, state bureaucrats had exploited the centralised planning machine to ensure they received as many favours and perks as possible, and administrative loopholes were abundant to perpetuate the mutual giving and receiving of rewards. Lewin (2005) cites the example of partying (in the literal and modern sense) in the small arms and machine manufacturing centre of Izhevsk, where in the 1968–69 period one state enterprise had hosted receptions and banquets involving the consumption of 350 bottles of cognac, twenty-five bottles of vodka and eighty bottles of champagne. The nomenklatura were not about to give up their rewards easily and soon Gorbachev was being nudged towards market solutions to consumer supply problems; these both increased opportunities for enterprising state officials and took on a momentum that became unstoppable.

In a 2001 interview Gorbachev spoke of the problems that centralised planning presented in the 1980s, and the impetus it gave to critics of the system :

> Imagine a country that flies into space, launches Sputniks, creates such a defence system, and it can't resolve the problem of women's pantyhose. There's no toothpaste, no soap powder, not the necessities of life. It was incredible and humiliating to work in such a government.
>
> Gorbachev 2001

As discussed in Chapter 4, the Soviet Military Industrial Complex was also out of control, not just in terms of its spending, but also in its actions. In 1976 the Poliburo (the ruling Party Committee of Government) approved on military grounds the deployment of SS-20 intermediate range missiles in 14 sites across Warsaw Pact countries to neutralise the threat of NATO tactical nuclear weapon use in any war. These missiles were targetable and would offer little warning that they were incoming, and so upset what NATO regarded as a balance of power. Politically, the Soviet leadership had not intended to breach détente, but it accelerated that process. Despite this growth of tension, the long negotiated second Strategic Arms Limitation Talks (SALT II) agreement was signed in Vienna in June 1979. Its impact was momentary: the US Senate refused to endorse it and by the end of the year the Soviet invasion of Afghanistan parked it to one side indefinitely. SALT II would have established numerical equality of nuclear delivery systems, a commitment honoured in practice until 1986 when the Soviets overtook NATO and the US, with an estimated 45,000 warheads, 20,000 of which were tactical (Ware 2016). This was costing up to 30 per cent of the USSR's entire GDP, the USA a more affordable but still astronomical 7 per cent of their own much more expansive GDP (Gorbachev 2000). Gorbachev's planned reforms would depend not just on international arms control agreements, but on gaining the support of his generals for a complete reappraisal of Soviet Foreign Policy and its place in the world. This hung in the balance all the way through until the failed coup in August 1991.

Reflecting on the changes he fought for in the 1980s to save socialism in the USSR, Gorbachev felt that the Soviet economic system had failed on several counts: it had not met ecological tests, and it had failed to give the people efficient production of quality goods in the quantities they wanted and required. It had, though, provided a minimum level of social security that was unknown in the West and had made impressive technological advances such as in space exploration. The market economies of the West had better met the material needs of their own populations but had failed to provide security and stability globally, and had divided the world between North and South (Gorbachev 2000). These are issues still being debated today.

The End of Détente and The USSR's Implosion

The hawks in the White House had started nudging President Carter in the direction of a more aggressive stance against the USSR in the late 1970s, sensing its economic weakness and the inert dissatisfaction of the population with the status-quo. If enough pressure could be applied the contradictions would either result in the collapse of communism, or a war that the USA might win. They were prepared to take the world to the brink to see through this strategy, and Ronald Reagan, the former Hollywood cowboy actor known for his anti-communism, was the right person to carry it out. He made this a central plank of his 1980 election campaign and won, assuming office in early 1981. In alliance with Britain's Margaret Thatcher, he began applying pressure on the USSR by increasing military spending to facilitate a successful tactical nuclear war in Europe. First planned under the Carter administration in 1979 to reduce the threat of the Soviet's SS-20, this involved the siting of new Cruise missile systems in Britain and Germany. The mobile Pershing-2 and BGM-109G missiles developed for this purpose were much more advanced than the SS-20s, proving again that the USA could outspend and outpace the USSR when it was so-minded. Reagan's trump card was to offer a 'zero option' – that the USA would hold back from its plans if the Soviets withdrew their SS-20s, a tactic that gave a peaceful cover to his escalation of Cold War confrontation. The move was seen as aggressive by many at home and brought about a massive resurgence of the peace movement in the Western world. CND (see Chapter 6) membership grew, and new forms of protest emerged – peace camps outside nuclear bases in the UK and elsewhere as a constant reminder of what lurked within. A massive 'Plowshares' protest in Central Park, New York, in 1982 attracted a million people.

The year 1983 marked a watershed. In March Reagan announced massive investment in the Strategic Defense Initiative (also called the 'Star Wars' programme) a largely aspirational space-based defence system. If it could ever be realised, this would eliminate the nuclear threat by destroying incoming nuclear missiles before they reached their targets. The accidental shooting down of Flight 103 finally signalled the end of détente.

The pressure was now on the Soviets to disarm and back down from the threat they were felt to pose to the West and its interests. Several events accelerated this process. In April 1986, an accident at the Chernobyl Nuclear plant in the north of Ukraine caused a chain reaction that was soon out of control, leading to the meltdown of one of its reactors. The results were catastrophic, but characteristically, the Soviets initially tried to hide and downplay the consequences. However, massive amounts of nuclear fallout were appearing over Northern Europe and the situation in the area around the plant was becoming highly dangerous. A huge operation commenced to evacuate the region around the plant and seal off the reactor – work that has continued since to make safe the consequences of the worst nuclear disaster in history. Workers who volunteered (or who were volunteered without being told of the possible consequences) and who took part in the initial response and later mop-up, died in their thousands, as did people – including children as yet unborn – in the years to follow. The impact on the USSR was profound in other ways; until then there had been reason to believe that Soviet scientific and engineering achievement was superior because it was not based on profit extraction but on other values. This was apparent in the early years of the space race, when the USSR were ahead of the Americans, and in the development of peaceful use of atomic energy – the 'Peaceful Atom' as it was described in the official literature. The Soviets built the world's first nuclear power station in 1954, a nuclear powered ice-breaker, the *Lenin*, and proudly showcased all these innovations in international exhibitions such as the Brussels World Fair event in 1958, where they contrasted strongly with the American emphasis on consumer items.

Chernobyl shattered what was left of the Soviet dream. The much-vaunted progressive and peaceful use of the atom turned out to be as illusory as other progress that successive Soviet leaders had promised. Like much else apparently, it was, according to Gorbachev, based on 'the concealing or hushing up of accidents and other bad news, irresponsibility and carelessness, slipshod work, wholesale drunkenness' (Gaddis 2005 p.231). One Soviet scientist recalls bitterly:

> In 1962, *Nine Days in One Year*, a film featuring Soviet atomic scientists was released. It was very popular. They earned large salaries and the secrecy added to the romanticism. The cult of physics! Even after it imploded at Chernobyl, how slow we were to part with that cult! Scientists were summoned. They arrived on a special flight, but many didn't even take razors with them, supposing they would be away for only a few hours. They were informed that there had been an explosion at an atomic power station, but all had faith in their physics. They were from the generation that shared that belief. The age of physics ended at Chernobyl.
>
> Alexievich 2016 p.220–1

Because of the way Soviet government worked at that time it was three weeks before Gorbachev addressed the nation on TV about the disaster; he later said that Chernobyl was the most significant single contributor to the downfall of the USSR (Woldman 2017).

Gorbachev's immediate reaction to Chernobyl was to convince the Politburo that Glasnost and Perestroika must proceed apace and they agreed. As already indicated, this had unintended consequences and opened the floodgates to Western influence and ideas about market solutions; these accentuated the contradictions between a command-and-control economy and one in which

Discarded doll in the abandoned zone near the Chernobyl Reactor site. (*S. Teschke via Wikimedia Commons*)

production to meet people's real (food shelter warmth etc) and perceived needs (that engendered by fashion and the marketplace itself) was controlled by other forces. Never keen on a turn to capitalism, Gorbachev was being dragged inexorably away from the socialism he wanted to save.

Other forces were at work in the USSR's satellites, where less progressive leaderships were still imbued with the ideologies and policies of Stalin and Brezhnev. In Poland especially, demands for reform and free elections could only be resisted by repression, and when it became clear that this could no longer be guaranteed by the USSR, the systems collapsed one by one. Limited free elections were announced in Poland for June 1989. Almost simultaneously, popular movements grew in the Baltic republics demanding independence, and mass movements in Hungary and Czechoslovakia were demanding free elections. This trend was fomented by Reagan, who fanned the flames of nationalism with his talk of the need for Russia to cease its imperialist domination of its own republics. Nationalist movements soon reappeared in the very largest republic, Ukraine, and many of the smaller ones in central Asia. In the momentous month of June 1989, the fortified border between Hungary and Austria was dismantled through simple agreement between the two countries. This enabled a by-pass of the Berlin Wall and East/West border for East Germans, so inevitably the Berlin Wall came tumbling down at the end of the year. The only country where there was a serious fightback by the old guard was Romania; here the Securitate fired on demonstrators until they were overwhelmed by popular revolt culminating in the execution after a rapid military trial of an unrepentant Ceausescu and his wife Elena on Christmas Day 1989.

The Afghanistan adventure had turned sour by 1985, when a decision was made by the Politburo to withdraw Soviet troops. However, it was to take another four years to achieve international agreement about the terms of withdrawal because of the complications arising from US and Western involvement with the forces fighting the Soviet presence. In 1987, after protracted talks over the previous two years, Gorbachev and Reagan signed an agreement that removed intermediate nuclear missiles from the Cold War front line in Europe. Gorbachev went even further by announcing that the Soviet military presence in Warsaw Pact countries would also be reduced, a strong signal that the future of these countries now lay in their own hands.

Gorbachev and Reagan pose beside a fragment of the former Berlin Wall, 1992. (*Ronald Reagan Library via Wikimedia Commons*)

Gorbachev and his supporters in the politburo hoped to save socialism in the USSR by freeing it from its responsibility

Soviet troops leaving Afghanistan, 1979. (*RIA Novosti via Wikimedia Commons*)

for the fate of other countries in the hope that peaceful settlement of differences could lead to a new world order where the values of socialism and communism could shine through on their own merit. In fact, the forces of capital outwitted him by taking advantage of his weaknesses, including those who opposed him from the old guard at home. In August 1991, while Gorbachev was on holiday, military and civil leaders incensed by the furtherance of devolvement plans that would break up the USSR, mounted a coup to try to turn the clock back with a return to the CPSU autocracy Gorbachev was rapidly abandoning. The leaders of the coup were poorly organised; ordinary people supported by loyal army units, and led by Boris Yeltsin, rallied in support of the government. The outcome was victory for Yeltsin, the side-lining of Gorbachev, and the furtherance of the aims of those who wanted to dismantle the socialist order entirely. The failed coup resulted in a loss of influence of the Moscow government, the secession of several republics and then agreement between Yeltsin and the leaders of Belarus and Ukraine that their relationship would be as independent states.

Having no further purpose, the Soviet federal government dissolved itself in December 1991. Soon after that the CPSU was abolished and outlawed. Yeltsin, the President of the newly declared Russian Federation, embarked on a 'shock-therapy' transformation to a free-market economy that enriched some, particularly those of his friends able to buy up and take over potentially profitable state industries such as gas production. Many others were impoverished as social security and previously secure jobs disappeared overnight. Ultimately Gorbachev's

Anti-coup demonstration, Moscow, August 1991. (*I. Simochkin via Wikimedia Commons*)

compromises in the name of peace and freedom had come up against a capitalist world order that never had any intention of compromise. Its attractions proved too much for most people in the Eastern Bloc and accommodation was not possible, so the communist project, in existence for seventy-four years, disappeared.

For many across the Eastern Bloc the sudden changes forced a rethink of everything they had ever known and been told to believe. Lea Ypi, an 11-year-old keen Young Pioneer in harshly repressive Albania, learned that private adult discussions about 'going to university', 'graduating', 'expulsion' and 'dropping out', were actually coded conversations about imprisonment, release, the death sentence and suicide (Ypi 2021). Adjustment involved shock-therapy in emotional lives, just as, they were now told, it would have to in economic terms.

Conclusion

Reagan and the White House hawks' risky strategy of exploiting the weaknesses of the Soviet Union through confrontational escalation of the Cold War, brought about the USSR's rapid demise and disintegration at the end of the 1980s. This meant unexpectedly sudden victory to the West after forty-five years of undeclared conflict, and achieved an outcome that might otherwise only have been possible through the worst of hot wars imaginable. The Cold War was over but the idea, as expounded by Francis Fukuyama in his book *The End of History and the Last Man* (1991), that liberal capitalism's triumph meant the end of humanity's ideological evolution, was somewhat premature. The impact of the USSR's disappearance will be touched upon in the next chapter which, as an Afterword, takes the book beyond its principal narrative.

Soviet 1957 postcard, imagined depiction of international friendship with dancing in the street in Red Square Moscow. (*Author's collection*)

Chapter 11

Afterword – the Legacy of the Cold War

> Considering past history and the events that have unfolded recently, it can be said that the Soviet Union was willing to find a way to arrive at genuinely democratic and peaceful international relations. In the West, particularly in the United States, no such willingness existed.... When the United States spoke about the new world order, it essentially meant a continuation of its previous policy with some corrections in methodology. The United States viewed the end of the Cold War as the removal of many substantial obstacles on the road to achieving long-standing goals of American policy.
>
> Mikhail Gorbachev, *On My Country and the World* (2000) p.210

Research for this book involved extensive reading and a viewpoint taken as far as possible from both sides of the Cold War divide (although there is no pretension of great academic depth). Despite the voluminous weight of Western narratives that blame the USSR for just about everything, I must draw a different conclusion. Stalin's bullying style and murderous policies towards his own peoples provided a convenient camouflage for American actions from 1945 onwards, and the absence of freedoms in the USSR and its satellites only served to justify their continuation after his death. The aggressor, both ideologically and militarily, was not the Soviet Union, whether under Stalin or any of his successors, it was always the USA and its allies. After 1945 the Americans were absolutely committed to destroying communism but there was no parallel drive from the other side to end capitalism. While an ideological aim of the USSR from 1917 onwards was to embed communism internationally across the world and replace the market and competition with trade and cooperation, the policy actuality was always pursuance of détente alongside border security. Soviet activity beyond its borders was always a reaction to events started by the Americans (as with Cuba in 1962) or a desire to win and hold onto socialist friends abroad (as with Africa in the 1970s and Afghanistan in the 1980s). In terms of aggression, these pale by comparison with the Vietnam war and American actions in Latin America during the Cold War. There is also no comparison when looking at American and Soviet military deployment across the world in the same period. The Soviets latterly developed a Navy that threatened to become an equal to that of the USA, but this costly attempt to keep up ultimately broke their economy and contributed heavily towards the USSR's collapse. Hence the graveyards of submarines, aircraft and other military equipment across the old USSR and Eastern Bloc after 1990.

The threat to the security of the USSR and its allies by the perpetual US attacks on their right to exist served to successfully embed paranoia and curtail freedoms. It took Reagan to finish the job by exploiting the problems inherited by Gorbachev in 1985. The end might have been a surprise to most of us who had been bought up in the West on notions of the USSR's mighty threat to our freedoms, but it was predictable too. Even Stalin recognised that his tanks alone could not deliver communism to the territories he liberated from the Nazis – that took popular will which was present across the world in 1945, but which diminished as economic progress engulfed the capitalist world in the post-war years. By 1989 only a small minority of people, East, and West, saw salvation for humanity emanating from the USSR, and that brought forward its demise.

Notions of legacy are inevitably linked to the interpretation of events that took place over thirty years ago, a theme that was discussed in the introduction and has run through this entire book. Memories arouse passions; during research I corresponded with someone who had been a child at the end of the Cold War, in the hope that I could include their stories in Chapter 8. Cooperation was withdrawn entirely after reading the draft Introduction on the basis that I had been unreasonably soft on communism. One of the reasons for exception taken was my assertion that while the Germans had been forgiven for their crimes in the Second World War as soon as it finished, the Soviets never had. The Soviets, I was told, had violently invaded the person's home country and communism is worse than fascism because it still exists. What seemed to be overlooked here was the well-established fact that the country concerned had entered the Second World War on the German side, had been involved in the murderous invasion of the USSR, and was complicit in the Holocaust.

I find this rewriting of history to place Nazi murderers in the same position as Stalin and the Red Army (in this case above them in terms of integrity), very worrying. It has aided a resurgence in far-right politics built on ignorance of the past. There is little doubt in my mind that notwithstanding the horrors inflicted by communist authorities on their own people, the elevation of fascist elements in some of the former socialist countries to the status of martyr is an inevitable consequence of the Prague Declaration, even if that was not its intention. Historical memory is an important factor in how we view the world, and it is neither inevitable nor immovable. As this is written there is concern about the impact of Coronavirus in former Eastern Bloc countries where vaccination levels are said to be low because of ingrained suspicion of government that goes back to pre-1991 times. I have no idea if this is accurate or whether there are other factors at play over thirty years after the last Eastern Bloc regime fell, but the point perhaps is that communism and really existing socialism continue to provide a convenient scapegoat for the West's failings long after their demise. I cannot help thinking that this rewriting of history might have the same long-term consequences as the historical depiction of the UK's role in slavery; while the background differs, the fact is that British people have seen themselves as the abolishers of slavery over a short period in the nineteenth century, rather than its principal beneficiary over a very long period, and this is only now coming under scrutiny and critical appraisal. In the future, will fascists be seen as a historically benign bulwark against the Twentieth Century evil of communism?

Socialist realism reduced to a theme park in Budapest. (*Dishual via Wikimedia Commons*)

Stalinism was certainly a terrible thing; as well as taking countless lives of those it was supposed to serve, it also besmirched the communist ideal. This had been genuinely fought for by individuals whose aim was the creation of a world that would be characterised by peace, justice, equality, and fair sharing internationally of the world's resources. Attacks by the Western powers on the USSR began soon after it was formed and long before the horrors of Stalinism offered humanitarian justification for the Cold War. The real reason for these attacks was not the behaviours at home (or abroad) of the Soviet Union, but its ideology that had challenged capitalism and imperialism. As noted throughout the book, the facts behind the Cold War suggest an emphasis on defensiveness on the part of the USSR and its allies, and aggression on the part of the US and Western powers, the opposite of what we have always been told.

The vacuum that the end of the Cold War and the balance of power that it involved that had put a brake on some aspects of international conflict, created its own problems. The reawakening of nationalism resulted in outbreaks of ethnic conflict not seen since the end of the Second World War. The break-up of the Yugoslav Republic soon descended into murderous ethnic war between neighbours who had lived peaceably together under Tito's relatively liberal post-war socialist regime. The same happened in several former Soviet republics where religious and ethnic difference had been buried by communist doctrine. The US were soon at war in the Middle East with their NATO allies in tow, ostensibly fighting dictatorship, but less interested in regime change than oil. Their later attempts to replace Saddam Hussein through the invasion of Iraq in 2003 set off ethnic conflict that persists in the region. Likewise, their efforts to bring peace on Western terms to Afghanistan saw the groups they had armed against the Soviets, become increasingly influenced by religious fundamentalism and turn on them. The US and its allies seemed to learn nothing from the Soviet experience and have recently abandoned the country to its own devices after a long and devastating war over a twenty-year period. Lasting peace in the world seems as distant as it did in the Cold War, only now there is no power to keep the USA in check. This should be no surprise; no sooner had the USSR ceased to be a reason for the Military Industrial Complex to continue to churn out their destructive wares, than new enemies were invented. Even where they did not exist, the arms industries had assumed such importance to economies that they did not even need to justify themselves. Most of the wars in which such hardware and equipment are used are far away from the countries of manufacture. The UK which regards itself as a morally upright nation, is complicit in this trade which continues to play a significant role in the economy (the UK was the world's second largest arms exporter in 2020). The *Guardian* newspaper reported in

Graves of ethnic cleansing victims Srebrenica, Bosnia. (*M. Buker via Wikipedia Commons*)

2021 that the UK is actually quite indiscriminate in its arms sales: of fifty-three countries considered by a leading human rights group to have a poor record for human rights abuses, thirty-nine had purchased UK-made military equipment, including twenty-one of thirty on the UK government's own list of 'human rights priority countries' (Townsend 2021). Nuclear arms continue to be owned by the USA, UK, China, France and Russia, with stocks limited by the 1968 Nuclear Non-Proliferation Treaty. Several other states are considered to have them including North Korea and Israel. So the link between the Cold War and the need for nuclear weapons was false, and the world remains a dangerous place as a result.

Another aspect of disappointment to many after the end of the Cold War was the continued role of NATO in the new world order. Initially promises had been made to the USSR during the negotiations of the late 1980s that NATO would not expand eastwards. While this was initially with reference to the prospect of German reunification it was considered that this commitment signalled the end of NATO as a Cold War organisation whose purpose had passed. However, not only did the enlarged FDR (unified Germany) remain within NATO, but soon other former Soviet satellites were asking to jump aboard. With a weakened Russian Federation raising few objections initially, most subsequently joined and many now host NATO military bases. A newly confident and assertive Russian Federation in the new millennium sees this as a threat and East/West tensions have increased. NATO continues to represent the military arm of American-led Western interests in the world, and operates as such independently of the United

US Marines in Iraq after the 2003 NATO invasion. (*US Marine Corps via Wikimedia Commons*)

Nations, the opportunity having passed for that organisation to have reasserted itself as the principal guarantor of worldwide security on behalf of all nations. Thus, it was NATO forces who, disastrously in the view of many, invaded Afghanistan in 2001 and Iraq in 2003. Of course, one of the justifications initially offered by Russia for the invasion of Ukraine was the threat of NATO expansion on its borders; they might, therefore, be considered to have scored a spectacular own-goal because their aggression has served only to enhance NATO's prestige; at the time of writing, the historically neutral countries of Sweden and Finland look set to join.

While an embrace of capitalism and the market, backed by US assistance, led to steady if unequal improvement in the economies of some former Eastern Bloc countries, others suffered from the start. Little Albania, whose austere Stalinist regime under the wartime partisan leader Enver Hoxha had regarded all the others as revisionist, had consequently spent many years in not very splendid isolation. Most of its oppressed population had endured grinding poverty under socialism, and the fall of the regime in 1990 only made things worse. A new language reflected new forms of oppression just as the old one had reflected those of the former regime: Lea Ypi (2021) discusses how 'Party' was replaced with 'civil society', 'democratic centralism' with 'liberalisation', 'collectivisation' with 'privatisation', 'self-criticism' with 'transparency', and 'anti-imperialist struggle' with 'fighting corruption'. As the economy collapsed, many tried to leave the country by any means they could, including up to 20,000 people, including families with children, who took over the cargo ship *Vlora* in August 1991 and forced it to sail from Durres to Bari in Italy. They were forcibly shipped home within weeks, a portent of the development of the borders of Europe as a barrier to the economic migration of the poor that would develop in the new millennium. The irony that Albanians had been previously welcomed in Western Europe if they could escape from communism, was not lost on many. Encouraged officially, many Albanians who stayed, invested their savings in pyramid schemes – entities that had few assets other than the ability to pay out from continued income from investors. They all collapsed in 1997 taking with them the savings of over 130,000 people, sparking demonstrations and riots in which people helped themselves to arms from the dumps that were a bequest of the previous regime. Law and order collapsed entirely and over 2,000 were killed in six months of civil war which was eventually ended through United Nations military intervention. The country remains desperately poor and its people unwelcome in most European Union countries including the UK.

And what of the former USSR that became the Russian Federation? There were many who felt humiliated at the terms of the ending of the Cold War, and led by Vladimir Putin, a former KGB agent in the USSR, have reasserted themselves through his United Russia Party. Although not communist (in fact communists, like other regime critics, are barely tolerated in the new Russia),

The cargo ship *Vlora* arrives in the Italian port of Bari heaving with Albanian economic migrants. (*Unknown origin via Wikimedia Commons*)

the new leaders are set on making Russia a world power once again, this time without the underlying ideology of peace and progress that drove the communist project of the twentieth century. The Russian Federation after 1991 quickly turned to neo-liberalism as the answer to everything, leaving behind the elderly and disadvantaged, many of whom had laboured to build an equal society under communism. Social security and health services were privatised or dismantled,

Second World War era discarded artillery pieces, Albania, 2011. (*Author*)

and social inequality widened on levels exceeding that in Western Europe in emulation of its old foes in the USA. The reduction in Russia's position as a world power had other enduring ramifications: Vladimir Putin revived notions of national pride and Russian greatness to stir up support among his people for the invasion of Ukraine in February 2022 (following territorial incursions in 2014 after the Maidan Revolution swept away a pro-Russian Ukrainian Government). The sight of Russian tanks invading Ukraine flying Soviet banners, and the use of the 1945 Victory banner which flew over the Berlin Reichstag, to mark the overrunning of Ukrainian communities, demonstrates a terrible distortion of history. This suits the Western narratives described in this book. However, the truth is that Russia today is not the USSR – that project died in 1991.

The story of neoliberal realities unfolded in the poorer former satellites in Eastern Europe – especially Bulgaria and Romania, and as related above, Albania. All have seen mass waves of emigration as did others like Poland.

> I was 90 per cent Soviet … I couldn't understand what was going on. I remember seeing Gadar on TV saying, 'Learn how to sell … The market will save us … you buy a bottle of perfume on one corner and sell it on another – that's business. The people listened, bewildered. I would come home, lock the door, weep … Maybe they wanted to do something good, but they didn't have enough compassion for their own people. All of it scared my mother so much, she ended up having a stroke. I'll never forget the rows of elderly begging for alms along the road.
>
> A recollection of the 1990s in Russia –
> from Alexievich 2013 p.66

Final Words

The Cold War was an ideological battle between two ideas about how human beings should conduct their affairs. On the one hand the West saw this in terms of freedom to engage in a global marketplace with as few restrictions as possible on an individual's right to accumulate wealth created by others. This involved free elections of government who facilitated perceptions of liberty and wealth creation. On the other hand, the Bolsheviks and their descendants believed that true progress for humanity involved collective endeavour, the abolition of profit as a motive for progress, and building a future based on notions of equality. If this meant restricting individual freedoms in the initial phases, the end would ultimately justify the means. The paradox for the USSR was that the process of building socialism (and the goal, communism) involved lofty ideals that the system was devoid of at everyday level. Soviet citizens got used to this; believing in the ideals and values of their state, at the same time as routinely reinterpreting them in their own practices (Yurchak 2005). Ultimately, as their state crumbled under international pressure and the failures of its self-appointed leaders to deliver on promises of a better life, it was inevitable that the material attractions of the West would shine through, and private practices become public ones. However, the story cannot end there; the years since the end of the Cold War have seen more wars and 'unfettered global capitalism [producing] misery, unemployment, inequality and hopelessness' (Ghodsee 2017). The threat of climate change and the absolute necessity of a global response has produced a new generation who are questioning the values of capitalism and its destructive processes; within their actions and commitment lie the hope of realising the ideals of the Bolsheviks – the actions of their USSR successors, many of which were deplorable, suggesting that perhaps they came before their time.

Soviet soldiers and T-55 tanks, 1970s. (*Author's collection*)

Appendix

Wilfred Burchett (1911–1983)

Wilfred Burchett was born in the rural community of Clifton Hill, near Melbourne, Australia, his family moving to Poowong and then Ballarat. The Burchetts, of English heritage, were close and Wilfred grew up in an environment where hardship and poverty went alongside religious-based socialist belief. He left school early to labour on his family farm before wandering to broaden his horizons through work on the land elsewhere. All the time he was educating himself though reading and involvement in socialist discussion groups. In 1934 he met by chance a socialist and anti-fascist orator Edgar Kisch, who was speaking in the open-air in Sydney to a crowd of 20,000. This, he later wrote, convinced him to become an active and campaigning socialist. In 1936 he embarked with his brother Winston for the UK. Wilfred travelled on to London where he tried to enlist in the International Brigade for service in Spain, but, lacking verifiable communist credentials, was turned

Wilfred Burchett in Paris, 1972. (*G. Burchett*)

down. Having married a Jewish refugee in England, he travelled to Germany to witness the ravages of Nazism first hand, becoming involved in journalism and attempts to help Jews emigrate to other countries. In 1940 Wilfred was sent by an Australian newspaper to report on Japanese aggression in China, and from there began reporting on the Pacific War as it spread with further Japanese invasion that brought war with Britain and the USA. Burchett gained a reputation for his war reporting from the front line and was able to use his credibility with the US Navy to gain unprecedented access to Hiroshima a few weeks after the Japanese surrender in August 1945. This unaccompanied adventure almost cost him his life – the first Western face to be seen after the atomic explosion over the city was hardly welcome by many.

After the war Wilfred returned to Europe and reported from Berlin, viewing developments there and the rapidly growing divisions between East and West from a very different perspective than most Western correspondents. He adopted a pro-communist perspective on the emerging Cold War and as a result, and through his contacts in China, ended up reporting the Korean War from the North. This happened when he was invited by French newspaper *Ce Soir* to cover the peace talks that presaged a further two and half years of fighting, a position that brought him disfavour with his own government. This gained momentum after he suggested that the reality over the treatment by the warring sides of their POWs was the opposite of that accepted by Western journalists – and the Western public. Based from the 1950s in Moscow, Wilfred adopted a similar stance over reporting of subsequent events in Indo-China and the war in Vietnam. In 1961 he obtained a scoop for the British *Daily Express* with detailed interviews with the first Soviet cosmonauts, Yuri Gagarin and German Titov. In 1955 Wilfred lost his Australian passport and reissue was refused on the basis of his journalistic activity, rendering him stateless until issued with travel documents by North Vietnam, and later a Cuban passport. With his second wife and family he subsequently moved between Moscow (1957–65). Phnom Penh (1965–69) and Paris (1969–82). Wilfred never joined the Communist Party and his political outlook rejected the blind loyalty and obedience expected with Party membership.

Wilfred returned to Australia by charter flight in 1970 to attend his brother's funeral and was issued with a new passport (issued by the newly elected Labour government) in 1972, after seventeen years of exile. The Australian government had considered putting him on trial for treason on various occasions over the years but by 1970 had given up. However, when Australian politician Senator Kane publicly accused him of being a KGB spy, Wilfred sued, and the court case in 1974 effectively became a treason trial. During the proceedings Wilfred's name was besmirched by his past associations with figures that included Chou En Lai of China, and Ho Chi Minh of North Vietnam. He was denounced by Australian veterans from Korea and Vietnam along with a host of other individual anti-communist witnesses from across the world. The jury eventually found in favour of Kane, and Wilfred was in exile once again. Now impoverished as a result of the court case, but still writing passionately, he was devastated by events in Cambodia where people he knew in the Khmer Rouge regime began a murderous policy of genocide aimed at their own people. Other developments in the communist world also disappointed him and in his final years he found solace only in the achievements of socialism in Vietnam. No slave to dogma, Wilfred was able to reflect and admit his errors of judgement in public, proof that he was no stooge for any regime but would criticise those East and West who were failing the cause of ordinary people. In failing health, Wilfred Burchett moved to Sofia, Bulgaria in 1982 and died there the following year. He left behind a legacy of journalistic writings, many written 'on the spot', and thirty books which demonstrate his commitment over forty-three years of work, to digging out uncomfortable truths.

Bibliography

Alexievich, S. (2016) *Second-Hand Time* London, Fitzcarraldo

Alexievich, S. (2016) *Chernobyl Prayer* London, Penguin

Anonymous (2005) *A Woman in Berlin* New York, Picador

Applebaum, A. (2004) *Gulag – a History* London, Penguin

Applebaum, A. (2012) *Iron Curtain – the Crushing of Eastern Europe* London, Allen Lane

Aust, S. (2008) *The Baader-Meinhof Complex* London, Bodley Head

Baldwin, J. (2018) *Dark Days* (originally published in *Esquire* 1980) London, Penguin

Barnett, N. (2018) *Britain's Cold War – Culture, Modernity and the Soviet Threat* London, Bloomsbury

Beckett, F. (1995) *Enemy Within – The Rise and Fall of the British Communist Party* London, Merlin

Beevor, A. (2003) *Berlin – The Downfall 1945* London, Penguin

Benton, G. & Loomes, G. (1976) *Big Red Joke Book* London, Pluto

Bidwell, S. (ed.) (1978) *World War 3 – a Military Projection Based on Today's Facts* London, Hamlyn

Blank, S. (1993) 'Soviet Foreign Policy and Conflict Resolution in the Third World: The Nicaraguan Civil War' *Conflict Quarterly* Autumn 1993

Blessing, B. (2006) *The Antifascist Classroom – Denazification in Soviet-occupied Germany 1945-1949* New York, Palgrave Macmillan

Brainerd, E. (2006) *Reassessing the Standard of Living in the Soviet Union: An Analysis Using Archival and Anthropometric Data* web.williams.edu/Economics/faculty/brainerd-ussr.pdf

Branson, N. (1997) *History of the Communist Party of Great Britain 1941-51)* London, Lawrence & Wishart

Burchett, W. (1950) *Cold War in Germany* Melbourne, World Unity Publications

Burchett, W. (1953) *This Monstrous War* Melbourne, Joseph Waters

Burchett, W. (1962) *Come East Young Man!* Berlin, Seven Seas

Burchett, W. (1980) *At the Barricades – the Memoirs of a Rebel Journalist* London, Quartet

Burchett, G. & Shimmin, N. (eds.) (2007) *Rebel Journalism – the Writings of Wilfred Burchett* Cambridge , CUP

Burds, J. (2009) 'Sexual Violence in Europe in World War Two' *Politics and Society* 37:35

Burleigh, M. (2013) *Small Wars, Faraway Places – The Genesis of the Modern World 1945-65* London, Macmillan

Calder, A. (1992) *The People's War* London, Pimlico
Callinicos, A. (1991) *The Revenge of History – Marxism and the Eastern European Revolutions* Cambridge, Polity
Campbell, D. (1982) *War Plan UK – The Truth About Civil Defence in Britain* London, Burnett Books
Carew, T. (1967) *Korea – The Commonwealth at War* London, Cassell
Chamberlain, W. (intro.) (1946) *Blueprint for World Conquest – The Official Communist Plan* Washington, Human Events
Chapman, J. (2006) 'The BBC and the Censorship of The War Game' *Journal of Contemporary History* 41(1) p.84
Chrystal, P. (2018) *British Army of the Rhine – The BAOR 1945-1993* Barnsley, Pen & Sword
CIA (1985) *A Comparison of the US and Soviet Economies* www.cia.gov/library/readingroom/docs/DOC_0000497165.pdf (accessed December 2021)
Clare, G. (1989) *Berlin Days 1946-1947* London, MacMillan
Clausewitz, C. von (2007 edition) *On War* Oxford, OUP
Cocks, C. (2018) *Fire Force: A Trooper's War in the Rhodesian Light Infantry* (5th edition), KDP self-published.
CPSU (1961) *Programme of the Communist Party of the Soviet Union* Moscow, Foreign Languages Publishing House
CPSU (1982) *Constitution (Fundamental Law) of the USSR Adopted October 7th 1977* Moscow, Novosti
Craig, W. (1973) *Enemy at the Gate – the Battle for Stalingrad* London, Penguin
Cross, G. (2017) *Dirty War – Rhodesia and Chemical Biological Warfare, 1975-1980* Solihull, Helion
Curtis, G. & Library of Congress Research Division (1998) *Russia – a Country Study* Washington, Library of Congress
Davis, A. (1974) *An Autobiography* New York, International Publishers
Deikin, A. (1973) *An Alliance of the Monopolies and the Military (On the US Military-Industrial Complex* Moscow, Novosti Agency Publishing House
Department of the Army (1950) *Russian Combat Methods in World War II* Washington, US Government Printing Office
Directorate of Army Education (1944) *The British Way and Purpose – Consolidated Edition* London, War Office
Donner, R. (2021) *All the Frequent Troubles of Our Days: The True Story of the Woman at the Heart of the German Resistance to Hitler* Edinburgh, Canongate
Dunstan, S. (2003) *Centurion Universal Tank 1943-2003* Oxford, Osprey
Durman, M. (and staff) (1977) *Threat – a Periodical Review of Developments in the Military Power of the Warsaw Pact* Vierson, 7 Intelligence Co. 1 Br Corps BAOR
Faid, R. (1988) *Gorbachev! Has the Real Antichrist Come?* Oklahoma, Victory House
Fleming, D.W. (1961) *The Cold War and its Origins 1917-1960* (2 volumes) New York, Doubleday
Ford, K. (2015) *Building the H Bomb* Singapore, World Scientific
Francois, D. (2018) *Chile 1973 – The Other 9/11* Solihull, Helion
Fryer, P. (1956) *Hungarian Tragedy* London, Dobson

Fukuyama, F. (1992) *The End of History and the Last Man* London, Hamish Hamilton

Funder, A. (2003) *Stasiland – Stories From Behind the Berlin Wall* London, Granta

Gaddis, J.L. (1997) *We Now Know – Rethinking Cold War History* Oxford, OUP

Gaddis, J.L. (2005) *The Cold War – The Deals, The Spies, The Lies, The Truth* London, Penguin

Gallacher, W. (1966) *Last Memoirs* London, Lawrence & Wishart

Garrison, J. & Shivpuri, P. (1983) *The Russian Threat – Its Myths and Realities* London, Gateway

Gavin, J. (1959) *War and Peace in the Space Age* London, Hutchinson

Geist, E. (2019) *Armageddon Insurance – Civil Defense in the United States and Soviet Union, 1945-91*

Gellately, R. (2013) *Stalin's Curse – battling for communism in war and cold war* Oxford, OUP

Gentry, K. (1991) *J.Edgar Hoover: The Man and the Secrets* New York, W.W. Norton

Ghodsee, K. (2015) *The Left Side of History – World War II and the Unfulfilled Promise of Communism in Eastern Europe* Durham, Duke University Press

Ghodsee, K. (2017) *Red Hangover – Legacies of Twentieth-Century Communism* Durham, Duke University Press

Ghodsee, K. (2018) *Why Women Have Better Sex Under Socialism – and Other Arguments for Economic Independence* London, Bodley Head

Gollan, J. (1960) *The German Menace – A Damning Exposure* (pamphlet) London, Communist Party

Gopal, P. (2019) *Insurgent Empire – Anti-Colonial Resistance and British Dissent* London, Verso

Gorbachev, M. (2000) *On My Country and the World* New York, Columbia University Press

Gorbachev, M. (2001) *Interview for the Public Broadcasting Service (PBS)* www.pbs.org/wgbh/commandingheights/shared/minitext/int_mikhailgorbachev.html (accessed December 2021)

Graf, W. (1984) 'Anti-Communism in the Federal Republic of Germany' *Socialist Register* Vol.21 https://socialistregister.com/index.php/srv/issue/view/420 (accessed December 2021)

Гражданская оборона СССР (1972) *Это должен знать каждый* (*Everyone Should Know This* – pamphlet) Москва, Военное издательство министерства обороны СССР.

Green, J. & de la Motte, B. (2009) *Stasi Hell or Workers' Paradise – Socialism in the German Democratic Republic – What Can We Learn From It?* London, Artery

Grierson, P. (1942) *Books on Soviet Russia 1917-1942* Twickenham, Hall

Griffiths, P. (1971) *Vietnam Inc.* New York, Collier

Grossman, V. (2006) *Life and Fate* London, Vintage

Grossman, V. (2019) *Stalingrad* London, Harvill Secker

Guardian Newspaper (6 August 2020) *Clive Ponting Obituary by David Leigh*

Hansard (22 October 1945) *House of Commons British Aircraft Industry Debate* UK Parliament https://hansard.parliament.uk/Commons/1945-10-22/debates/

dc2b782f-f7fa-4262-bf58-160e107f3cf9/BritishAircraftIndustry (accessed October 2021)
Haraszti, M. (1975) *A Worker in a Worker's State* Harmondsworth, Penguin
Harris, J. & Paxman, J. (1982) *A Higher Form of Killing: the Secret History of Chemical and Biological Warfare* New York, Hill & Wang
Hartung, W. (2011) *Prophets of War – Lockheed Martin and the Making of the Military Industrial Complex* New York, Bold Books
Haslam, J. (2011) *Russia's Cold war – From the October Revolution to the Fall of the Wall* Michigan, Yale
Heller, J. (1961) *Catch-22* New York, Simon & Schuster
Heller, J. (1977) 'Reeling in Catch 22' in Rosen, L. (ed) *The Sixties* New York, Random House
Herring, G. (2008) *From Colony to Superpower – US Foreign Relations since 1776* New York, OUP
Hertle, H. (2011) *The Berlin Wall Story – Biography of a Monument* Berlin, Ch.Links
Herz, J. (1948) 'The Fiasco of Denazification in Germany' *Political Science Quarterly* 63.4
Higham, C. (1983) *Trading With the Enemy – An Expose of the Nazi-American Money Plot 1933-1949* London, Robert Hale
Woldman, B. (2017) 'Why Did the USSR Collapse? Chernobyl, Gorbachev and Glasnost.' *History is Now* Magazine (August 21st 2017) http://www.historyisnowmagazine.com/blog/2017/8/21/the-reason-the-ussr-collapsed-chernobyl-gorbachev-and-glasnost#.YcNODmjP3IU= accessed December 2021
Hobsbawm, E. (1995) *Age of Extremes: The Short Twentieth Century 1914-1991* London, Abacus
Home Office (1957) *The Hydrogen Bomb* (pamphlet) London, HMSO
Home Office (1980 2nd edition) *Protect and Survive* (pamphlet) London, HMSO
Hoole, R. (2007) 'The Buster Crabb Enigma' *Warship World* Jan./Feb. 2007
Horrabin, J. (1944) *An Atlas History of the Second World War Volume 9* London, Thomas Nelson
Howell, E. (1956) *The Soviet Partisan Movement 1941-1944* Washington, Department of the Army
Hughes, J. (2014) 'Frank Kitson in Northern Ireland and the 'British Way' of Counterinsurgency' *History Ireland* Volume 22
Human Rights Watch (1990) *The Legacy of Psychiatric Abuse in the USSR* https://www.hrw.org/reports/pdfs/u/ussr2905.pdf (accessed November 2021)
Inkeles, A. & Geigher, D. (eds.) (1961) *Soviet Society – a Book of Readings* Boston, Houghton Mifflin
Jackson, R. (1991) *The Malayan Emergency and Indonesian Confrontation* London, Routledge
Joly, C. (1980) *Silent Night – the Defeat of NATO* London, Cassell
Jones, S. (1999) 'When Chemical Weapons Were First Dropped From the Air, North Russia 1919' *Imperial War Museum Review* 12, 1999
Kahner, L. (2007) *AK-47 – The Weapon that Changed the Face of War* New Jersey, John Wiley

Kaldor, M. (1983) *The Baroque Arsenal* London, Andre Deutsch

Kaldor, M. (1990) *The Imaginary War – Understanding the East-West Conflict* Oxford, Blackwell

Kiely, D. (ed.) (1991) *The Future for the Defence Industry* Portsmouth, Carmichael & Sweet

Kitson, F. (1971) *Low Intensity Operations: Subversion, Insurgency and Peacekeeping* London, Faber & Faber

Kendall, B. (2017) *The Cold War – A New Oral History* London, BBC Books

Kenez, P. (2006 2nd edition) *A History of the Soviet Union from the Beginning to the End* Cambridge, CUP

Киселев, А., Ребров, М (1967) уходят в космос корабли (Ships Go Into Space) Москва, Военное Издательство Министерства Обороны СССР

Kolarz, W. (ed.) (1963 2nd edition) *Books on Communism* London, Ampersand

Kolko, G. (1990) *The Politics of War – the World and United States Foreign Policy 1943-45* New York, Pantheon

Laugesen, A. (2010) 'Books for the World – American Book Programmes in the Developing World, 1948-1968.' in Barnhisel, G. & Turner, C. (eds.) *Pressing the Fight – Print, Propaganda, and the Cold War* Amherst, University of Massachusetts Press

Lewis, D. & N. (2018) *Cold War Germany – Travels of the Most Reluctant Draftee* Washington DC, self-published

Lewkovicz, N. (2020) *The German Question and the Origins of the Cold War* UK, Lulu.Com

Lowe, K. (2013) *Savage Continent – Europe in the Aftermath of World War II* London. Penguin

MacIntyre, B. (2018) *The Spy and the Traitor – The Greatest Espionage Story of the Cold War* London, Viking

McKee, A. (1982) *Dresden – 1945: The Devil's Tinderbox* London, Souvenir Press

McNamara, R. (1970) *The Essence of Security – Reflections in Office* London, Hodder

Magee, A. (2021) The Cold War Wilderness of Mirrors – U.S. and Soviet Military Liaison Missions 1947–1990 Havertown Pa., Casemate

Mastny, V. (2005) 'Was 1968 a Strategic Watershed Year of the Cold War?' *Diplomatic History* 29 (1) pp.149–177

Medvedev, Z. (1980) Nuclear Disaster in the Urals New York, Vintage

Merridale, C. (2006) *Ivan's War – Inside the Red Army 1939-45* London, Faber & Faber

Meyers, S. & Biderman, A. (eds.) (1968) *Mass Behaviour in Battle and Captivity – the Communist Soldier in the Korean War* Chicago, University of Chicago Press

Miller, W. (1960) *Russians as People* London, Letterpress

Ministry of Defence (1955) *Treatment of British Prisoners of War in Korea* London HMSO

Montagu, I. (Nov.1946) *Soviet Soldier in Europe* (pamphlet) London, British-Soviet Society

Mutambara, A. (2013) *The Rebel in Me* Durban, 30 Degrees South

NATO (undated) *A Short History of NATO* https://www.nato.int/cps/en/natohq/declassified_139339.htm (accessed September 2021)

NATO Information Services (October & November 1969) 'Life in the Soviet Union' *NATO Letter* Brussels, NATO
NATO Information Services (1984 & 1984) *NATO and the Warsaw Pact – Force Comparisons* Brussels, NATO
Nelson, M. (1997) *War of the Black Heavens – The Battles of Western Broadcasting in the Cold War* London, Brassey's
Newsinger, J. (2nd edition 2015) *British Counterinsurgency* Basingstoke, Palgrave Macmillan
Noel-Baker, P. (1958) *The Arms Race* London, Atlantic
Norman, N. (1967) *Armour in Profile – Centurion 5* Surrey, Profile Publications
Novosti Press Agency (1973) *Radio Stations of the Cold War* Moscow, Novosti
Nutt, R. (2000) 'For Truth and Liberty – Presbyterians and McCarthyism.' *Journal of Presbyterian History* 78(1)
Osborne, M. (2015) ' "The Rooting Out of Mau Mau From the Minds of the Kikuyu is a Formidable Task" : Propaganda and the Mau Mau War.' *The Journal of African History* 56(1), pp.77–97
Pauwels, J. (2002) *The Myth of the Good War – America in the Second World War* Toronto, Lorimer
Pembroke, M. (2018) *Korea – Where the American Century Began* Melbourne, Hardie Grant
Perry, R. (1988) *The Exile – Burchett: Reporter of Conflict* Victoria, Heinemann Australia
Pollack, D, & Wielgohs, J. (eds.) (2004) *Dissent and Opposition in Communist Eastern Europe – Origins of Civil Society and Democratic Transition* Aldershot, Ashgate,
Posner, C. (ed.) (1970) *Reflections on the Revolution in France: 1968* Harmondsworth, Pelican
Rethly, A. (2006) *The Hungarian Revolution 1956* Budapest, Premier
Pyadyshev, B. (1977) *The Military Industrial Complex of the USA* Moscow, Progress Publishers
Rice, B. (1971) *The C-5a Scandal – An Inside Story of the Military-Industrial Complex* Boston, Houghlin-Mifflin
Rivero, D. (2009) *Soviet and Western Bloc Competition in the Less Developed World and the Collapse of Détente* FIU Electronic Theses and Dissertations. Paper 213. http://digitalcommons.fiu.edu/etd/213 (accessed November 2021)
Roberts, P. (2012) *Cuban Missile Crisis – The Essential Reference Guide* Santa Barbara Cal, ABC-CLIO
Roman, M. (2018) 'Soviet 'renegades', Black Panthers, and Angela Davis: the politics of dissent in the Soviet press, 1968–73' *Cold War History* 18:4, pp.503-519
Rossiter, C. (1996) *The Chimes of Freedom Flashing – A Personal History of the Vietnam Anti-War Movement and the 1960s* Washington, TCA
Rzepecka, M. (2012) 'Richard Nixon's Campaign Rhetoric of Anti-Communism' *Polish Journal for American Studies* (6) p.49–62
Sampson, A. (1976) 'Lockheed's Foreign Policy – Who in the End Corrupted Whom?' *New Yorker Magazine* 15 March 1976

Samuelson, L. (2011) *Tankograd – the Formation of a Soviet Company Town – Chelyabinsk 1900s–1950s* Basingstoke, Palgrave Macmillan

Shanina, R. (undated) *Roza Shanina's War Diaries* https://rozasdiary.com/ (accessed September 2021)

Shaposhnikov, V. (ed.) (1984) *Problems of Common Security* Moscow, Progress Publishers

Shaw, W. & Pryce, D. (1990) *Encyclopaedia of the USSR* London, Cassell

Shindler, C. (2012) *National Service – From Aldershot to Aden: Tales from the Conscripts 1946-62* London, Sphere

Shubin, V. (2008) *The Hot Cold War – The USSR in Southern Africa* London, Pluto Press

Smith, J. (2010) 'The British Information Research Department and Cold War Propaganda Publishing' in Barnhisel, G. & Turner, C. (eds.) *Pressing the Fight – Print, Propaganda, and the Cold War* Amherst, University of Massachusetts Press

Smith, S. (2014) 'Centurions and Chieftains: Tank Sales and British Policy Towards Israel in the Aftermath of the Six Day War' *Journal of Contemporary History* June 2014, pp.219–39

Sumner, G. (2011) *Unstuck in Time – A Journey Through Kurt Vonnegut's Life and Novels* New York, Seven Stories

Swanson, M. (2013) *The War State – The Cold War Origins of the Military-Industrial Complex and the Power Elite 1945–63* North Charleston, Creative Space

Sykes, G., Mercer, H. & Woolf, J. (1985) *Deadly Persuasion: Teaching the Cold War, a Study of School History Textbooks* London, Teaching the Cold War Study Group

Taylor, F. (2011) *Exorcising Hitler – The Occupation and De-Nazification of Germany* London, Bloomsbury

Thedailyvonnegut.com (2021) *Vonnegut as Cultural Guide – Kurt Vonnegut in the Soviet Union: An Interview with Sarah D. Phillips* https://thedailyvonnegut.com/interviews/vonnegut-as-cultural-guide-kurt-vonnegut-in-the-soviet-union-an-interview-with-sarah-d-phillips/ accessed November 2021

Thompson, E.P. (1980) *Protest and Survive* (pamphlet) London, Campaign for Nuclear Disarmament

Thompson E.P. (1982) *Beyond the Cold War* (pamphlet) London, Merlin

Titarenko, S. (1950) *The Peaceful Co-Existence of the Capitalist and Socialist Systems* London, Soviet News

Townsend, M. (2021) '£17bn of UK arms sold to rights abusers' *Guardian* newspaper June 27th 2021

Turbett, C. (2017) *Playing With The Boys – Olga Kevelos Motorcycle Sportswoman* Isle of Arran, Beinn Nuis (Self-Published)

Turbett, C. (2018) *Motorcycles & Motorcycling in the USSR from 1939 – a Social & Technical History* Dorchester, Veloce

Turbett, C. (2020) *Red Star at War – Victory at all Costs* Barnsley, Pen & Sword

Turbett, C. (2021a) *The Anglo- Soviet Alliance – Comrades and Allies in World War II* Barnsley, Pen & Sword

Turbett, C. (2021b) *Soviets in Space – the People of the USSR and the Race to the Moon* Barnsley, Pen & Sword

US Navy (1981) *Understanding Soviet Naval Developments* Washington, US Govt. Printing Office

United States Senate archive *'Communists in Government Service,' McCarthy Says* https://www.senate.gov/about/powers-procedures/investigations/mccarthy-hearings/communists-in-government-service.htm (accessed October 2021)

Vonnegut, K. (2005) *A Man Without a Country* London, Bloomsbury

War Office (1960) *Infantry Training Volume IV Tactics – The Infantry Platoon in Battle* UK, War Office Publications

Ware, P. (2016) *Cold War 1946-1991 Operations Manual* Yeovil, Haynes

Washington Post (11 August 1981) 'The New Neutron Bomb Crisis'

Wesson, A. (1962) *The American Peace Movement: A Study of its Themes and Political Potential* RAND Corporation https://www.rand.org/pubs/papers/P2679.html (accessed November 2021)

Wilford, H. (2003) *The CIA, the British Left and the Cold War* London, Frank Cass

Wilczynski, J. (1981) *An Encyclopaedic Dictionary of Socialism & Communism* London, Macmillan

Williams, V.,, Peace, R. & Kuzmarov, J. (2018) *Central America Wars 1980s* United States Foreign Policy History and Resource Guide online: http://peacehistory-usfp.org/central-america-wars (accessed November 2021)

Wilson, S. (1995) *Sabre, MiG-15 & Hunter* Fyshwick Aus., Aerospace Publications

Ypi, L. (2021) *Free – Coming of Age at the End of History* London, Allen Lane

Yurchak, A. (2005) *Everything was Forever, Until it Was No More – The Last Soviet Generation* Princeton, PUP

Zaitsev, I. (1979) *The Second Front – The Great Soviet Encyclopaedia 3rd Edition* The Gale Group, Inc. https://www.encyclopedia2.thefreedictionary.com/Second+Front (accessed May 2021)

Zappa, F. (1990) *The Real Frank Zappa Book* New York, Simon & Schuster

Index